Seward's Folly

Seward's Folly
A New Look at the Alaska Purchase

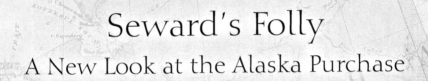

Lee A. Farrow

University of Alaska Press
Fairbanks, Alaska

Published by
University of Alaska Press
P.O. Box 756240
Fairbanks, AK 99775-6240

Library of Congress Cataloging-in-Publication Data

Names: Farrow, Lee A., 1966– author.
Title: Seward's folly : a new look at the Alaska Purchase / Lee A. Farrow.
Description: Fairbanks : University of Alaska Press, 2016. | Includes bibliographical
references and index.
Identifiers: LCCN 2016002210 | ISBN 9781602233034 (pbk. : alk. paper)
Subjects: LCSH: Alaska—Annexation to the United States. | Seward, William H.
(William Henry), 1801–1872. | United States—Foreign relations—Russia. | Russia—
Foreign relations—United States.
Classification: LCC E669 .F38 2016 | DDC 327.73047—dc23
LC record available at http://lccn.loc.gov/2016002210

Cover and interior design by Paula Elmes

Cover credits:
Alexander Baranof: Sitka, Alaska. Statue of Alexander Baranof, First Colonial
Governor of Russian America, 1790–1818. Copyright: © Charles O. Cecil / Alamy
Stock Photo.

Map of Alaska: Public domain. U.S. Coast and Geodetic Survey. Created/published
Washington, D.C., 1867.

Contents

Acknowledgments

I am very grateful to many people who helped make this project possible. Auburn University at Montgomery provided funding for research at the National Archives and Records Administration through its Faculty-Grant-in-Aid award. The Kennan Institute at the Woodrow Wilson Center covered my expenses to participate in a conference on the history of Russian America in Moscow, allowing me to present some of the material in this book. I thank both of these organizations for their support. I also need to thank the crew at AUM's Interlibrary Loan Department and our new dean, Phill Johnson, who helped me acquire a variety of documents and images. Finally, Heather Adams, a graduate student here at AUM, worked diligently to collect newspaper articles from the period for this research; I greatly appreciate her time and reliability as a research assistant.

I would also like to thank the family and friends who supported me through this process, including, but not limited to, Karen Racine, Heather Thiessen Reily, Angela Mitchell, Dana Bice, and Michael

Samerdyke, as well as Neela Banerjee and her daughter, Radha, who gave me a place to sleep in Washington, D.C., on more than one occasion. My parents, husband, and children also deserve thanks for being constant cheerleaders in every new research project.

Introduction

*I*n 1872 Appleton and Company's *Hand-Book of American Travel* included Alaska for the first time, explaining, "Alaska is the newest accession to the territory of the United States, and, though it is not likely to prove very inviting to travelers, a brief sketch seems necessary to complete the Hand-Book." The travel guide went on to say that the popular ignorance about Alaska had produced the most exaggerated claims on both ends of the spectrum, but the guide's own assessment of the region was also a mixed bag and did little to promote the likelihood of settlement or tourism. On the one hand, it praised the scenery of waterfalls and icebergs as "an inconceivably magnificent sight" but then described Sitka as "beyond doubt, the dirtiest and most squalid collection of log-houses on the Pacific slope" and noted that the governor's house was protected from the local Natives by a guard "constantly on the alert with rifles loaded, and a field-battery of Parrott guns kept constantly trained on the Indian village, adjoining the town." During roughly the same period, U.S. Treasury Agent H. A. McIntyre sgave another pessimistic evaluation of Alaska and its resources, reporting "nor can we look for any material increase of revenue for many years, except in the event of extraordinary circumstances, such as the discovery of so large deposits of valuable minerals as would produce an influx of population."

Appleton's guidebook and McIntyre's opinion could hardly have been more wrong in their dire predictions of Alaska's future. But one can hardly blame them. In the first years after the purchase, Alaska's enormous size, its geographic diversity, the variations in climate, and the lack of reliable information made it difficult to understand and assess Alaska's full potential. Eventually, gold would be discovered in the Klondike region and a population tidal wave would bring prospectors and settlers from around the globe who would build towns and establish a transportation network to facilitate travel and trade. Much later, Alaska would become famous for its oil reserves. But even in the dark days, before these rich resources had been unearthed, some of Alaska's most spectacular physical features had been discovered and praised by early explorers. Many would echo the sentiments of the geographer Henry Gannett who wrote, "Its grandeur is more valuable than the gold or the fish, or the timber, for it will never be exhausted. This value measured by direct returns in money from tourists will be enormous; measured in health and pleasure it will be incalculable." Gannett's prediction was far more accurate than those of Daniel Appleton and McIntyre. Today Alaska is a premier tourist destination, and tourism is an important part of the state's economy; between October 2013 and September 2014, nearly two million people visited Alaska, half of them on cruise ships, spending nearly $2 billion while in the state.

· · · ● · ·

The story of how Alaska became one of America's most valuable treasures begins with a hurried and secret deal in March 1867 that was executed in the dark of night and announced to the American public the following day as a fait accompli. Most Americans know that the

United States bought Alaska from Russia for $7.2 million and that there were naysayers and doubters who called the new acquisition the Russian American Folly, Seward's Icebox, or Walrussia. Few, however, are aware of the details—Russia's reasons for selling and America's reasons for buying, the intricacies of the deal, the complexities of the transfer, the debates and derision in the press and on Capitol Hill, the persistent lawsuit that threatened to ruin the sale, and the scandal that followed. In fact, the story of how Russian America became Alaska is far more interesting and complex than the simple history that most of us were taught.

Russia and the United States both had good reasons to want the sale of Alaska. For Russia, the sale would mean letting go of an unprofitable and hard-to-manage colony, freeing up money and other resources for domestic reform, and pursuing expansion into Russia's Far East along the Amur River near China. The United States had other motives. In conjunction with its desire for territorial growth, the purchase of Russian America would accomplish two things: it would expand the United States' control on the North American continent, and, many believed, it would eventually lead to the absorption of British Columbia. It also promised to facilitate and expand commercial relations with Asia, making new ports and routes available for the Pacific trade. Though little was known about the true economic value of Alaska at the time, many believed that it would prove to be a profitable acquisition in the end. There were also diplomatic dimensions to the deal. Both countries recognized that this deal would likely trouble Great Britain, but British diplomacy over the previous decades had done little to warm Russian or American hearts. Finally, though the Russian-American friendship was highlighted in diplomatic and media circles in many places, the Alaska purchase was not an act of benevolence between two countries on favorable terms; it was a mutually beneficial deal, carefully negotiated, with very specific aims and aspirations for both parties.

There is another facet of the Alaska Purchase that has been underappreciated—its interpretation on the international stage. Most histories of the Alaska Purchase examine it in a domestic context, but the treaty also had international implications. Some countries feared the possibility of a Russian-American alliance and the ways that such an alliance could affect European affairs, particularly the fate of the Ottoman Empire. Some in Europe were convinced that the treaty must include some sort of quid pro quo arrangement by which Russia sold Alaska to America with the expectation of either assistance or simply a free hand elsewhere. It was also widely believed that the treaty was aimed specifically at interfering with the interests of Great Britain and included plans to annex portions, or even all, of Canada. At the very least, many were suspicious of American expansionism and the ideology of Manifest Destiny. At a time when the balance of power in Europe was threatened by the unification of Germany and Italy, the fracturing of the Ottoman Empire, and the growing tide of nationalism, the Alaska Purchase was viewed as much more than a simple exchange of territory.

· · · · ● · ·

This book began on an Alaskan cruise with my family. As our ship docked in Sitka, I decided that I should know more about the Alaska Purchase. Though a Russian historian by trade, I knew very little of the details of this major event in Russian-American relations. I popped into the independent bookstore in town only to find that there was not a single book on the purchase. When I returned home, I began to research this glaring hole in the literature on Alaska and Russian-American relations and discovered that although there were several recent children's books on Seward's Folly, the most recent book for an adult audience had been published in 1975. Recognizing the need for a new study of the purchase, one that would appeal to a broad readership, I approached the University of Alaska Press with my idea to write such a book and they agreed to work with me.

The research for this book came from a variety of sources. There are a number of books that contained published primary sources on the purchase, and these were invaluable to completing this study. I also used quotes from several secondary sources when I could not reasonably gain access to the original documents myself, particularly when it came to newspapers and foreign documents. I did, however, conduct a great deal of research online and in person. There are many newspapers, including European papers, that are accessible online in scanned form—so there is no question of reliability—and I used these whenever possible. I also spent a week at the National Archives and Record Administration microfilm division in Maryland looking at diplomatic correspondence between the United States Department of State and its representatives in various European cities at the time of the purchase to gauge international reaction. To that end, a number of published memoirs and collections of letters were also helpful. The chapter endnotes indicate the source of all quoted material. Finally, I relied on my own research on the Perkins Claim from my earlier book, *Alexis in America*, as well as on a number of excellent secondary sources on the Alaska Purchase and various aspects of the history of Russian-American relations. I am greatly indebted to those who have come before me in studying and telling the story of this fascinating episode in American and Russian history.

Eduard de Stoeckl, Russian minister to the United States at the time of the purchase. Baron de Stoeckl. [Between and 1855 and 1865] Retrieved from the Library of Congress, (LC-BH82-5273 A).

CHAPTER I

Some Mysterious Sympathy: The Foundations of the Russian-American Friendship

*I*n the second half of the nineteenth century, Russia and the United States had a significantly different relationship than the one future generations would come to know. During this pivotal period in American and Russian history, the two great nations were on friendly terms, and many in Europe worried that they might become allies. Situated on opposite sides of the globe, they were an unlikely pair in many ways—one was a conservative monarchy, the other a young republic—yet over the course of a century the bond had developed from hesitant and uncertain beginnings to a mature and complex friendship that both countries sought to protect and expand. Repeated encounters in trade, diplomacy, and technological matters had brought the two countries closer, while events on the international scene—war, trade disputes, and the shifting balance of power in Europe—often pushed them together as well. To a large extent, this unusual friendship must be understood in a broader diplomatic context; since the end of the eighteenth century, Russian-American relations were both a reaction to and a facet of other interactions, particularly those between Great Britain and Russia and Great Britain and the United States. The constant, if sometimes dormant, tension between these nations over maritime power, fishing rights, and territorial expansion repeatedly drove Russia and the United States into one another's arms. The end result was that by the time those two nations exchanged that stretch of wild territory in North America, they already had a surprisingly long and active relationship, much of which was built at the expense of and in opposition to that imperial powerhouse of the nineteenth century, Great Britain.

· · · ● · · ·

It was during the reign of Catherine the Great (1762–96) that the earliest foundations of the Russian-American relationship were laid. The first recorded contact between Russians and "Americans" came in 1763 when the ship of a prominent Boston merchant, loaded with rum, sugar, sassafras, mahogany, and indigo from the West Indies, landed outside of St. Petersburg at Kronstadt and returned home with linen, hemp, and iron from Russia. This began a period of active trade, though the connection remained exclusively a commercial one. The spirit of the Enlightenment and ominous international events eventually tested the strength and sincerity of that early relationship. Catherine considered herself an enlightened monarch, embracing many of the ideas of the Enlightenment and even corresponding with a number of the philosophers, but when these same ideas inspired the American revolutionaries to action, Catherine was unwilling to offer support to the rebels. Instead, she issued the famous Declaration of Armed Neutrality in March 1780, which avoided direct involvement but effectively aided the colonies by pronouncing the right of neutral ships to enter American ports.

Catherine's declaration also encouraged leaders in the American colonies to consider a formal mission to Russia. In 1781 Francis Dana, accompanied by fourteen-year-old John Quincy Adams, traveled to St. Petersburg. Though the complexities of the war and Catherine's hope of convincing Britain to accept her mediation prevented Dana from being received in any official capacity, he did meet with important Russian and foreign diplomats and tried to alleviate concerns that an independent United States would be harmful to Russian commercial interests, specifically its trade in naval stores. Dana's efforts at persuading Russia to assist the colonies were a failure, and it would be twenty years before the United States could establish an official representative at St. Petersburg. Nonetheless, the American Revolution did have an impact in Russia. Educated Russians enamored with the ideas of the Enlightenment were intrigued by the American colonists' establishment of a new nation based on republican values. Though none traveled to the United States, several Russian writers made reference to America, including Alexander Radishchev, the proto-revolutionary and author of one of the earliest condemnations of serfdom, *Journey from St. Petersburg to Moscow*.

There were other contacts during Catherine's reign as well. In 1788 the famous American seaman John Paul Jones secured an appointment in the Russian navy and served in the Black Sea under one of Catherine's favorites, the talented soldier Prince Grigorii Potemkin. Jones's period of service, however, did not go well. He did not speak Russian or get along well with the British officers in the Russian navy, and in the spring of 1789 he was accused of raping a twelve-year-old girl. Whether or not the accusation was true, Catherine took the opportunity to get rid of Jones; he was given leave and made his way as far as Paris, where he died there three years later. Despite this rather disastrous episode, Russian-American ties continued to grow, particularly in the commercial sphere. At the end of the eighteenth century, at least four hundred ships from Boston, New York, Philadelphia, and other American ports brought goods to Russia, and "most New England houses and ships were put together with Russian nails, and it would be a rare vessel that did not have sails, tackle, and anchors of Russian origin." More formal commercial relations were hindered by the lack of an official diplomatic relationship. Catherine's own fears about the radicalization of the French Revolution, which had begun in 1789, also slowed such a development, as she became wary of republican ideas and sought to draw closer to Britain. Her son and heir, Paul I (1796–1801), a true conservative, proved even less inclined to pursue concrete ties with the young republic.

Russia and the United States finally established full diplomatic relations under Catherine's grandson, Alexander I (1801–25). When Alexander became tsar, he and his small circle of liberal advisors were more receptive to establishing a diplomatic friendship with the United States, despite its very different political system. There were strategic diplomatic reasons, as well. When President Thomas Jefferson proposed the idea of an official minister in 1807, both the United States and Russia had become increasingly isolated as France under Napoleon Bonaparte proved its superiority on land and Great Britain dominated the seas. In June 1809 the U.S. Senate approved the nomination of John Quincy Adams as minister to Russia; Alexander I had already selected Fedor Pahlen as the first Russian minister to the United States. This new diplomatic bond was strengthened when, in 1813, Alexander I offered to mediate an end to the war between the United States and Britain. Britain refused and so it was not until the Treaty of Ghent in early 1815 that the war ended, but the Russian offer of assistance impressed the American government as a sign of goodwill.

In the following years, however, a series of small complications threatened the developing friendship. In November 1815, in an episode oddly reminiscent of the John Paul Jones affair, Nikolai Kozlov, the Russian consul-general in Philadelphia, was accused of raping a twelve-year-old girl. A Pennsylvania court denied Kozlov's claim of diplomatic immunity and decided that crimes by foreign diplomats fell within the purview of federal courts. In response, Andrei Dashkov, who had become Russian minister in 1811, demanded that Kozlov be cleared of all charges, and when this did not happen, he ceased all communication with the U.S. government. The Russian government retaliated by declaring the American chargé d'affaires in St. Petersburg, Levett Harris, to be persona non grata, though he was permitted to carry out his official duties. The crisis settled in late 1816 when Alexander I and his cabinet, eager to maintain good relations with the United States, accepted the argument that diplomats were answerable to the laws of the country where they resided at the time of the offense.

· · · ● · · ·

There is one other major point of contact between Russia and America during this period, of course—the birth of that territory called Russian America, what would eventually come to be known as Alaska. Even as the Russian and American governments were taking the first steps toward building an official diplomatic relationship, there were other contacts and conflicts between traders and settlers in the Pacific Northwest that created challenges to that fledgling friendship. As Russia tried to establish a sound footing and stake its claim to Russian America and its commercial possibilities, it repeatedly ran afoul of American traders of various kinds eager to exploit those same natural resources. These disagreements went on for decades and contributed to the later conversations about the future of Russian America. Russia may have gotten there first, but the persistent intrusions of American traders made it a difficult road with an uncertain outcome.

Russian presence in the Pacific Northwest had slow and tentative beginnings. By the mid-1660s geographical information of some kind had reached Moscow, suggesting that beyond the farthest reaches of Siberia one would find the northwestern tip of North America, but at the time no one knew if the two continents were one. In the eighteenth century, through a combination of government-sponsored exploration and individual entrepreneurship, Russia established a presence, not only on the islands leading up to the mainland, but on the North American mainland itself. As early as 1741, Vitus Bering's expedition made Russians aware of the rich possibilities of the seal and sea otter fur trade, and this discovery fueled the increase in Russian traffic in the second half of the century, which eventually led to the establishment of a Russian trading company. The Russian-American Company evolved over a period of roughly twenty years as one private trading company transformed into another. Though these early iterations of the Russian-American Company received some assistance from the Imperial government, the company's ultimate success can largely be credited to the efforts of the merchant Grigory I. Shelikhov, who recognized the potential for the fur trade in Alaska in the 1770s. Shelikhov continuously agitated for government support and a permanent settlement in North America, and he proposed the organization of a trading company along the lines of the British East India Company that would have a monopoly on the fur trade. Though he did not live to see his plan come to fruition, he did establish a permanent settlement on Kodiak Island. Finally, in 1799, Paul I granted the Russian-American Company a charter and a monopoly on all hunting, trading, and mining of the northwest coast of North America from 55 degrees latitude north, just north of present-day Prince Rupert, British Columbia, to the Bering Strait and including the island approaches, such as the Aleutians. The company was also permitted to sell its stock. That same year Alexander Baranov, who had served as Shelikhov's assistant and then manager of the company in his own right, founded a permanent settlement to serve as his headquarters and named it Novo-Arkhangelsk (later, Sitka). Over the next seventy years, the Russian-American Company would serve as the primary representative of Russia's commercial interests in the Pacific Northwest.

The Russians were not alone in their pursuit of the lucrative fur trade, however. At the end of the eighteenth century, Boston merchants began to send ships to the area hoping to acquire sea otter furs from Natives that would then be taken to the port of Canton in China. Within a few years a trading route from Boston to the Pacific Northwest to Canton to Boston was well established, and by 1801 sixteen American vessels were enjoying the profits of the sea otter trade. Beginning in 1803 this desire for a secure supply of pelts led American sea captains to strike deals with the Russian settlement in Alaska; in these arrangements, the Russian-American colony would supply the Americans with furs in exchange for supplies and the occasional manpower when needed. Since Russian vessels were not allowed in Chinese ports, the deal seemed to benefit both parties.

For the most part, this system worked well for several years, but in reality Russia had already been looking for a way to cut out its American middlemen. In 1805 Nikolai Rezanov, a Russian nobleman and longtime supporter of the trading company, arrived in Sitka as an inspector for the Imperial government. Rezanov was troubled by American encroachment in the sea otter trade, but Baranov pointed out that it was better to work through the Americans than simply have them strike their own deals with the local hunters. Nonetheless, Rezanov urged the Russian-American Company to build a settlement on the Columbia River. Baranov took Rezanov's concerns seriously and during the next few years tried to extend Russia's control over the sea otter trade in the Pacific Northwest. In addition to a failed attempt to establish a trading post in the Sandwich Islands, Baranov also sent a vessel to Northern California to find a Russian base for hunting and agricultural production that could then be used to support the Alaskan settlements. First established at Bodega Bay, the base was later relocated to the north and named Fort Ross. The settlement, situated eighty-five miles north of present-day San Francisco, served as the headquarters of Russian California for thirty years.

Meanwhile, in response to complaints from the Russian-American Company about the intrusion of American fur traders, Minister of Foreign Affairs Count Nikita Rumiantsev wrote to Levett Harris, the American consul in St. Petersburg, in May 1808 asking that American traders use only Russian-American Company agents at Kodiak and refrain from trading firearms with the locals, a practice that had enabled the Tlingit uprising that had destroyed

Sitka several years earlier. It was partly this ongoing conflict over the sea otter trade that made Russia realize that it was necessary to place a permanent representative in the United States. Alexander I appointed Fedor Pahlen as the first Russian minister in 1809, and he selected Andrei Dashkov to serve as the Russian consul-general in Philadelphia. Dashkov arrived in the United States months ahead of Pahlen, however, and so it was he who served as Russia's representative on all matters initially. When Dashkov, arrived in Washington in the summer of 1809, one of his first challenges was to tackle the problem of American vessels illicitly trading with local tribes in the Pacific Northwest, referring to it as a violation of Russian territorial rights. When Secretary of State Robert Smith asked Dashkov to specify the boundaries of what Russia considered to be its territory, Dashkov had to admit that he could not, making it easy for the American government to ignore the complaint for the time being. But the issue was far from settled, and in subsequent years, the debate continued. While Russia attempted to claim territory down to the mouth of the Columbia River, both Secretary of State Smith and President James Madison realized that signing any convention with Russia on this subject would be tantamount to recognizing Russian rights over territory in North America.

The War of 1812 disrupted trade in the Pacific Northwest, but by this point the Russian-American Company had grown dependent on American traders for its sustenance and for the shipment of furs to Canton. When the war ended in 1815, the fur trade was revived and with it appeared a number of discussions and resolutions in Congress demanding the protection of American fur interests. Though Russian activity in the area was of great concern, American traders and the politicians who supported them also worried about the British presence in the region. Russia viewed the situation quite differently, of course, and decided to take more aggressive steps to protect its business concerns. In September 1821, Tsar Alexander I issued an imperial *ukaz* (proclamation) that closed the entire area along the Pacific Northwest coast to trade by anyone other than the

Russian-American Company and claimed Russian territorial waters for a hundred miles from the coastline. At the same time, Alexander renewed the charter of the Russian-American Company and re-affirmed the southern boundary of the colony at 51 degrees north latitude, the upper edge of current Vancouver Island. Alexander explained that the ukaz was a reaction to the illicit activities of foreigners along the Russian-American coast. In response, a congressional committee urged the United States to occupy the Pacific Northwest before Russia took it all and proposed a bill to that effect. This bold suggestion found strong support among American traders who stood to lose a great deal if the tsar's ukaz remained in force.

Ultimately, the United States made it clear to Russia that it could never accept Alexander's decree and that the presence of American traders in the Pacific Northwest was a permanent reality. Secretary of State John Quincy Adams had long supported the notion of an American continental empire, and in fact believed it to be an inevitability, but one that, in his view, required patience and caution. There was no need to obtain something by force that would eventually be gained by providence. Adams also understood that America's relationship with Russia could serve as a useful counterbalance to British sea power. In March 1822 Adams informed the Russian minister in Washington, D.C., Pierre de Politica, that the United States could neither accept Russian claims to the Northwest coast nor could it abide by the regulations in the ukaz. At the same time, Adams instructed the U.S. minister to Russia, Henry Middleton, to press American rights in St. Petersburg. Middleton did so, implying the possibility of war between the two nations should the matter not be resolved soon, and the Russian government decided to back down.

As the slow wheels of diplomacy turned, the issue of jurisdiction in the Pacific Northwest became tied to the growing threat of European interference in Latin America to help Spain regain its lost colonies. By the fall of 1823, the U.S. government anticipated the possibility that the European monarchies of the conservative Holy Alliance might tamper with affairs in the Western Hemisphere and said so in a strongly worded note to the Russian minister. Only days later, President James Monroe delivered his famous message to Congress that gave birth to the Monroe Doctrine, stating that any further actions by European nations to establish colonies or interfere with states in North or South America would be perceived as acts of aggression, thus prompting U.S. intervention. The United States had staked out a firm position on spheres of influence. Meanwhile, the Russian government suffered pressure from within. The tsar's ukaz had been devastating to the Russian-American colony, resulting in an annual average loss of 300,000 rubles. In 1823 Matvei Muraviev, the governor of Russian America, begged the board of directors in St. Petersburg to lay aside the trade restriction with Americans, and a group of stockholders petitioned the Russian government to reopen Sitka to foreign vessels.

Finally, in February 1824, formal negotiations opened between the two governments on the issue, and a treaty was signed two months later that provided that both nations could fish, navigate waters, or trade with Natives along the Northwest coast at points not yet occupied. Consequently, it was expected that both Russian and American citizens would request permission before entering each other's ports. For the first ten years after this agreement, however, both countries would have free movement in the area, with the notable exception that the trade of firearms, gun powder, and alcohol was prohibited. Finally, the two governments settled on 54 degrees 40 minutes north latitude as the dividing point between Russian and American territory. While American officials viewed the treaty as a complete victory, the Russian government believed it had executed a successful maneuver to stop further U.S. penetration into Russian territory. In ten years Russia believed it could rightfully forbid Americans from trading and fishing in the entire area. At the same time, the dispute and its temporary resolution made one thing clear—Russia's ability to defend its Pacific Northwest colony was questionable, as was the political and economic value of its distant investment.

· · · ● ● ● ●

The temporary resolution of the conflict in the Pacific Northwest was not the only bright spot in this period; there were other positive interactions between the two countries in the 1820s and 1830s. Though there was no official commercial treaty, an impressive number of American ships traveled to Kronstadt and St. Petersburg with a variety of valuable goods, including sugar from the West Indies, and as much as 90 percent of America's linen imports came from Russia. More significant purchases occurred as well. In 1829 Nicholas I (1825–55) sought to modernize the Russian navy and sent a naval mission to the United States to visit various shipyards and naval facilities, resulting in the purchase of one steam corvette. The deal was wrecked, however, by anti-Russian sentiment in Washington, D.C., over the Russian government's suppression of the 1830–31 Polish uprising. Luckily, American ire was short-lived, and by 1832, many Americans had lost interest in the Polish cause and the two countries signed a commercial treaty.

The developing railroad industry also benefitted from the two countries' friendly interactions. In 1838 a group of Russian railroad proponents persuaded Nicholas to create a special committee to consider ideas for a Moscow–St. Petersburg rail line. Once the tsar decided that the idea had merit and potential benefits, he established an official construction committee and approved the proposal to bring an American railroad expert, George Washington Whistler, to oversee construction. Whistler, an army major and one-time chief engineer for the Baltimore and Ohio Railroad, had demonstrated his considerable skills in overcoming the challenging curves and steep grades in the Berkshire Range of Massachusetts on what would become the Boston and Albany Railroad. Similarly, the Russian government brought in American locomotive builders to set up a factory and educate locals in the art. These men all lived in Russia for several years, and Whistler even brought his family, which included his son James, the future painter.

Meanwhile, the situation in the Pacific Northwest continued to be problematic. The freedom of trade allowed by the treaty of 1824 created a situation in which the Russian colony became more dependent on American traders for necessary supplies of food and other items, while these same Americans traded with the Natives for furs, depleting the colony of its most valuable resource. As the presence of American traders increased, the Russian-American Company's profits declined. Meanwhile, a number of American politicians continued to agitate for U.S. occupation of the mouth of the Columbia River before it fell into Russian or British hands. The Russian-American Company's fears intensified with the declining success of the Russian settlement at Fort Ross as much of the trade in that area was taken over by American traders. By 1834 the Russian government no longer viewed Fort Ross as a viable possession and simply waited for an opportunity to divest itself of the failed colony, which it did in 1841 in a sale to John Sutter, a California pioneer.

Tensions continued to mount as the ten-year free-trade clause of the 1824 treaty expired. Though American traders ignored the resurrected restriction and continued to do as they pleased, the Russian government was eager to assert its control and press its interpretation of the treaty that all American vessels were now excluded from areas north of 54 degrees 40 minutes latitude, even those unsettled by Russians. Without such protection, the Russian-American Company faced inevitable ruin. Tsar Nicholas and Foreign Minister Karl Nesselrode realized that refusing American demands for open trade in the area could jeopardize the Russian-American relationship that they relied on as a counterweight to British commercial power and expansion. Indeed, Nicholas said to U.S. Minister George Dallas in St. Petersburg in 1839 that the amity between Russia and the United States was derived from the fact that "not only are our interests alike, but (with emphasis in his tone) our enemies are the same." The U.S. administration, for its part, would not back down nor was it willing to provoke war over the matter, being mindful of its other great commercial enemy, Great Britain. Nonetheless, in his annual message of December 1838, President Martin van Buren stated in no uncertain terms that "the citizens of the United States have, independent of the provisions of the Convention of 1824, a right to trade with the natives upon the coast in question at unoccupied points."

In 1836, at the same time that Russia and the United States were haggling over the question of open trade in the Pacific Northwest, Russia saw an opportunity to pit Great Britain and the United States against one another. After several employees of the Russian-American Company crossed into the British sphere, the Russian government offered the Hudson's Bay Company a ten-year lease on a strip of land running from Cape Spencer (west of present-day Juneau, at the southern tip of Glacier Bay National Park and Preserve) south to 54 degrees 40 minutes north latitude in lieu of the $250,000 demanded by the British company. Russian foreign minister Nesselrode hoped that the arrangement would halt American penetration and force the United States to find other outlets for its expansionist energies, but in fact it did little, if anything, to deter American traders, least of all whalers.

By 1845 more than 250 American whaling vessels were hunting off the coast of Russian America and in the Bering Sea, and Russian-American Company officials complained to their government that these whalers stole oil, food, and women from the local Natives and left behind only bad liquor and syphilis. In response, the Russian government agreed to send several armed cruisers to the area, but only as a show of force to protect residents there. Eventually, the Russian complaints produced results. In September 1845, Secretary of State James Buchanan published a statement in the *Washington Daily Union* that American vessels were "not to violate the existing treaty . . . by resorting to any point on the Russian coast where there is a Russia establishment . . . nor to frequent the interior seas, gulfs, harbors and creeks upon that coast at any point north of the latitude of 54° 40'."

It was nearly a decade before the Russian-American relationship faced another serious challenge. The Crimean War, which broke out in 1853 between Russia and an alliance of the British, French, and Ottoman Empires, threatened to damage the comfortable understanding that had been reached in recent years. Though the theater of war was far away and not an area of strategic interest for the United States, there was much about the conflict that proved relevant. On the one hand, American officials saw Russia as a friend and Britain as a constant irritant; on the other, British trade was too profitable to cast aside. Soon, however, American ambiguity shifted in favor of Russia. In the summer of 1854, the United States offered to mediate the conflict between Russia and Britain, but when the effort came to nothing, Russia and the United States subsequently signed a maritime neutrality agreement that was so friendly that it was close to an actual alliance. This did not stop the British from recruiting soldiers in the United States, an activity that angered Russian officials who viewed it as a violation of the American position of neutrality. In fact, several British recruiters were arrested and put on trial, and the British minister to the United States, John F. Crampton, was dismissed over the matter. Many Russians would have welcomed a fallout between the United States and Great Britain. Constantin Catacazy, the secretary to the Russian legation in the United States, for example, suggested that American merchant vessels should be encouraged to set sail for Russia, hoping that if they were stopped by the British it might push America into the war.

The American government had no intention of being drawn into the Crimean War, but it did take the opportunity to study the military tactics and experiences of the participants. In the summer of 1854, the War Department sent Maj. Richard Delafield, Maj. Alfred Mordecai, and Capt. George McClellan to act as observers. The men began their sojourn in St. Petersburg, where they stayed for six weeks, touring military installations and learning more about the Russian army, as they waited for permission to head south. Ultimately, the American observers never made it to the Russian front; they were refused under the official claim that other groups had been denied the same request, so they were forced to observe the war from the British side. A considerable number of private citizens traveled from the United States to the Crimea as well, including thirty-five American doctors who traveled to the region to offer medical aid, some out of sympathy for Russia, others for adventure, experience, or money. Pure capitalist incentive was the motive for many others. Though the United States remained neutral, more than one man took the opportunity to profit from the Crimean War, selling guns, powder, coal, and cotton to Russia and, in some cases, also to its enemies.

The Crimean War concluded in March 1856 with the Treaty of Paris. When Tsar Nicholas I died in 1855, his son, the more liberal Alexander II, took the opportunity to remove Russia from a war that had exposed many of its weaknesses, particularly the poor physical condition of its peasant conscripts. Russia's attitude toward the United States, however, remained positive, and the period between the end of the Crimean War in 1856 and the beginning of the Civil War in 1861 was one of the most active periods in Russian-American trade, with the continuation of old business deals and the development of many new contracts. During these few years, shipments of cotton from the United States to Russia rose steadily. In 1857, about 45 percent of Russia's cotton imports came from the United States and that figure rose to 80 percent in the following year. Russia also imported American sugar, rice, and lumber. Military trade flourished as well. In the late 1850s, the William H. Webb Shipyards began building warships for the Russian navy, and Samuel Colt, who had already been selling guns to Russia, secured a lucrative business deal to supply machinery and designs for Colt-style revolvers to be manufactured there.

In the domestic arena, however, both Russia and the United States faced difficult times. In early 1861, civil war erupted in the United States over the issue of slavery at the same moment that Alexander II declared an end to the centuries-old practice of serfdom in Russia. American newspapers praised the tsar for this liberal reform and for decades politicians and the press would refer to the serf emancipation in discussions about Russian-American relations. It would be a constant theme in the speeches welcoming Alexander II's son, Grand Duke Alexis, a decade later. Once America had emancipated its own slaves, the two nations perceived a new special bond, and Lincoln and Alexander were often spoken of in the same breath.

Sadly, America's path to emancipation was more difficult. While liberal Russians applauded the abolition of slavery, the violence of the American process saddened them. Meanwhile, Russian officials, anxious about the fate of the Russian-American friendship, were even more dismayed by the Civil War. Russia needed a strong ally in its ongoing rivalry with Great Britain and in reestablishing itself as a European power after the disastrous Crimean War. By 1862 Russian Minister of Foreign Affairs Alexander Gorchakov and others in St. Petersburg were frustrated with the American Civil War and worried that a permanent split in the American union might occur. Consequently, Gorchakov pledged Russia's support for the Union, a declaration that was widely circulated in Washington and published in all the major Northern newspapers. At the same time, the Russian government refused to join mediation attempts by France and, to a lesser extent, Britain, unless the North and South expressed a willingness to negotiate. The possibility of any Russian mediation effectively ended, however, with the internal distraction of the Polish revolt of 1863. Despite decades of foreign rule, the Poles of the Russian Empire had retained a strong sense of national identity, and Polish nationalists still held out hope for independence. In January 1863 this desire for autonomy manifested itself in a sudden and violent uprising. The Russian government, however, was not interested in an independent Poland and suppressed the rebellion, leaving dreams of Polish independence unfulfilled once again.

It was at this complex moment that Alexander II decided to send a squadron of his Baltic fleet to the United States. Though historians have disagreed about Russia's motives, it is widely believed that the tsar wanted to prevent his best warships from being trapped in

Baltic ports in the event of a general European war over the Polish issue. Russia also may have simply wanted to demonstrate its growing naval capability. In any event, when some three thousand Russian sailors and officers arrived in the United States in September 1863, they enjoyed a hearty welcome and during the next two months they attended numerous dinners, receptions, balls, and parades in New York, Philadelphia, Baltimore, and Washington. A separate group of ships from the Pacific squadron visited the West Coast, docking in San Francisco. These sailors were fewer in number and their visit was longer, about ten months. Whatever the primary motive may have been, for many Americans, then and later, the arrival of the Russian fleet was a sign of friendship and a show of support for the North, and one that may have discouraged Britain and France from recognizing the Confederate government.

The visit of the Russian squadron in 1863 also inspired two men to learn more about Russia, leading to careers in Russian-American diplomacy. Eugene Schuyler had only recently completed a law degree at Columbia University when he visited one of the Russian warships, befriended several of the officers, and decided to learn Russian. A few years later, he got a consular post in Moscow and later in St. Petersburg and in 1867 became the first to translate Ivan Turgenev's *Fathers and Sons* into English. Similarly, Jeremiah Curtin had begun to study Russian while in college and developed a love of Russian literature, a passion further stimulated by the visit of the Russian fleet. Curtin subsequently obtained the position of secretary of the American legation in St. Petersburg, working there until the fall of 1869.

One other point of Russian-American contact during the Civil War years deserves mention—the plan to build a telegraph line connecting the two continents. In 1865 Western Union sent four men to Kamchatka in the far eastern region of the Russian Empire to explore the possibility of building a Pacific telegraphic cable. One of these men was George Kennan, the uncle of the later political advisor of the same name who became well-known during the Cold War era as the "father of containment." The men made their way up the Kamchatka Peninsula with the help of native guides to explore the route for the proposed cable, and according to Kennan's memoir of the expedition, the terrain was difficult and uncharted, and the men suffered greatly from the intense conditions. Ultimately, the expedition was a failure; in 1866, when an Atlantic cable was successfully completed, the Pacific project was suspended. Nonetheless, the project was an example of Russian-American cooperation and stimulated Kennan's interest in Russia, which would eventually result in a number of publications about that country.

Russians and Americans continued to feel connected by other shared experiences, as well. In April 1865, when President Abraham Lincoln was assassinated by John Wilkes Booth, Russia expressed sympathy for America's loss in both official and unofficial circles, and throughout Russia pictures of Lincoln were displayed next to those of Grand Duke Nicholas, the tsar's eldest and recently deceased son. Not long after Lincoln's assassination, Alexander II had his own brush with death. In April 1866, a suicidal and disturbed student named Dmitry Karakazov fired a shot at Alexander near one of the royal gardens in St. Petersburg. Though the attempt was unsuccessful, such an attack so soon after the American president's murder resonated in both nations. In response, Congress approved a joint resolution to congratulate Alexander on his narrow escape, and the new president, Andrew Johnson, selected Gustavus Vasa Fox, assistant secretary to the navy, to deliver it. The mission also had another purpose—to thank Russia for its continuing support and to flaunt this friendship by stopping in France and Britain on the way. Fox and the naval officers were received and welcomed in St. Petersburg, Moscow, and several cities along the Volga River and feted with dinners and receptions. As minor celebrities they had their photographs taken many times and their images were in great demand, and the Russian press reported widely on the visit. Fox met Alexander II personally to present the congressional declaration and took home many mementoes of his time in Russia that he would proudly display when the tsar's son visited America five years later.

••••••

Overall, then, the Russian-American friendship was on solid footing when the first serious conversations began about the possibility of the sale of Russian America. The two nations had faced and overcome numerous domestic and international crises and had remained on good terms. They represented fundamentally different political systems but had found common ground in their suspicions about Great Britain. Nonetheless, there were still challenges ahead before Russian America would become Alaska.

William Henry Seward, the primary actor behind the Alaska Purchase. [No Date Recorded] Retrieved from the Library of Congress, (LC-USZ62-21907).

CHAPTER II

Evident Advantages:
Origins and Objectives

*I*n the wee hours of the morning of March 30, 1867, the United States signed a treaty to purchase Russia's North American possessions, adding some 580,000 square miles of new land to the ever-expanding nation. Over the next few days, as the American press reported that its government had agreed to pay more than $7 million for a chunk of frozen coastline, there were mixed feelings and considerable surprise. Over the years, there had been blustery talk about the eventual acquisition of Russian America, of course, but in recent months no public discussion or debate had occurred that might suggest such a transaction was in the works nor had the country's largest newspapers given any indication that such a possibility was likely. The whole deal seemed to have transpired overnight. And, indeed, in some ways the agreement between Russia and the United States had come together very quickly. But there also was a long history behind the purchase, a history of which few Americans, or Russians, were aware.

• • • • • • •

The man whose name is most closely associated with the Alaska Purchase is William H. Seward. Born in 1801 in the town of Florida, New York, Seward studied law and practiced for several years before moving into politics, eventually serving as New York state senator, governor of New York, and secretary of state under Abraham Lincoln and Andrew Johnson. Slight of frame, with a large nose and thick, unruly hair and usually dressed in a plain, baggy suit, Seward was not an impressive physical specimen, but what he lacked in appearances, he made up in personality and character. His friends and colleagues often described him as courteous and genial, with a good sense of humor and a propensity for profanity. A supporter of emancipation, Seward had harbored fugitives in his home and had given financial support to Frederick Douglass's abolitionist newspaper, the *North Star*. During the Civil War, he displayed impressive skills in diplomacy, above all working to keep France and Britain from recognizing the Confederacy, an acknowledgment that would have surely lengthened and altered the evolution of the Civil War. He worked with Lincoln for four years, and the two men developed a close personal relationship and a deep mutual respect. Like Lincoln, Seward recognized that he might sometimes be forced to set aside his own beliefs about human rights in the face of political necessity. Seward was also instrumental in maintaining good relations between Russia and the United States. Grateful for Russia's noninterventionist stance in the Civil War, Seward was able to repay the favor during the Polish rebellion in the Russian Empire in 1863 when he rejected French requests to join an international declaration of protest to the tsar. Seward was sympathetic to the Poles but had faith in Alexander's liberalism and wisdom. The United States would not interfere in Russia's domestic affairs.

Seward was also a true expansionist, and his vision of empire and America's destiny dominated U.S. policy even after his departure from government life. He had long made it known that he believed that America's fate was to expand and take over the entire continent. In 1846 Seward wrote that while he would not support annexation of British North America at the expense of war and loss of human life, he could not deny his conviction that "the popular passion for territorial aggrandizement is irresistible. . . . The monarchs of Europe are to have no rest while they have a colony remaining on this continent. France has already sold out. Spain has sold out. We shall see how long before England inclines to follow their example." Fourteen years later, speaking in St. Paul, Minnesota, during the campaign of 1860, Seward directly addressed the presence of Russia and Great Britain in the Pacific Northwest: "Standing here and looking far off into the northwest, I see the Russian as he busily occupies himself in establishing seaports, and towns, and fortifications, on the verge of this continent, as the outposts of St. Petersburg, and I can say, 'Go on and build up your outposts all along the coast, up even to the Arctic Ocean—they will yet become the outposts of my own country . . .'" In the same vein, he added, "I look off on Prince Rupert's Land and Canada, and see there an ingenious, enterprising and ambitious people, occupied with bridging rivers and constructing canals, railroads and telegraphs . . . and I am able to say, 'It is very well, you are building excellent states to be hereafter admitted into the American union.'" Seward's grand vision of a massive American empire also included territory beyond the North American continent. He was eager to obtain Hawaii and tried to establish a reciprocity treaty in 1867 with the possibility of eventual annexation. He wanted Alaska, as well, to sandwich British Columbia between American territories and to create a foothold for naval and commercial operations in that area, creating an access point to Asia. Finally, it was under Seward that the United Stated acquired the Midway Islands.

Seward did not pull off the Alaska deal alone, however. He had a steadfast ally in Eduard Stoeckl, Russia's minister to the United States between 1854 and 1868. Stoeckl, who was married to an American woman, was personally popular and active in the social activities of

Washington D.C. He was a strong advocate of the Russian-American friendship, placing great importance on the shared experience of emancipation and faithfully reporting all examples of American friendliness and sympathy to his government. The Russian minister was also an early supporter of the idea of selling Alaska to the United States. Recognizing the many problems and diminishing returns of the Russian-American colony, he believed that Russia should sell while that was still an option. Both before and after the sale was completed, Stoeckl worked tirelessly to ensure that everything went as planned. His role in the sale involved travel to Russia, graceful diplomacy, and, it would seem, bribery. Ultimately, the experience left him exhausted and ready to retire, but he did so with a sense of accomplishment.

There were others, of course, who played important roles in the making of the Alaska deal—Russian Grand Duke Constantine, who advocated the sale of Russian America for more than a decade and worked to convince his brother, Tsar Alexander II, that it was not worth retaining, and Senator Charles Sumner, who, despite his own misgivings, persuaded the Senate to ratify the treaty. But it was Seward and Stoeckl who made it happen, drafting the treaty, negotiating its terms, and securing its ratification by both nations.

· · · ● · · ·

The fate of Russian America had become a subject of concern and debate in Russia even before the outbreak of the Crimean War (1853–56), and there were some within the inner circle of the Russian government who believed that Russian America would never survive the slow but steady creep of American expansion. In 1853 Nikolai Muraviev, a Russian statesman who had been instrumental in extending Russian territory to the east into the Amur region, advised Tsar Nicholas I to cede the Russian-American colony to the United States. The Americans, Muraviev warned, would soon spread all over North America. A peaceful withdrawal by Russia would allow it to reconsolidate its forces in the Far East, while potentially building a closer relationship with the United States, despite the efforts of Great Britain and its agents. Ultimately, before Muraviev's suggestion could be considered, Russia's entry into the Crimean War in 1853 and Nicholas I's death in 1854 put any further discussion of this idea on hold.

Serious discussions of the future of Russian America began in the following year. Embroiled in the Crimean War, the Russian government was worried that Great Britain would use this opportunity to seize its North American holdings. In reaction to this fear, an agent for the Russian-American Company came up with the idea of executing a fictitious sale to a group of San Francisco merchants, the American-Russian Commercial Company. The contract for the fake transaction was drawn up in January 1854 and sent to Russian Minister Stoeckl in Washington, D.C., for approval. Stoeckl sought advice from Secretary of State William L. Marcy and California senator William M. Gwin, both of whom thought the sale was too transparent a scheme, one that might provoke the British to simply seize the Russian territory. In any case, before Stoeckl could send his response, other circumstances intervened. In late March, Great Britain agreed to exclude Russian America from the war, acting on its own fear that Russia might simply give the area to the United States.

Though this first exploration of an Alaskan sale went nowhere, it stimulated interest and curiosity in the United States and raised the possibility that Russia might indeed contemplate such a transfer in the future. In February 1854, for example, Seward hinted in a Senate speech on Kansas and Nebraska that the United States might one day purchase or conquer Russia's possessions in North America. Only a few months later, in the spring and summer of 1854, several American newspapers took a fresh look at Russian America and its potential role in international diplomacy. The *New York Daily Times,* for example, stressed Russia's weakness in holding on to this distant territory and reported that although Britain hoped to seize Sitka, there might be a deal in the works between Russia and the United

States for the transfer of Russian America. The paper advised the U.S. government to keep a "jealous eye" on the spread of British power in the Northwest and take advantage of "the concessions which Russia finds herself forced to make." Meanwhile, the *New York Herald* urged the United States to purchase Russian America immediately, warning, "Delay will preclude the possibility of our acquiring it, and will in all probability have the effect of aiding Great Britain in its promised conquest, and adding further strength to a rival whose power is already but too formidable on this continent."

The rumors inspired several American politicians to press the issue. Both Secretary of State Marcy and Senator Gwin, the same two men who had been consulted about the fictitious sale, were interested in developing American interests in the Pacific, the former pursuing the annexation of Hawaii and the latter advocating a greater American presence in the North Pacific. Though they knew that the rumors about Russian America were based on a complete fabrication, eventually they approached Stoeckl about the possibility of a genuine purchase. Stoeckl firmly declared that Russian America was not for sale, and his description of the incident makes it clear that it was nothing more than an inquiry and that no senior government official in the United States was involved in any way.

The Crimean War, which ended in 1856, was a humiliating defeat for the Russian Empire and shone a bright light on many of its shortcomings, particularly in the supplying and training of its military. It also caused some Russian officials to reevaluate Russia's imperial ambitions. In the spring of 1857, Grand Duke Constantine, brother of the new tsar, Alexander II, wrote to Minister of Foreign Affairs Alexander Gorchakov that Russia should sell its North American territories to the United States. The grand duke emphasized the needs of the Russian treasury, the declining value of the colony, and his belief that the Americans were eager to control the whole of North America. Gorchakov, who was cool on the idea of a sale, solicited the opinion of Baron Ferdinand von Wrangell, a former governor of Russian America. Wrangell estimated the colony's value at $7.4

million, though he recognized that circumstances might make the sale a wise move: "If it were not for the *fears of the future*, there could be no doubt that even 20 million silver rubles could not be regarded as a complete remuneration for the loss of possessions which promise important results in the development of industrial activity." In response to this advice, the foreign minister reported to Constantine that while a sale might indeed be possible, it should not take place until 1861, when the Russian-American Company's charter expired.

Even the Russian minister to the United States began to believe that selling Russia's North American holdings might be the best idea. In late 1857 Stoeckl expressed concern that the actions of the Russian-American Company would eventually lead to conflict between the Russian and American governments. He also wrote to Gorchakov of rumors that Brigham Young and his Mormon followers were planning to relocate to either Hudson's Bay or Russian America. Stoeckl worried that a Mormon invasion would present the Russian government with a dangerous dilemma—either use armed force to stop the influx of unwelcome guests or surrender part of the North American possessions. Tsar Alexander's response to this somber prediction was a notation in the margin of Stoeckl's letter that said, "This supports the idea of settling henceforth the question of our American possessions."

Grand Duke Constantine raised the issue once again in December 1857. Constantine believed that Russia's postwar recovery and financial stability were connected to the future of Russian America. In a long memo to Gorchakov, Constantine echoed Stoeckl's concerns about the problems of the Russian-American Company leading to future conflicts. He argued that the United States would eventually expand into the region in question and Russia should seize the opportunity to sell while it could. Believing that Russia's energy and resources should be focused on maintaining and improving its center, Constantine stressed that a North American colony was a luxury that Russia could ill afford. Despite the views of these Russian officials and the tsar's own inclination to sell, Gorchakov was still reluctant to pursue the sale and instructed Stoeckl to proceed cautiously and to wait for the Americans to make the first move. Consequently, nothing more occurred on the subject during the next year.

At the end of 1859, however, the Alaska question resurfaced. Senator Gwin received permission from President James Buchanan to approach Stoeckl informally about purchasing Russian America, using the assistant secretary of state as a liaison specifically to keep the conversation on an unofficial status. The suggested sale price was $5 million. Stoeckl was at first unsure about this tentative probing, but Secretary of State John Appleton assured him that if Russia was interested, the United States was eager to talk. Stoeckl passed this information on to his government in early 1860 and made his own opinion clear: it was time to let the North American holdings go. Echoing the views of other Russian officials, Stoeckl stated that the Russian-American Company was not profitable and, more importantly, was a threat to peaceful Russian-American relations. Moreover, the colony was vulnerable: "Any maritime power with which we shall be at war, could take them from us." The Russian minister advocated Russian expansion in Asia rather than North America and added one other significant point, that selling Alaska to the Americans would serve as a barrier to British interests in the region.

Only a few days after Stoeckl's memo reached Gorchakov and the tsar, another Russian official weighed in. This was Admiral Andrei Popov, commander of the Pacific Fleet, who in a memo to the Ministry of Foreign Affairs harshly criticized the administration of the Russian-American Company and stated unequivocally that Russia should sell if it had the chance to do so. Emphasizing the inevitability of American possession of Alaska and the centrality of the notion of manifest destiny to the American people, Popov declared, "Anyone who has lived in the North American life cannot fail to understand instinctively that this principle is entering more and more into the blood of the people and that new generations are sucking it in with their mother's milk." Though Gorchakov was still reluctant, he instructed Stoeckl to investigate the possibility of a sale, but added that it would have to be for more than $5 million. Before any of this could go further, however, American domestic affairs interfered. While President Buchanan may have hoped that a dose of expansion might be just the thing to distract the nation from the crisis of growing sectionalism, the timing was not right. Congress was hostile to Buchanan and any proposal he made would be soundly rejected. The president consequently dropped a number of foreign pursuits, including Russian America. Within months, Buchanan's Democratic Party was split and his efforts to maintain peace between the North and the South had alienated him from both sides. Any hope of purchasing Russian America would have to wait until the election of a new president.

On March 4, 1861, Abraham Lincoln took office in the midst of an immense crisis with a dangerous momentum. Five weeks later, the American Civil War began with the attack on Fort Sumter. Needless to say, the events of 1861 put all thoughts about the acquisition of Russian America on hold. But there were other consequences of the conflict that, in the long run, would make the cession more likely to occur. Russia's sympathy with the North during the Civil War, the common experience of emancipation, and the visit of the Russian fleet in 1863 strengthened the Russian-American bond. At the same time, the actions of Great Britain and its citizens drove a wedge between the two great English-speaking nations. During the Crimean War a decade earlier, the British tried to recruit American citizens for their army, the so-called Crampton affair, and later, during the Civil War, Great Britain sold ships to the Confederacy, resulting in the *Alabama* claims. These actions by British representatives intensified anti-British feelings in the United States and made some American officials view British expansion in North America even more suspiciously.

Though negotiations for the sale of Alaska may have stopped on the American side, the Russian government had continued to plan as though a sale would eventually take place. In 1860 Grand Duke Constantine initiated an investigation into the administration of the Russian-American Company. The final report harshly criticized the company's operations, noting in particular its inattention to the needs of the local population and its inability to sustain itself as a colony, and cited the company's problems with American smugglers and whalers. Subsequently, in 1863, Tsar Alexander convened a special commission to make recommendations on the future of Russian America. Although its stated purpose was not to decide the issue of sale, the commission's conclusions clearly addressed that question. While the report admitted that the Russian-American Company was problematic and the cost of maintaining the colony was not worth the amount it earned, it proposed that the colony's political significance might outweigh its shortcomings. Russia's presence in North America was key to its strength as an empire and its success in the Far East. Consequently, the committee made a group of recommendations to revise the policies and practices of the Russian-American Company, specifically calling for the end of its trade monopoly and advocating that it be placed under the Russian government's direct supervision. The suggested reforms, however, were very expensive, and the Russian-American Company threatened to dissolve if it lost its monopoly, leaving the Russian government to bear the full burden of administration. In the same vein, when the Russian State Council drafted a new charter for the company that reflected the recommendations of the special commission, the company rejected it completely. The Russian-American Company was not only difficult to deal with but also failing to turn a significant profit. In 1866, for example, it could only afford to pay its stockholders a dividend of one ruble forty-five kopecks, a paltry amount. (For a point of comparison, consider that in Fyodor Dostoevsky's novel *Crime and Punishment*, which appeared in the same year, the poor student Raskolnikov pawns a watch for one ruble fifteen kopecks.) The company needed a substantial loan to reinvigorate itself. There were London banks willing to come to the rescue, but in return they expected a guarantee that the company would not be liquidated through a sale to the United States.

This price was too high for the Russian Foreign Office and so the idea of British loans was abandoned.

In addition to these concerns, there was one final factor that encouraged Russian officials to rid themselves of the burdensome colony. In 1863 there were rumors that gold had been found along the Russian section of the Stikine River in Russian America. Fearing the discovery would attract a flood of American miners, the Russian-American Company asked St. Petersburg for a man-o-war. Though that particular gold rush never transpired, Stoeckl wrote to Gorchakov that he believed that the discovery of more gold in the area was inevitable; he had spoken with a geologist who confirmed the favorable geological conditions of the region. Indeed, in 1866, a man struck gold while digging a hole for a telegraph post for the Collins Overland Telegraph Line Company in Sitka. Neither the Russian-American Company nor the Russian government was in the position to manage the problems that would come with a large-scale gold rush.

· · · · · · ·

There was one other issue that brought Russia and the United States together in the Alaska deal: a shared distrust of Great Britain. Although Russia and Great Britain had joined forces with the great alliance that defeated Napoleon in 1814 and 1815, in subsequent years, and for the remainder of the century, the two nations were often at odds. Britain feared that Russia and the United States would sign an alliance and collaborate together against British interests, particularly in the Pacific Northwest, and this concern affected the Canadian colonies as well. Russia and Britain also eyed one another nervously in the Near East, as Britain anticipated that Russian expansion into Central Asia would threaten its security in the Indian subcontinent, the so-called Great Game. Britain had also, of course, fought against Russia in the Crimean War, so there was no love lost between the two governments.

The United States similarly had conflicts with Great Britain. The British presence in North America has a long history, of course, beginning with the first successful English settlement at Jamestown in 1607 and the subsequent conquest of New Netherland, which was renamed the Province of New York. The story of how these meager beginnings developed into the British-American colonies need not be repeated here. British influence remained south of the Canadian border for the most part, however. There was one notable exception: the formation and expansion of the Hudson's Bay Company and its operations. Founded in 1670 by a royal charter of King Charles II, the Hudson's Bay Company was granted exclusive rights to all natural resources and trade in the Hudson's Bay watershed, an enormous area that the company named Rupert's Land. Here, the company comfortably ran its business for decades, using Natives to catch and deliver pelts to the company's posts, posing a serious challenge to the well-established fur trade empire of France.

In the eighteenth century, however, British interests in North America changed dramatically. In 1713 Great Britain acquired Nova Scotia from the French at the conclusion of the War of Spanish Succession (1701–14), and thirty years later, the War of Austrian Succession (1744–48), known as King George's War in America, made it clear to the French authorities in Quebec that their empire was in a precarious position, facing both the threat of the British navy and the uncertain allegiance of the Native Americans. Ultimately, the Seven Years' War (1756–63) sealed the fate of the French empire in North America. The war resulted in the British conquest of New France, territory that stretched from Hudson's Bay down to the Gulf of Mexico and from Newfoundland to the Rocky Mountains.

The glow of Imperial victory was short lived, however, for a little more than a decade later, Great Britain faced a much more serious challenge: the rebellion of its American colonies. The outcome of the American Revolution had important consequences farther north as well. The British government realized it could no longer operate its Canadian possessions as a collection of separately functioning entities. Instead, it was decided that British North America, in its new strictly Canadian form, should be consolidated under a single government. Thus, Parliament passed the Constitutional Act of 1791, creating Upper Canada and Lower Canada, granting all citizens the same rights and privileges of other loyal subjects in North America and allowing colonial assemblies the right to collect taxes to pay for local administrative needs.

No sooner had Great Britain gotten its house in order regarding Canada than it faced another major challenge closer to home, but one that would have consequences abroad as well: war against France—first Revolutionary France and then Napoleonic France. Before this protracted series of wars had ended, London found itself in a war across the Atlantic as well. The War of 1812 lasted some two and a half years and pitted Great Britain and its Native American allies against the young United States. Though there were certainly many reasons that led the United States to declare war in 1812, including the impressment of Americans into the British navy and the seizure of ships—both consequences of Britain's war with France—one other significant factor was British support of the Native American nations in the Ohio Valley, who resisted American expansion beyond the Appalachians. The conclusion of the war in 1814 by the Treaty of Ghent made no territorial changes, but it did confirm a long section of the boundary between the United States and British America that had been agreed upon some years earlier. The War of 1812 did not resolve all of the problems between the United States and Great Britain, however. The two nations soon clashed again over other issues, such as fishing rights off the coast of the Atlantic provinces. Moreover, the Canadian-American border remained fortified and garrisoned as the British continued to suspect American dreams of annexing Canada. And, in fact, there were still boundary questions in the East. The boundary between the United States and British North America along the Maine, New Hampshire, New York, and Vermont borders was only settled in August 20, 1842, by the Webster-Ashburton Treaty.

Great Britain and the United States also clashed over competition in the Pacific Northwest. In 1779 a group of merchants in Montreal who hoped to establish a monopoly over the fur trade in the West formed the North West Company. During the course of the next forty years they expanded their trade area all the way to the Pacific Ocean, but by 1821 the North West Company was facing financial ruin. Having established no permanent trade posts out west and unable to sustain its trade interests over such great distances, the North West Company decided to merge with the Hudson's Bay Company, thereby extending the latter's reach all the way to the Pacific. Henceforth, British interests in the Pacific Northwest would largely coincide with those of the Hudson's Bay Company.

American merchants, of course, had arrived in the Pacific Northwest in the 1780s, about the same time that the North West Company had been established, and Russians had arrived even earlier. Consequently, from the first days of settlement in the Pacific Northwest there was a three-way rivalry between Russian, British, and American merchants over trading rights and boundaries, disputes that would eventually involve the governments that represented their interests. In 1818 the United States and Great Britain had signed a treaty that set the boundary between the United States and British North America in the Pacific Northwest at the forty-ninth parallel from present-day Minnesota to the Rocky Mountains. The region to the west of those mountains, known as Oregon Country to the Americans and as the Columbia Department (or Columbia District) to the British, would be jointly controlled by the two countries for a period of ten years. The treaty left an important question unanswered: what would the final boundary be? In the ensuing years, joint control became more and more difficult to manage and aggressive expansionists in the United States began to call loudly for annexation of the entire region, even if it meant war with Great Britain. President James Polk boldly stated in his inaugural address in March 1845 that America had a clear and unquestionable title to the entire Oregon territory but offered Great Britain a compromise, the extension of the forty-ninth parallel boundary all the way to the Pacific coast. When Great Britain refused, Polk rescinded his offer and renewed his demands for the entire area. Ultimately, the outbreak of war with Mexico in the spring of 1846 led American politicians to seek a new compromise. The result was the Oregon Treaty, which extended the boundary along the forty-ninth parallel and through the channel south of Vancouver Island. Eventually the British territories there were joined to form the Colony of British Columbia, and when the colony joined Canada in 1871, the forty-ninth parallel remained the border between Canada and the United States.

Border disputes were not the only source of tension between the two English-speaking giants. Great Britain and the United States also did not see eye to eye over the future of Texas. In 1840 Great Britain recognized Texas independence with several goals in mind. The British hoped that an independent, slave-free Texas would serve as a check on American expansion in the Southwest and could halt the spread of slavery farther westward. In addition to this goal of containment, Britain also hoped that Texas could become a serious rival to the Southern domination of the cotton market, while simultaneously providing a safe market for British manufactured goods. British foreign secretary Lord George Hamilton-Gordon Aberdeen was willing to take Great Britain to the brink of war with the United States in order to accomplish these goals, but not beyond, and in the end, the United States annexed Texas in 1845.

American expansionism led to conflicts in Central and South America as well. In 1840 Britain proclaimed Belize as a crown colony and hoped to use the Caribbean islands of the region as a hedge to block American expansion. Great Britain had also established a protectorate over the Mosquito Coast in 1848, and the following year butted heads with the United States over Tigre Island near Nicaragua. In 1850 after American businessman Cornelius Vanderbilt signed a contract with the Nicaraguan government to construct a canal through Nicaragua to connect the Pacific to the Atlantic, the United States and Great Britain signed the Clayton-Bulwer Treaty to clarify each nation's rights and limitations in the area. The treaty declared that neither the United States nor Britain would attempt to control exclusively any ship canal that might be built through Central America, nor would either nation move to fortify, colonize, or dominate the region. Finally, Britain and America competed to control Hawaii. Britain had signed a treaty guaranteeing the integrity of Hawaii in 1843, but within a few short years American missionaries, who had become landowners and advisors to the Hawaiian king, became worried about the rivalry of Great Britain and France over Hawaii. In response, they proposed annexation to the United States, asking for immediate statehood. The United States would not agree to statehood and rejected the offer, but Great Britain had cause to be concerned over the possibility.

Over the next two decades, Great Britain and the United States would find themselves in two major wars, threatening Anglo-American relations while strengthening Russian-American relations. The first of these was the Crimean War. Though the United States never joined the war, American sympathy for Russia and the signing of a maritime neutrality agreement alarmed Great Britain. America's offer to mediate a settlement did nothing to lessen these fears. The British were also vexed by the open anti-British sentiment expressed in American newspapers. Meanwhile, the British recruitment of soldiers in the United States angered both Russian and America officials and resulted in the arrest of several British recruiters and the dismissal of the British minister to the United States, John F. Crampton.

Relations between Great Britain and the United States declined further during the American Civil War and the years immediately after. It was widely feared in the United States that British dependence on American cotton would bring it into the war on the side of the South. For their part, the other powers of Europe were concerned that they might reluctantly be drawn into the conflict through some sort of incident at sea or a dispute over protection of sea lanes and international commerce. Moreover, the Union's declaration of a blockade of the entire Confederate coast raised problematic questions, for if the Union did not possess enough ships to suffocate Southern trade, as many in Europe suspected, then the attempted blockade would be considered a "paper blockade," allowing other powers to disregard it. Questions about the definition of neutrality and to what degree recruiting and commissioning ships abroad was a violation by other nations only made matters worse. From this vantage point, the American Civil War, which has been viewed through a domestic lens, was a crisis with serious international implications.

The threat of British intervention was highest early in the war, partly because it was widely believed that reunion between the North and South was impossible and that the war was destined to end in Southern independence. Many British politicians, consequently, favored some sort of mediation or intervention to bring the bloodshed, and loss of trade, to a quick end. The possibility that Great Britain might recognize the Confederacy was the most challenging issue in Anglo-American relations during the war. If the British formally acknowledged Southern independence, the Confederacy could declare nationhood and claim legal access to British ports and the right to negotiate military and commercial treaties. For Lincoln, Seward, and other policy makers in the North, mediation was equivalent to defeat.

There were several specific episodes during the Civil War that nearly pushed the United States and Great Britain into war with one another. Two of these deserve elaboration. The so-called *Trent* affair in the fall and winter of 1861–62 began when Union naval captain Charles Wilkes stopped the *Trent*, a British mail steamer, off the coast of Cuba and forcibly removed James M. Mason and John Slidell, the new Confederate commissioners to Great Britain and France, respectively. Though Wilkes became a hero in the North for this action, it was a serious breach of international law and an insult to British honor. In the words of historian Frank J. Merli, the seizure of the *Trent* "had stirred up that deep pool of anti-Americanism that lurked just under the surface." In the midst of the *Trent* crisis,

Great Britain enlarged its fleet in the Atlantic and sent more troops to Canada, a reminder that protection of British America was always a factor in Anglo-American relations in this period.

The second incident was the *Alabama* affair. Though Great Britain was officially neutral, many British merchants continued to do business with the South by selling ships to the Confederate government. The most notorious example was the *Alabama*, which was built in Liverpool in 1862. For two years the warship terrorized the seas, confiscating goods and burning ships headed to or from the North until it sank off the coast of France in 1864. Subsequently, the United States accused Britain of failing to enforce its own laws of neutrality and demanded reparations. The matter dragged on for years and was not settled until the Washington Treaty of 1871 in which London agreed to pay $15.5 million in damages.

Finally, there is one other point of contention between the United States and Great Britain that deserves greater attention—the status of Canada and British fears of annexation movements on both sides of the border. The history of these annexation proposals is a distinct yet interwoven part of the narrative of Anglo-American relations in this period before Canadian Confederation. In 1775, during the American Revolution, a detachment of revolutionary soldiers made a failed attempt to seize Quebec, and when the war ended, Benjamin Franklin tried to persuade the British ministry to cede the territory to the United States. The young American nation feared Canada as "a British knife poised for a thrust" against the northern states. In the War of 1812, the American military struck again, this time in the western part of Canada, believing that the inhabitants of the area would rise up to support them. They were wrong. During the next few decades, there was little talk about annexation, but the suggestion did resurface periodically. In 1837 and 1838, for example, armed rebellions erupted in Upper and Lower Canada with demands for more responsible government. Though these rebellions were quickly put down, they also gave birth to a series of secret organizations called Hunters' Lodges, many of which were formed in the United States. In

1838 delegates from these lodges met in Cleveland and, claiming to form a provisional government for Canada, launched a series of attacks on Canadian soil. Known as the Patriot War, this brief episode was unsuccessful, but it appealed to the national myth that America's spirit of republicanism and free enterprise was an irresistible magnetic force. Moreover, some Americans thought that these provincial rebellions were proof that British America would one day free itself from British control, either as an independent country or as a part of the United States.

Talk of annexation became more serious in the 1840s. In 1846 the British Parliament repealed the Corn Laws—which set duties on all grain imports into Britain for the protection of British agriculture—bringing an end to the preferential treatment of Canadian wheat in its home market of Great Britain. The result was economic depression, which Canadians blamed on the removal of imperial preference. Over the next few years, as efforts to negotiate a reciprocity treaty with the United States floundered, many Canadians began to seriously ponder the benefits of annexation. Still, most were not yet ready to make such a significant change of course. In 1849, however, a group of businessmen took the leap, forming the Montreal Annexation Association and demanding political union with the United States as the answer to Canada's financial woes. Fortunately for British officials, the movement remained geographically limited and was hampered by competing concerns about the guarantee of religious freedom in America. The annexation movement of 1849 did accomplish one significant thing: It convinced British officials that Canada must have a reciprocity treaty with the United States. The governor general of the Province of Canada, Lord Elgin, was deeply concerned. Elgin wrote to Colonial Secretary Lord Grey: "A great deal of this talk is, however, bravado . . . but if England will not make the sacrifices which are absolutely necessary to the put the colonists here in as good a position commercially as the citizens of the States . . . the end may be nearer at hand than we wot [sic] of." Several months later, he again warned Lord Grey that if the commercial imbalance was not corrected, "there is nothing before us but violent agitation, ending in convulsion on annexation." To British prime minister Lord John Russell, he added, that without a reciprocity treaty, "arguments will not be wanting to those who seek to seduce Canadians from their allegiance." Elgin had reason to be concerned. In 1853, in a speech dedicating a university in Columbus, Ohio, Seward said, "Canada, although a province of Great Britain, is already half annexed to the United States. She will ultimately become a member of this confederacy, if we will consent—an ally, if we will not allow her to come nearer." Ultimately, Elgin succeeded in getting the treaty. After several failed attempts, an agreement was finally hammered out in June 1854. The Elgin-Marcy Treaty eliminated tariffs between the United States and Canada and increased exports from British North America to the United States. But the treaty also created a situation quite the opposite from what British officials had expected. Instead of killing the annexation movement, the new trade arrangement led Canadians to become increasingly dependent on the American market, so much so, it was feared, that another depression might reignite the annexation flame.

And, in fact, there continued to be calls for annexation on both sides, especially in an area north of Minnesota called the Red River settlement. Scotch settlers had established a community here in 1812, and as the settlement grew and formed a government, it sought to become a crown colony. In 1858–59 residents of the Red River settlement petitioned to join Canada, but British officials were not interested in expanding farther west and turned them down. Politicians in Minnesota then seized the opportunity to appeal for the absorption of the settlement into the United States, and there were many residents who supported this idea. In 1860 the legislature of Minnesota presented the idea to Congress, and murmurings about annexation of the region continued for several more years. Ultimately, the Red River settlement would become part of the province of Manitoba during the process of Canadian confederation.

Before any of this could occur, however, the American Civil War erupted and Canada became a pawn in a bloody game. As tensions between the federal American government and Great Britain rose over the possible recognition of the Confederacy and specific incidents like the *Trent* affair and the *Alabama* dispute, there were also more direct attempts by Confederate agents to organize riots in Canada, as well as actual incursions from Canada into the Northern states. In addition, British America became a refuge for slaves, Union deserters, and escaped Confederate prisoners. All of this finally led the American government to terminate the reciprocity treaty at the conclusion of the war. Some Canadians believed, however, that Seward had ended the treaty to starve the provinces into submission and toward annexation. For about a year, the Canadian government attempted to resurrect the treaty with the United States, but when it became apparent that there was no hope, another wave of annexationist sentiment arose in Canada. The new movement was strongest in big cities like Toronto and Montreal, but it lacked the vigor and organization of previous movements and soon died out. Still, concerns about annexation persisted. In March 1865, Robert Walker, a former senator from Mississippi, visited Canada, giving birth to rumors that he had been sent there by the American government to stimulate an interest in political union. Later that year, John Potter, the American consul-general at Montreal, seemed to confirm these suspicions when he made a statement at a commercial convention in Detroit indicating that Canadians wanted annexation. Meanwhile, an ad in the *Brooklyn Eagle* called for volunteers to invade either Canada or Mexico.

The British had other reasons to fear for the future of their North American colony. The Fenian Brotherhood, a secret organization of Irish republicans, threatened to invade Canada in order to divert British troops so that a simultaneous revolt in Ireland could succeed. The Fenians had approximately a hundred thousand members in the United States, but it was also from America, specifically New

York and Vermont, that they launched raids in 1866. In the spring of 1867, the American consul in Montreal, William Woods Averell, reported that the Canadians were on constant alert regarding Fenian movements and warned that "no more prejudicial event could at this time transpire than a Fenian invasion . . . thousands of people [Canadians] who are now indifferent would be aroused against the United States and asperities and prejudices awakened in the minds of all, even our friends, that would defeat every legitimate effort of the liberal party."

There was one region of Canada that was especially vulnerable to annexation sentiments, the colony of British Columbia. Sparsely populated and underdeveloped until 1858, the colony had enjoyed a brief boom with the discovery of gold, but by 1865 residents were struggling and began to believe their future rested with their relationship with the United States rather than Great Britain or Canada. During the Civil War, Great Britain had left British Columbia undefended, apparently deciding that it was in Britain's best interests to divest itself of the colony as soon as it could responsibly and honorably do so. Not surprisingly, beginning in 1866, colonists in British Columbia began to agitate for annexation, with Vancouver Island at the center of the movement. Newspapers in the colony acknowledged that British Columbia's relationship to the United States was closer than to either Canada or Britain and expressed support for annexation, and in mid-September a group of citizens met in Victoria and voted to ask the British government for permission to join the United States. American officials, of course, took notice of this movement and some, like Seward, sought to exploit it. In early 1866 E. H. Derby, a congressional investigator, informed Seward of the rising discontent in British Columbia and suggested to Seward that Great Britain settle the *Alabama* claims by giving the United States its Pacific territory. Seward supported this suggestion and forwarded it to the Senate for consideration. He then approached the British government with the idea and continued to push it over the next year or so.

All of these threats and rumors, combined with other issues motivated the British government to explore confederation. The discussion of Canadian confederation had, in fact, been around as long as the idea of annexation. Ironically, British officials had hesitated to pursue the idea because they worried that confederation would lead to independence and then absorption by the United States. Now, in the 1860s, in the face of American expansionism and Canadian economic distress, confederation seemed like a good idea to stop annexation movements on both sides and create a Canadian national economy. In particular, British officials were fearful of the possibility of a renewed American interest in expansion at the conclusion of the Civil War, and this concern was specifically mentioned in the debates and discussion about confederation. In 1864 the maritime provinces of Nova Scotia, New Brunswick, and Prince Edward Island met to discuss creating their own federation. Other Canadian provinces soon joined the conversation, and the process of confederation was underway. Even in the midst of these discussions, the fear of American sprawl continued, as noted in the words of George Brown, president of the executive council of Canada: "The inclusion of British Columbia and Vancouver Island is rather an extreme proposition, but it would be wrong to exclude them in the formation of the scheme. The Americans are encroaching."

Brown had reason to be anxious. In 1866 Nathanial P. Banks, a representative from Massachusetts, and Congressman Henry J. Raymond, editor of the *New York Times*, introduced a bill that called for annexation of British North America. The bill went nowhere, but it did not go unnoticed. Moreover, by the spring of 1867, the American consul William Averell was reporting from Montreal that not all Canadians supported the idea of confederation and that some viewed it as a creation "for the political and pecuniary benefit of the ruling aristocratic class." Averell had it on good authority that if the liberals should attain a majority in the House of Commons in the upcoming elections, they would immediately appeal to the queen, "praying for a change of many features of the Confederation Bill or a discontinuation of their relations with the Empire and permission to act for themselves . . . asking permission to join the United States at once."

On March 29, 1867, the day before the Alaska treaty was signed, Queen Victoria approved the British North America Act. The Dominion of Canada came into existence on July 1, 1867, and comprised four provinces: Ontario, Quebec, New Brunswick, and Nova Scotia. Confederation did not end all fears about American expansion and annexation, however. In 1867 Nathanial Banks once again introduced a bill calling for Canadian annexation. Although Banks's appeal did not represent majority views, it was alarming nonetheless to British ears. Moreover, as the battle over the *Alabama* claims continued, it became evident to some, particularly the American minister to Great Britain Charles Francis Adams, that Seward's obstinate stand was intended to drive the British to the point of surrendering British Columbia. In fact, there were those in British Columbia who saw the purchase of Alaska as an opportunity to push from the other side of the border. Allen Francis, U.S. consul in Victoria, reported that many locals, "those claiming to be loyal subjects included, are now urging with great unanimity annexation to the United States as their only salvation—as the only means of retrieving the Colonies from their present embarrassment and decline." Though annexation sentiment in British Columbia remained strong through 1867, Seward's dreams were not borne out. Nonetheless, it should come as no surprise that both Canada and Great Britain would be less than thrilled about the Alaska Purchase and its potential impact on their interests.

· · · · · · ·

There was one more reason that the United States was interested in purchasing Alaska—the Asian trade market. Though America had been involved in the trade of furs with China since the late eighteenth century, two major events heightened American interest in this part of the world. In 1844 the United States and China signed their first commercial treaty, negotiated by Caleb Cushing. This was followed by U.S. territorial expansion in the West, first the annexation of Oregon territory in 1846 through a treaty with England and then the absorption of California in 1848 after war with Mexico. These acquisitions meant new ports on the Pacific coast and correspondingly led to a greater interest in the trade possibilities of Asia. Consequently, once the door to China had been opened, Japan was the next target. In 1853 Commodore Matthew Perry arrived in Japan with a letter from President Millard Fillmore asking the emperor for the opening of trade but also for friendly relations, particularly with regard to shipwrecked sailors or ships in need. When Perry returned to Japan a year later, a treaty was signed, but it did not mention trade. The United States finally signed its first trade agreement with Japan in 1858. By 1867 the U.S. government had already opened the way for steady commercial relations with China and Japan, and the purchase of Russian America would facilitate the expansion of this trade while potentially reducing the time and cost invested in Pacific trade routes. During the debates over ratification and appropriation for the Alaska deal, many would point to these benefits.

· · • • · ·

When Stoeckl returned to St. Petersburg in the autumn of 1866, the Russian minister was immediately approached by both Grand Duke Constantine and Finance Minister Mikhail Reutern, each of whom was eager to find out if the Americans were still interested in purchasing Russian America. When Stoeckl answered in the affirmative, Constantine and Reutern moved to get Alexander's approval. In December 1866, Alexander received a report containing the opinions of several important men—Minister of Finance Reutern, Grand Duke Constantine, and Russian Minister Stoeckl. Though the men differed slightly in their precise reasons, all of them agreed that it was in Russia's best interest to cede Russian America to the United States.

The tsar received this proposal and, at Minister of Foreign Affairs Gorchakov's suggestion, immediately called together a meeting of Reutern, Constantine, Stoeckl, and Vice Admiral Nicholas Krabbe, head of the Naval Ministry. At the conclusion of their discussion on that mid-December day, Alexander approved the sale of Alaska and authorized Stoeckl to begin negotiations.

Stoeckl returned to New York on February 15, 1867, after a rough transatlantic journey that had caused him to fall and injure his ankle. As a consequence, the Russian minister did not proceed directly to the capital, staying instead in New York to recuperate. Stoeckl made good use of his time, however, locating someone who could serve as a go-between with Seward. Gorchakov's instructions had not changed since the previous attempt; the idea of a sale must be initiated by the Americans. Though Stoeckl never revealed who served as his liaison, it has generally been assumed by historians that it was Thurlow Weed who was a friend of Seward's and in New York at the time to purchase the *Commercial Advertiser*. It is presumably through Weed that Stoeckl requested a meeting with Steward.

By the weekend of March 9, Stoeckl's ankle had healed enough to travel, and upon his arrival in Washington his first order of business was a meeting with Seward. On Monday morning, March 11, the two men met in Seward's office at the State Department, dancing carefully around the subject of Russian America, speaking of some of the conflicts in the area over fishing rights and American incursions. Since the Russian government would not lease the property nor offer greater fishing rights, Seward raised the subject of sale. Once Seward had opened the conversation, Stoeckl was free to proceed and informed the secretary of state that he had been given permission to begin negotiations for the sale of Russian America. Seward was no doubt elated by this news but reminded Stoeckl that he did not have authority to negotiate without the approval of President Andrew Johnson and the cabinet. Though Johnson often deferred to him in matters of foreign policy, the president still expected to be consulted. Seward was also aware that given the current mood of Congress, it would be critical to have the support of the cabinet. The following day, Seward presented the idea to Johnson and received his approval.

On Thursday, March 14, Seward and Stoeckl met again, and Seward informed the Russian minister of the president's support. Stoeckl was eager to move forward, even suggesting that he could begin to approach members of Congress, but Seward insisted that the negotiations must be kept secret for the time being. Stoeckl was a bit offended by Seward's refusal to accept his help, writing to Gorchakov some days later that Seward had selfishly wanted to claim all the glory for himself. It was also in this second meeting that the men began to talk about price. Seward began with $5 million, the number that had been bandied about in 1860, adding that the United States might be able to go as high as $5.5 million. Though little had been accomplished in any concrete sense at this point, Stoeckl was encouraged. The fact that Seward was already talking about price gave Stoeckl the confidence to cable the Russian government about the meeting, adding that he would try to get the highest price possible, $6 million or even $6.5 million.

The next step for Seward was to win over the members of the cabinet who he planned to see at their regular meeting on Friday. Seward prepared a draft treaty and a proposal to offer Russia as much as $7 million for Alaska and the Aleutian Islands. Though Seward had only offered Stoeckl $5.5 million the last time they met, he clearly anticipated more negotiation on price before the deal was complete. The meeting with the cabinet was surprisingly unremarkable. With the exception of a few small complaints about the draft treaty, there was little discussion and the proposal was unanimously approved. Seward could resume negotiations in earnest.

In the following days, Seward and Stoeckl hammered out the specifics of the treaty, including questions about the standing obligations of the Russian-American Company with other entities, such as the Hudson's Bay Company and the American Russian Commercial Company, which had been selling Alaskan ice in California for more than a decade. At some point during these negotiations the price climbed to $6.5 million. There were also deliberations about the immovable property left behind by the Russian-American Company. In discussing this point, Seward and Stoeckl came to an agreement that the warehouses and other buildings belonging to the company would be included. Stoeckl later described to Gorchakov that he conceded this point to Seward in return for the selling price being raised from $6.5 million to $7 million. Stoeckl felt safe in making this deal since he estimated the value of the company's buildings to be less than $500,000. With these issues settled, Seward insisted that Stoeckl cable the treaty to St. Petersburg immediately for approval, which he did on March 25. Only a few days later, the Russian minister received word that Tsar Alexander had agreed to the treaty with two amendments. The proposed treaty stated that the United States would pay for Alaska ten months after the signing of the treaty; the tsar wanted to receive payment sooner, and he also requested that the payment would be made in London instead of Washington. Finally, Alexander desired that the United States respect the American Russian Commercial Company's exclusive right to export ice from Russian America.

Within twenty-four hours, the proposal was formalized. Stoeckl, eager to deliver the good news immediately, walked over to Seward's home, only a few minutes away. Interrupting the Seward family at a game of whist, Stoeckl offered to meet the secretary at his office the following day, but Seward would have none of it. Ready to wrap up the deal, Seward declared that he could summon together his staff that evening if the Russian minister could do the same. As the two men called together their secretaries and clerks, Seward also sent his son, Frederick, who served as assistant secretary of state, to find Charles Sumner, chairman of the Senate Foreign Relations Committee, who still had no idea that the Alaska Purchase was in process. Sometime later that evening, Sumner received the note Frederick had left and rushed over to Seward's house where Stoeckl and Frederick explained the terms of the treaty and asked for his support. Sumner was noncommittal and returned home.

Shortly after midnight, Stoeckl met Seward at the State Department where the two men worked out a few final details. In keeping with the tsar's request, Stoeckl asked that the payment date be pushed up and that the deposit be made in London, which would be more convenient for the Russians. He also made an additional request, that the contract to provide ice to San Francisco be honored until its expiration the following year. None of Stoeckl's requests were met. Seward pointed out that the House of Representatives would not meet again until December, so the appropriation could only occur then. He promised, however, that the payment would be made. Stoeckl had also been assured by Finance Committee Chairman Thaddeus Stevens that he would have the appropriation passed on the very day that Congress reconvened. As for the question of payment in London, he declared this was also impossible. Finally, the secretary made it clear that the United States could not be held accountable for obligations made by the Russian-American Company before the purchase. Stoeckl was in no position to challenge any of these points, but as a consolation, Seward added $200,000 to the purchase price. The revised treaty was written out in two copies, and at about 4:00 a.m. on March 30, the men gathered in Seward's office and signed the famous document in the presence of Assistant Secretary William Hunter and secretary to the Russian legation, Vladimir Bodisco. Though the famous commemorative painting by Edward Leutze shows the presence of Charles Sumner, he was not, in fact, there. Sumner's great role would be played in the months that followed.

The treaty that the United States and Russia concluded for the sale of Russian America was fairly brief and straightforward, consisting of seven articles and a preamble that spoke of the two countries wishing to "strengthen [sic], if possible, the good understanding which exists between them." The first article laid out the boundaries of the territory to be ceded. The eastern boundary would be that established by the Russian-British convention of 1825 at 54 degrees 40 minutes north latitude, just south of present-day Ketchikan. The western limit would pass through the Bering Strait on the parallel of

65 degrees 30 minutes north latitude, just north of where Fairbanks sits today, and ultimately would include the Aleutian Islands. Several other articles dealt with the particulars regarding people and property in the territory to be transferred. Article Three, for example, stated that Russian inhabitants had the option to return to Russia or remain in the territory and enjoy the rights of American citizens. Native inhabitants—"the uncivilized tribes"—would be subject to the laws and regulations that the United States government saw fit to impose. Stoeckl later wrote to Gorchakov that he was in no position to argue in favor of any particular points regarding the Natives since to do so would imply continued interference in the ceded territory. The Russian minister felt, however, that the Natives were peaceable and would be well treated by the Americans. Article Two stipulated that the purchase included all lands and public buildings that were not private individual property but excluded the Orthodox churches built by the Russian government, which would remain the property of the congregations. As for fortifications and military posts, those would be given over to the United States, and Russian troops would be withdrawn as soon as possible. One other sticking point that had ultimately affected the final selling price concerned the commitments of the Russian-American Company to other entities. In the end, the treaty stated that the territory would be free and unencumbered by any previous obligations established by or with other companies.

For all of this the United States agreed to pay $7.2 million in gold at the Treasury in Washington within ten months after ratification, though the cession and assumption of full possession of the territory would occur immediately after the ratification by both parties. Stoeckl was concerned about the delay in payment, but he believed he had no choice but to trust the promises he had been given. He admitted to Gorchakov that his only other option would have been to change the date at which the property would be officially ceded. In the end, he chose not to do this, noting, "The American agents and our own will not arrive on the spot until toward the end of the year and not until then will there take place the actual delivery of the territory, which will in fact coincide with the payment of the indemnity." Stoeckl miscalculated here, and it would be this last point— the actual payment—that would prove to be one of the most difficult parts of the treaty to execute.

"THE BIG THING"

OLD MOTHER SEWARD: I 'll rub some of this on his sore spot:
it may soothe him a little.

NAST'S CARTOON ON THE ALASKA PURCHASE

From " Harper's Weekly " for April 30, 1867.

CHAPTER III

Seward's Chimerical Project:
Public Reaction and Ratification

*T*hough the treaty to acquire Russian America was signed in March 1867, it would be well over a year before the purchase would be completely approved and paid for, and during the course of those seventeen months, there would be a great deal of debate over the wisdom of the acquisition, the prerogative of the House to approve the appropriation of funds, and the integrity of those involved in the deliberations. Interestingly, the majority of the opposition came from politicians in Washington, not the American public. Though history has often repeated the humorous names assigned to America's new acquisition—the Russian American Folly, Seward's Icebox, Walrussia—in truth, most newspapers voiced support for the treaty, or at least remained relatively neutral. Even the loudest critic, Horace Greeley's *New York Tribune*, eventually toned down its indignation and came around to a more positive view. In the end, the bitterest arguments took place in Congress where politicians were at war with one another over a whole host of issues, some of which were directly connected to the recent civil war.

· · · ● ● ● · ·

The Alaska treaty was presented to the Senate at ten o'clock in the morning on March 30, 1867, six hours after it was signed and two hours before the first session of the fortieth Congress was set to adjourn for three months. Seward arrived at the Capitol and immediately approached a number of individuals to win them over to his cause, hoping that the Senate would ratify the treaty immediately. Gideon Welles, secretary of the navy, was one of the first men informed of the treaty that day. Welles wrote in his diary that as he watched Seward buttonhole various senators, he was "somewhat amused and not a little disgusted with the little acts and overpowering egotism he [Seward] exhibited." He added, "The last is a growing infirmity." When the Senate convened, President Johnson presented the treaty for approval, and immediately Charles Sumner of Massachusetts moved to refer the treaty and its relevant documents to the Committee on Foreign Relations, which he chaired. Meanwhile, though Congress adjourned at noon, it was decided to hold a special session of the Senate from April 1 to April 20. At this point, Sumner, who had learned about the treaty only hours before, had not yet declared his support. In fact, Stoeckl confided to Gorchakov that Sumner had asked him to withdraw the treaty. Stoeckl believed that had a vote been taken immediately, it would have failed. Lucky for Seward and Stoeckl, there was a brief period of time between the initial presentation of the treaty and the official Senate vote.

Seward wasted no time in marshalling his forces on all fronts. Seward's friend Thurlow Weed owned the *New York Commercial Advertiser*, which reported the treaty in its March 30 afternoon edition and continued to print favorable articles over the following week that praised the territory's abundant resources and possibilities. Seward also received assistance from the *New York Times*, whose editor was another friend. There were also a number of letters published in the press by notable Civil War heroes—such as Montgomery Meigs, John Rodgers, and Henry Halleck—in support of the treaty. Meigs, for example, applauded the acquisition of Alaska and stated, "I can conceive of no greater boon to our Pacific States. . . . As a lover of my country and anxious for the growth and prosperity and strength and virtue of the nation, I should value Russian America, its fisheries and mines beyond the hot plains of Mexico or the fertile plantations of Cuba." Rodgers and Halleck expressed similar sentiments. Rodgers noted with humor that the cost of Alaska should not be a deterrent since "a few houses of Broadway would amount to as much." Not all of these were clearly solicited by Seward, but it is likely that some of them were.

Meanwhile, Seward used other methods to promote his project. The State Department published a pamphlet that consisted largely of reprints of the letters by Meigs, Rodgers, and others, along with additional information from the naturalist and scientist Spencer Baird of the Smithsonian Institution. Though Baird had not been to Alaska himself, in his capacity as assistant secretary of the Smithsonian, he had helped to oversee the study of its natural resources for about five years and had extensive correspondence with field observers. The secretary of state also began a series of dinners during which he tried to persuade his guests—senators and cabinet members—that the purchase of Russian America was a good move. Seward had also won the support of Republican Congressman Thaddeus Stevens who, despite his disagreements with Seward in the past, was an ardent expansionist.

Seward indeed had a challenge ahead of him. Leaving aside the fact that most senators knew nothing about Russian America, it was also the case that the Foreign Relations Committee was composed largely of men from the East who might not fully appreciate the benefit of this western acquisition. The rushed and secretive evolution of the treaty was also an obstacle to ratification; some senators thought it suspicious and unsettling. "Happily," Stoeckl reported to

Gorchakov, "there was an interval of some ten days during which Senators had time to reflect." Indeed, the *Sacramento Daily Union* made a similar observation in the second week of April, suggesting that if the two-thirds vote needed to ratify the treaty had not been reached yet, then the Senate should have more time to investigate. "Votes have been gained by delay and inquiry," the paper noted. In fact, it was during this time that Seward and other supporters went to work and, in the words of the Russian minister, "the Senators were converted one by one."

· · · ● · · ·

As the Senate debated the merits of the treaty, the American press and its readership engaged in some of the same conversations. The first report of the purchase appeared in the afternoon edition of the *New York Commercial Advertiser* on March 30, and on the following day, the story appeared across the country. Seward's deal with Russia had been concluded quickly and in secret, and there had been no previous discussions of such an acquisition in public or official venues. Despite their surprise, many of the early newspaper articles were positive and tended to focus on the same arguments to explain why Seward's deal was a good thing.

The most popular argument in favor of the purchase was the economic one. Proponents of the treaty declared that Russian America would bring great financial benefits to the United States. On April 1, the *Times* pronounced in an article entitled "Important Annexation" that the purchase was "hailed with delight" by Americans for its addition of "valuable fur country." In subsequent days, the *Times* continued to praise the Alaska treaty and to print information from other sources that backed that assessment. Moreover, various reports clearly indicated that Russian America was not the "dreary waste of glaciers, icebergs, white bears and walrus" that some had made it out to be. In fact, the land was rich with gold, copper, iron ore, fish, timber, and fur-bearing animals, and even the ice, so central to many of the critics' jokes, could be harvested and sold. The editors acknowledged that people in the eastern United States might not recognize how important this purchase was for the western part of the country. It added that the secretary of war, Edwin Stanton, had received many telegrams from people who had been to Russian America testifying to its value.

Indeed, newspapers on the West Coast, especially those from San Francisco, Sacramento, Portland, and Seattle, were particularly enthusiastic about the possibilities of the new territory. A number of them focused on the fisheries, while others concentrated on the reports of copper, silver, gold, and fur. The *Sacramento Daily Union* wholeheartedly embraced the treaty and confirmed that on the West Coast there was "a remarkable unanimity of sentiment on the subject." The paper also criticized those who opposed the purchase because of ignorance or outdated and irrelevant arguments. For example, while the expansion of slavery had once been a reason for some to oppose the acquisition of new territory, the Civil War had eliminated that concern. Moreover, the sheer remoteness of Russian America should cause no objection since steamers easily traveled from Sitka to San Francisco and the development of the telegraph allowed easy communication with Washington, D.C., so that San Francisco was "nearer the Capital [*sic*] of the nation than Boston was before Morse harnessed the lightning." The paper predicted that the extension of telegraph communication and railroads would only make this more true in the years to come and would "bring the people of the most widely separated sections into intimate intercourse, until the desire to form part of one grand, free nationality will stir the minds of all, from Behring Straits to Yucatan."

Though the West Coast may have been more unanimous and favorable in its assessments, many other newspapers, even those on the East Coast, applauded the acquisition. Both the *Boston Daily Evening Transcript* and the *Boston Advertiser* wrote of Russian America's abundant resources, the latter also noting that it would serve as a good location for a naval station. Similarly, the *Philadelphia Inquirer* predicted that this new possession might give the United States command over the Pacific, while the *National Intelligencer* in Washington, D.C., wrote of the abundant furs, fish, and lumber. Newspapers in cities across the nation—for example, Albany, Louisville, Chicago, Memphis, and New Orleans—expressed similar sentiments.

Another popular reason to support the treaty was the idea of manifest destiny. The *New York Times* argued that in addition to Russian America's commercial benefits, its acquisition was also part of the natural course of events for the growth of the United States: "The American people are not ambitious of conquest, but they are ambitious of growth and greatness. . . . A young nation can no more arrest its growth, without death, than can a young man. When a nation ceases to grow, it begins to decline." The United States, moreover, had other reasons to expand. The *Times* asked, "We believe that republican institutions are the best for the happiness of mankind. Why not extend them if we can do it without injustice?" Finally, the *Times* reasoned that although the American principle of avoiding entangling alliances was certainly wise, "It would be most absurd in this great nation to check its growth in any direction by fears of foreign interference or too great extension." Other papers concurred. The *New York Herald* wrote of an "inevitable destiny which, in time, must give us the whole of North America," while the *Bangor Daily Times* declared, "We grow and swell out naturally . . . and without expansion we should burst."

Many supporters assumed that the acquisition of Russian America could eventually lead to the absorption of British Columbia. The *New York World* favored the treaty in part because it was "an advancing step in that manifest destiny which is yet to give us British North America." Many other papers agreed that the treaty would likely lead to the annexation of British Columbia. The desire by many in the United States to absorb British Columbia was tied to an overall wish to thwart Great Britain more generally. The *Times* joked that if Great Britain had loudly opposed the Alaska Purchase, then the Senate would have ratified the treaty immediately. In fact, many people saw the blocking of Great Britain as one of the chief benefits of the treaty. The *New York Times* declared that since the time of independence, England had sought to exclude America's fisherman from the fertile waters of Newfoundland and the surrounding seas. Consequently, should the Senate fail to ratify the Alaska treaty, it would "abdicate ... the empire of the sea, which the United States ought naturally to hold; and to render ourselves inferior in one full half of the strength of nations, to our most persevering and only formidable rival." The *Herald* similarly noted that the treaty placed "British possessions on the Pacific coast in the uncomfortable position of a hostile cockney with a watchful Yankee on each side of him," and suggested that "it will be well enough for England if she is discreet enough to profit by the example of Russia and to withdraw gracefully from a continent where institutions are out of place and where her intrigues can only bring trouble upon her colonies and humiliation to her government at home." Other papers, including the *St. Paul (MN) Pioneer*, the *San Francisco Daily Alta California*, the *San Francisco Bulletin*, and the *Sacramento Daily Union*, reiterated these jingoist notions. There were those, however, who thought the treaty might have the opposite effect, hastening the process of Canadian Confederation and driving British Columbia into Canadian arms.

There was one other potential benefit of purchasing Russian America that appeared in the discussions—greater access to the Asian market. The *New York Times* reported on March 31 that Russian America possessed a number of good harbors and added that "the lines of commercial intercourse between our Western ports and China, Japan, &c., . . . could hardly fail to profit by the additional feeders from a new quarter." A week later, the paper noted, "The main importance of this acquisition grows out of its bearing upon our future trade with Japan, China and the other countries of Eastern Asia" and continued to cite this benefit throughout the month of April and into early summer. Seward underscored this notion in a speech he gave in Annapolis that summer. According to the *New York Times*, Seward said, "In acquiring Russian America we get not only her products but a market for them. . . . China is one of the best markets for furs; and the ease of transportation from the Aleutian Isles to China is too well known to need comment."

Finally, many newspapers cited Russia's historic friendship with the United States. The *New York Herald* referred to the treaty as a "spontaneous offer of the Emperor," concluding "Russia in her friendship for this country, from a desire to contribute to its progress and power, and for the purpose of perpetuating intimate relations with it ceded these vast possessions for an insignificant sum." The *Chicago Republican* similarly believed that the treaty's chief significance was as "evidence of the good will of the Russian Government towards the United States." Newspapers in Philadelphia, Baltimore, and San Francisco echoed these same ideas about the importance of the Russian-American relationship.

Not everyone supported the acquisition. Initially, the *New York Tribune* was the loudest critic of the treaty, but even it initially assessed the treaty in largely favorable terms. On April 1 the *Tribune* declared Russian America "a vast section of territory, the possession of which will influence in our favor the vast trade of the Pacific." The *Tribune* also acknowledged the value of the area's fisheries and fur trade. It was only after the Senate had ratified the treaty that Greeley began to attack the purchase. Of those newspapers that came out against the Alaska treaty, there were three major lines of argument. The first and most common reason cited by the opposition was the perceived worthlessness of Russian America. Papers all over the country, including those in Louisville, San Antonio, Indianapolis, Chicago, New York, and Milwaukee, called the land a barren tract of ice. The *Nation* referred to the Alaska Purchase as "Mr. Seward's chimerical project of saddling us with a frozen desert of a colony." Lest there be any confusion about the magazine's viewpoint, the editor elaborated, "We do not want far-distant, detached colonies, nor ice and snow territories, nor Esquimaux fellow-citizens, nor Mt. Saint Elias, and there is nothing else to be had from Alaska and Barrow's Point, so far as we are informed." Doubtful that the territory's climate could be overcome, the *New York Tribune* used sarcasm more than once to register its disapproval, describing polar bears lounging among roses and barley growing on icebergs. The editor added, "We have heard of people going to Russian America, but never heard of anybody staying there except those who were frozen in the snow." The *New York Evening Gazette* called the purchase the "Russian American folly."

There were also concerns that the cost of Russian America was too high and that the United States' treasury was in no condition to spend so much money. The *New York Tribune* declared that the territory was "certainly not worth seven millions of dollars to a nation already possessed of more territory than it can decently govern, and burdened with debt." Though the *New York World* recognized some strategic benefits in the new acquisition, it did not believe in its potential riches, describing it as a "sucked orange." Though most Southern newspapers were neutral on the issue, several did suggest that the money could be better spent on the restoration of the South.

Finally, some editors attacked the treaty on principle because they opposed expansionism. The *New York Sun* warned that the idea of territorial expansion due to manifest destiny "contains an element of danger against which we cannot too carefully guard." The paper gave examples of nations such as Spain that had grown too big and had declined as a result. Acquiring new territory could be beneficial, if done with purpose. But, the current supporters of the Alaska treaty were like "the young frogs in the fable, who induced their mother to try the experiment of puffing herself up to the dimension of a cow. The old frog failed to accomplish the feat, but she burst in the process." *Harper's Weekly* was similarly unhappy with the prospect of territorial gain to satisfy "that vulgar sense of national honor which mistakes size for splendor." The United States, the *Harper's* editor suggested, should strengthen and secure the country's current possessions before seeking to expand. Referring to the South, the editor added, "The rule which, in the present alienated condition of a part of the country, should govern the policy of extension is not hard to discover. Mere expansion is undesirable." The editor was also upset by the secrecy of the treaty, which was "hurried through the Senate before there was fair opportunity for its intelligent discussion by the country," but it was the reckless acquisition of "the new national ice-house" that was most galling.

The *New York Times* took to task those who criticized the treaty. In particular, the *Times* attacked the *Tribune*, which had come out strongly against Seward's acquisition. Reiterating its own arguments in favor of the treaty, it added that though some newspapermen might fail to appreciate Seward's efforts, "the people, we believe, will neither undervalue his services, nor depreciate the importance of the acquisition to which they have led." The *Times* also attacked the *Evening Post*. Though it was not as guilty as the *Tribune* of "inventing all sorts of malicious absurdities" about Seward and his acquisition, it was "quite as prolific in suggesting motives why the Senate should refuse to sanction the purchase."

Supporters of the treaty believed that the initial opposition came largely from hatred of Johnson and Seward. In early April, the *New York Times* asserted, "While narrow-minded political bigots have been exhausting all their resources in branding him [Seward] as a traitor to his party, he has been quietly pursuing great objects of permanent and paramount interest to his country." Papers in Sacramento, San Francisco, and Detroit expressed similar suspicions. The *Sacramento Daily Union* harshly condemned those who let personal or political biases blur their vision, proclaiming, "The people don't care who negotiated this bargain. They can have no respect for a Senator who votes against the ratification simply because he dislikes the Secretary of State. The interests of the nation should be set above all partisan considerations when an issue of this nature is presented so that to the outside world, however fiercely we engage in faction fights, we shall always appear consolidated in favor of that which tends to enhance the power and glory of the republic."

There was one other comment, neither positive nor negative, that several papers made, an observation that anticipated some of the greatest concerns of the European powers about the Alaska deal.

Many believed that the purchase was related to Russia's interests in the Middle East and southeastern Europe, specifically, the eventual collapse of the Ottoman Empire and the international scrambling that would likely take place to seize the territory. Immediately after the signing of the purchase treaty, the *New York Times* reported that "influential parties regard it as significant of Russian policy, in view of impending European complications on the Eastern Question." The *New York World* and the *San Francisco Alta California* more pointedly stated that the treaty was tied to Russian preparations for war over the Eastern Question.

••••••

While the press debated the value of Russian America and Seward worked to get the votes on his side, the Senate Committee on Foreign Relations met to discuss the treaty. The members of the committee were mostly from the East Coast: the chair, Charles Sumner, of Massachusetts; William Fessenden of Maine; Reverdy Johnson of Maryland; Simon Cameron of Pennsylvania; James Patterson of New Hampshire; James Harlan of Iowa; and Oliver Morton of Indiana. The only record of what occurred in those meetings is the memorandum written by Sumner's secretary, Charles Beamon. The memo is brief and in Beamon's own shorthand and not all quotes are attributed, but it gives some indication of the deliberations that took place over the course of eight hours of meetings.

At the first meeting, Sumner presented a brief history of the treaty and shared the positive assessments of Professor Baird of the Smithsonian Institution, as well as letters from Gustavus Vasa Fox and General Meigs. He indicated that while he hoped the United States would eventually come to occupy the whole continent, it would be "better without pressure than with pressure." He acknowledged that one of the political advantages of the purchase would be "to squeeze England out of the continent." Sumner was clear about his reservations, however. He declared that Russian America had "some scientific value for minerals," but little else except for fisheries. Though Sumner personally did not approve of the rushed and secretive methods used by Seward, he recognized the desirability and potential gain in the endeavor and the likely fallout if the Senate rejected a proposal so important to the West. He openly took Seward to task for not consulting the Senate and was unhappy to be put in this uncomfortable position, but he acknowledged that if the committee voted against the treaty, the fact that the men were mostly New Englanders would raise criticisms.

Others in the committee expressed their own doubts about the purchase and used the forum to air political grievances. Reverdy Johnson joked, "Must have been whiskey not champagne that made this treaty." Someone, who Beamon did not identify, asked whether it was better to spend money on purchasing Alaska or on helping the South, a valid question only two years after the end of the Civil War. Another member commented that the land was worthless, while access to the fisheries could likely be gained at no expense. The men discussed the possibility of putting off the decision until December, and all members except one expressed a desire to delay. William Fessenden, the most outspoken opponent on the committee, had another idea and proposed, "I'll go for it with an extra condition be put in that Mr. Secretary of State be compelled to live there and the Russian government be required to keep him there." Johnson replied, "That will be carried unanimously," and promised to lead off the vote.

Despite these significant reservations, on April 8 the Committee on Foreign Relations reported to the Senate as a whole to recommend that the treaty be considered without amendment. Sumner gave a notable speech advocating ratification that, according to several newspapers, lasted between two and three hours. Unfortunately, it is not known what was said in that speech since no one recorded it, and the version that was later published was of considerable length and would have taken twice as long to deliver. Based on this document, however, some of what he must have said can be surmised. Sumner introduced his fellow senators to the geography and history of the territory, as well as how the discussion of a sale transpired, and he then laid out reasons for supporting the treaty. In enumerating the advantages of the Alaska treaty, Sumner began with America's access to the Asian market. Pointing out that the distance between Sitka and Hong Kong was much shorter than between San Francisco and Hong Kong, Sumner argued that "to unite the east of Asia with the west of America is the aspiration of commerce." He added that the relationship between the West Coast and Asia should be as strong as the one enjoyed between the Atlantic states and Europe. Ultimately, the benefits to the Pacific coast would contribute to the general welfare of the whole nation. Sumner also addressed the importance of "extension of dominion," but he believed that the treaty meant more than just the acquisition of new territory: "By it we dismiss one more monarch from this continent." Sumner also mentioned the possibility that the treaty would thwart British plans in the area, an issue of little concern to him, but something that was certainly of interest to many. Finally, he addressed the economic potential of the territory, enumerating its many valuable natural resources. Sumner claimed to have presented his information on Russian America "plainly and impartially," and he admitted that his support was not without some reservations. He wished that the Senate had been consulted before the treaty was signed and hoped that this would not serve as a precedent, adding, "I would save to the Senate an important power that justly belongs to it." Although he supported American expansion, the treaty must not initiate a pattern of "indiscriminate and costly annexation."

Sumner's speech must have been sufficiently persuasive. On the following day, April 9, the treaty was ratified with a vote of thirty-seven to two and was submitted to Russia for ratification. Secretary of the Navy Gideon Welles observed in his diary that while only William Fessenden of Maine and Justin Morrill of Vermont had voted against the treaty, many others had spoken violently against it. Welles judged these men as "mere partisans wanting in legislative wisdom and moral courage." In the days that followed, many papers printed the text of the treaty, and the debates about the purchase continued. The *New York Times* joked that "the sapient critics who have been so sorely distressed because of Mr. Seward's dinners" would be glad to know that he had just served "the last Russian-American codfish taken in those waters. . . . Henceforth they are all American cod."

Interestingly, the Senate approval of the treaty did not curb criticism of the purchase that, in some cases, became more intense. On April 10, the *Tribune* reported that the treaty had been ratified by a secret vote, adding, "We do not understand the reasons for this secrecy in regard to a matter claimed to be perfectly frank and just." Greeley also seemed to believe that the decision had been made hastily, observing, "As sailors are sometimes seized with a passion for the land, and insanely run their ships on the nearest shore, so with the Senate." The following day, the *Tribune* described Russian America's "impassable deserts of snow . . . frozen rivers, inaccessible mountain ranges." And he noted, "We may make a treaty with Russia, but we cannot make a treaty with the North Wind, or the Snow King." In late April, *Farmer's Cabinet* described Russian America's harsh climate and mountainous terrain and concluded that "commercially speaking, the country is hardly worth accepting as a gift."

Others crowed about the deal. The *New York Times* continued to proclaim that the acquisition would pay off and predicted that "time will justify the wisdom of President Johnson's administration in making the treaty." The *Times* also argued that, although Russian America had not been successful under Russian supervision, it would be profitable now that it would receive America's attention and care. In the following months, numerous articles in the *Times* contained descriptions of Russian America and information about its valuable resources. In early May, the *Times* printed more "Notes on Russian America," describing its "beautiful and picturesque islands" and noting that in the summer, it is a paradise. Once again the paper emphasized the territory's material wealth and stressed that "the political and strategical advantages of acquiring a foothold on this portion of the continent will doubtless be rated by statesmen as of more importance than any material wealth which they might afford to citizens of the Republic." Later that month, it was reported that "Californians are irrepressibly anxious to get up into the new territory in order that they may go to work 'prospecting' it."

· · · ● ● ● · ·

With the ratification of the Senate completed, there was one other significant step to be taken—the selection of a name for the territory. The Russian use of the name Alaska originated in the 1700s, sometimes as Alaeksu, Alachschak, and Alaxa, and, subsequently, Captain Cook referred to Alaschka in the report of his voyage to the Pacific Ocean in 1778. In these early documents, the name, or some variant of it, was used to refer both to one or more islands and the mainland itself, and it was often attributed to the Aleut root meaning "mainland" or "continent". Once Russia took possession of the region, of course, the area was referred to as Russian America, and the name Alaska (sometimes spelled Aliaska) was used mostly with reference to the peninsula. So it largely remained until the United States purchased the territory and it became necessary to decide on a permanent name.

No one was sure what to call the new territory, however. The *San Francisco Daily Alta California* is a good example of how that uncertainty played itself out in the press. Between April and July 1867, it referred to the territory as Russian America, Alaska, and even reported at one point, "Russian America—we shall call it the Territory of Alexander." In fact, since the announcement of the treaty, the press had had a field day imagining names for the territory, many of them clearly intended only for humor, including Polario, Frigidia, Seward's Icebox, Johnson's Polar Bear Garden, and Behringia. Other names suggested were Sitka, Knitchpek, Behring, Norland, and Isickles (for Gen. Daniel Sickles). There were also articles that humorously referred to the new territory as Walrussia or Esquimaux.

Sumner had suggested the name Alaska in the printed version of his speech, declaring that the name "should come from the country itself . . . should be indigenous, aboriginal, one of the autochthons of the soil," but it is not known if he mentioned the name when he delivered his speech in April. Maj. Gen. H. W. Halleck, commander of the Military Division of the Pacific, similarly recommended the name of Alaska in a letter to Gen. E. D. Townsend in the adjutant general's office in May, after Sumner's famous speech but before the published version appeared. The name also can be found in some early correspondence about the territory, so it is not clear who actually deserves credit for the idea. Regardless, during the summer of 1867, the name Alaska gradually took hold in the press and began to be used regularly in various government documents.

· · · ● · ·

Seward had fulfilled his dream of expanding the American empire, and the United States gained a valuable piece of territory with a wealth of natural resources that might also serve as a stepping-stone to Asia. For its part, Russia had divested itself of a possession that had become too expensive and too complicated to maintain. Both parties walked away from the treaty signed in the wee hours of March 30, 1867, with a sense of accomplishment and satisfaction. Stoeckl especially could heave a sigh of relief that this complex negotiation was complete. In an April 19 letter to Gorchakov, Stoeckl described, perhaps with some exaggeration, the task faced by a diplomatic representative charged with negotiating a treaty with the United States. The matter was not so simple as it was in Europe, where one need only consult the minister of foreign affairs and the sovereign. In America, Stoeckl wrote, one must consult the administration, the Senate, and the House of Representatives: "It is necessary to confer with some hundreds of individuals, to know almost all of them, to give on one side and another explanations and information, to speak to each one and to talk his language to him." Given the current tensions between the administration and Congress, Stoeckl had found it very challenging to get all parties in agreement. The 25,000 silver rubles he received did not seem sufficient compensation for all the difficulties he had endured, and Stoeckl felt he should have received more, writing to a friend that summer that he would have expected the tsar to be more generous in light of the fact that he (Stoeckl) got a higher purchase price for Alaska than anyone in his government expected.

PREPARING FOR THE HEATED TERM.

King Andy and his man Billy lay in a great stock of Russian ice in order to cool down the Congress-

This commentary on the possible challenges that lay ahead in the process of securing appropriations appeared in *Frank Leslie's Illustrated* on April 20, 1867. RETRIEVED FROM THE LIBRARY OF CONGRESS, (LC-US262-61346). ILLUS. IN AP@.L52 (1867) (CASE Y) (P&P).

CHAPTER IV

No Longer Russian America: Taking Possession of Alaska

The transfer of Russian America occurred on the afternoon of October 18, 1867, in a relatively small and understated ceremony, but long before this day arrived, preparations for the American occupation were already underway. Seward was eager to begin gathering information and laying the groundwork for the occupation of his newly acquired territory as soon as the agreement had been signed, but he recognized that it would be tactless to make any moves in that direction until the official exchange of ratifications. Consequently, as he waited for the appropriate time, Seward proceeded cautiously and quietly, gathering information that would assist in a smooth transfer and occupation. In March he contacted the U.S. Coast Survey Office to arrange for the preparation of a map of the territory. This map would later be printed in numerous copies and would be included in the published version of Sumner's persuasive ratification speech. Per Seward's request, the secretary of the treasury began to arrange for a ship to make its way to Russian

America for the purpose of looking after the interests of the U.S. Customs service and to oversee and regulate the commerce that was already springing up in that area. To make the most of this expedition and to satisfy the needs of the secretary of state, there would also be a team of surveyors and naturalists. This information would be critical for the battle over appropriation that lay ahead. Since there were already discussions in the American press and elsewhere that labeled the new territory a barren wasteland, Seward needed testimony to the contrary.

The U.S. Senate ratified the treaty on Alaska on April 9, 1867, and with this step accomplished, Seward and Stoeckl made haste to have the treaty signed by the tsar. According to Article VII of the treaty, both parties had to ratify it by June 30. With that deadline in mind, Vladimir Bodisco, first secretary of the Russian legation, left Washington on April 19 with an original copy of the treaty and arrived in St. Petersburg about two and a half weeks later. In mid-May, Stoeckl informed Seward that the tsar had signed the treaty and that Bodisco was on his way back to the United States with the signed document in hand. When Bodisco returned in mid-June, he gave the signed treaty to Stoeckl, who promptly took it to Seward. This exchange of signed treaties between the United States and Russia took place on June 20, 1867.

With this formal exchange of ratifications, the treaty was now official, and other arrangements to oversee American interests in the new territory could begin. On July 21, the *Lincoln*, a revenue cutter, departed San Francisco for the northern coast under instructions to protect U.S. Customs interests, examine the harbors, and report on the conditions of the local inhabitants. It also would gather information about the latitude, longitude, and magnetic declination of various places; the presence or absence of lighthouses; and collect various botanical and conchological specimens.

As the American government made arrangements for the establishment of U.S. offices and the ceremonial transfer of ownership, problems arose due to the territory's hazy legal status. In theory,

Russian law still applied, but at the same time the United States now owned it, and a number of enterprising individuals saw the potential for gain in this situation. Even before the ratifications were exchanged, people from the United States and from Victoria, British Columbia, had begun to move to the region and claim plots of land in anticipation of the extension of preemptive rights. Locals were frustrated with these interlopers who were staking out lots around town, even on church property. A correspondent from the *Daily British Colonist* reported the seizing of land and the possibility of violence: "Parties who came here in schooners are talking of jumping lots. They believe might is right. Those who recorded lots and left will have them jumped. I am afraid there will be blood spilled about the same lots."

There was also the matter of trade regulation. Seward wanted American goods to arrive freely in Sitka during these interim months, and Stoeckl agreed. The vessels of all other nations would be expected to stop in an American port of entry to pay duties before continuing on to Alaska. At the same time, the American government also wanted to prevent the importation of guns and alcohol, but this was no easy task. When the *Lincoln* arrived in Sitka in the late summer, Capt. W. A. Howard of the Revenue Service discovered that small boats were arriving regularly with alcohol, weapons, and foreign goods, and no one was in the position to stop them. Seward was eager to execute the transfer and establish American control over the territory before these problems worsened.

In late July and early August, Seward and Stoeckl worked hard to address these difficulties. As the representatives of the Russian government and the Russian-American Company arrived in New York, Seward had Maj. Gen. Lovell H. Rousseau commissioned as the American representative to receive the territory during the official transfer. Seward and Stoeckl then made arrangements for the commissioners of both countries to travel to Alaska via San Francisco on a vessel of the Pacific Mail Steamship Company, which had offered to transport the men for free. Subsequently, Secretary of the Navy Gideon Welles sent orders to prepare the USS *Ossipee* or some other ship to transport the commissioners from San Francisco to Sitka. Major General Halleck, commander of the Division of the Pacific, also announced that the territory would be established as the Military District of Alaska, attached to the Department of California but with its headquarters located at Sitka. Meanwhile, Brevet Maj. Gen. Jefferson C. Davis was informed that he had been assigned to command the Military District of Alaska after the transfer had been completed. Davis was not related to the former Confederate president by the same name but had a checkered past of his own. In 1862 Davis shot and killed a fellow officer, Maj. Gen. William Nelson, at the Galt House hotel in Louisville, Kentucky, after an argument over a perceived insult. Davis was never charged with murder and five years later was tapped for this important position in Alaska.

The instructions Davis received from Major General Halleck, commander of the Division of the Pacific, were lengthy, some thirty-nine paragraphs, and covered a variety of topics. Halleck projected that the period of military supervision would be short, but he made it clear that Davis's job was an enormous one. Halleck ordered that immediately after the exchange of flags the America troops should take possession of all the property and buildings ceded by the treaty, but the Russian officers and troops who currently occupied those places should be allowed to stay "until such time as may be reasonably and conveniently practicable" for their departure. Halleck instructed Davis to tread lightly with the local inhabitants, both Native and Russian, and reminded him that the Russian citizens there had the option to return home to Russia or to stay in Sitka, and to those who chose to stay he should extend his "official protection and encouragement." Halleck added, "Whatever may be the future for those who go, and for those who stay, and for us who are to occupy and possess this new territory, I am sure that we shall, one and all, now and hereafter, hold inmost respectful and kind remembrance the people of Russia and their august Sovereign—the best and most constant friend of the Republic of the United States."

Halleck took a less charitable view of the local Native population. He warned Davis that he should be particularly careful with the Natives who resided on the nearby islands since they were known to be both "warlike and treacherous." While both the British and the Russians had lived among these people for years with only a very few instances of violence, there were some interactions that were certain to cause problems, particularly "a violation of tribal laws or rules in regards to the rights and duties of their females." He instructed Davis to do what he could to prevent conflict in this area. It was best to be always vigilant; for example, the Natives should be prohibited from entering or remaining within the garrison during the night and, Halleck advised, "It may be well to have guns charged with grape and canister always bearing on their village, ready, at an instant's warning, to destroy them."

Meanwhile, Gen. Ulysses Grant, who was serving as acting secretary of war, asked Seward to acquire information about the facilities in Sitka that would be available to house troops; in October the weather would already be cold. Stoeckl indicated that there were barracks that would be turned over to the Americans at the transfer and that these could hold 100 to 120 men, roughly the number in a company of soldiers. This information may have influenced the American decision to send out only two companies of troops instead of four, as had been proposed earlier by Major General Halleck. At about the same time, the U.S. postmaster general appointed a postmaster to Sitka and announced that mail would be delivered weekly from San Francisco. Soon after, Halleck ordered Davis to proceed to Sitka with his two companies of soldiers. In late September, the *John L. Stevens* of the California, Oregon, and Mexican Steamship Company departed San Francisco for Alaska. On board were Davis and his wife, Marietta, his troops (a total of 271 enlisted men and officers), a number of blacksmiths, carpenters, and laundry women, as well as supplies and livestock, including chickens, pigs, cows, mules, sheep, and horses.

While American officials were making preparations for the transfer, the chief manager for the Russian-American Company, Prince Dmitry Petrovich Maksutov, had been given the unenviable task of liquidating the possessions of the Russian government. Though there is very little surviving information about what Maksutov sold, to whom and for how much, some records do exist and provide a glimpse into what this liquidation process involved. Sometime in the summer of 1867, for example, Maksutov sold a 160-acre tract of land near Sitka to the American Russian Commercial Company of San Francisco for $15,000. He also sold sixteen thousand furs at forty cents apiece to a Victoria fur merchant who shipped them home to British Columbia and sold them for two to three dollars each. In early October, the prince exchanged one of the company's brigs for $4,000 and unloaded the bulk of the company's assets, including several steamers, harbor vessels, coal, furs, and buildings to the newly formed Hutchinson, Kohl, and Company for about $350,000. This latter sale would only be announced after the transfer had taken place.

While Maksutov attempted to dispose of the Russian government's property through legitimate channels, there was also a great deal of opportunism and unethical behavior. C. D. Bloodgood, who spent almost a year in Sitka with the U.S. Navy, commented on the flood of fortune seekers who came to Alaska before and after the official transfer hoping to build their futures in this new frontier. He complained of their "schemes" and "squatter claims," and the price gouging on the "veriest necessities of life" that followed. Bloodgood admitted that such circumstances were not unheard of "in the incipiency of colonization," but he commented that it reflected poorly on America. William Healey Dall, a naturalist who would later write a book on Alaska, described some of the early abuses he witnessed as well. One party of opportunists that Dall described as "several German Jews, one Russian, and some other foreigners" had staked out some pieces of land on St. George Island where the fur seals usually came on shore and "declared their intention of holding these tracts of beach under the homestead laws (!) by force, if necessary."

....

At the time of the transfer, Sitka was a settlement of less than a thousand and was described by one visitor of the period as "totally un-American" in its arrangement and appearance. Another traveler provided a more detailed description: "The houses yellow, with sheet-iron roofs painted red; the bright green spire and dome of the Greek church . . . with the antiquated buildings of the Russian Fur Company, gave Sitka an original, foreign, and fossilized kind of appearance." Others noted the wet climate of Sitka, calling it the most rainy place in the world. Davis arrived at Sitka on October 9 and immediately went ashore to meet Prince Maksutov while his soldiers remained on board according to Halleck's instructions and grew increasingly uncomfortable and restless as the days passed. Finally, Rousseau arrived on October 18, and the American troops were allowed to go ashore for the transfer ceremony. At almost the same time, a company of Russian troops marched toward the governor's house; known as Baranov's Castle, it was named for the first governor of Russian America, Alexander Baranov.

A little after 3:00 p.m. on October 18 the formal transfer took place in a brief and modest ceremony. George Foster Emmons, commander of the USS *Ossipee*, which had transported the American commissioners to Alaska, reported the weather that day was cool and unusually pleasant, and he estimated that some three hundred people were present for the occasion. American and Russian officials and residents assembled in front of the governor's house, including Prince Maksutov and his wife who, it was reported, wept. There were no lengthy speeches, no presentations or pomp. As the Russian flag was lowered, the *Ossipee* fired its nine-inch guns and a Russian battery on the wharf answered in kind with a twenty-one gun salute. But before the Russian flag completed its descent, it became tangled in the ropes and tore. As an impatient crowd observed from below, several Russians climbed up the pole in an attempt to dislodge it but were unsuccessful. In the meantime, those on the ground shuffled uncomfortably and watched the awkward drama unfolding above them. Finally, one soldier was able to rip the flag free but, Emmons recorded, instead of carrying it down with him "as was evidently the wish and expectation of the R. [Russian] authorities present, [he] threw it down upon the bayonets of their own soldiers presenting arms underneath." One source reported that Maksutov's wife fainted at the sight of her country's flag defiled in such a way, but if this actually occurred, Emmons made no mention of it in his journal.

Once the Russian flag was removed, Rousseau's fifteen-year-old son, who served as his private secretary, raised the American flag that had been provided by Washington for that precise purpose. The *Ossipee* fired once again, and the Russian commissioner stepped forward and concisely stated, "Genl Rosseau, by authority from His Majesty the Emperor of Russia, I transfer to the United States, the Territory of Alaska." Rousseau replied with a brief acceptance and the ceremony was over. Commander Emmons remarked in his diary that a number of reporters were undoubtedly disappointed by the brevity of the ceremony, having expected "a spread eagle speech to report to their papers." After this brief exchange of words, all the officers assembled in Prince Maksutov's quarters for a quick toast of champagne. At sunset the American and Russian flags were lowered together on the three American ships. Clearly moved by the events of the day, Emmons reflected, "No longer Russian America, the Am. (U.S.) emblem which has this day been hoisted here sends a National salute and in the presence of nearly all the civil and military present—I hope will hereafter be the emblem that will embrace all of N. Am. [North America]."

With the transfer complete, Davis and his wife moved into the governor's house, the largest and most prominent structure in town. The impressive two-story building included spacious living quarters and offices, as well as a library, billiard room, and ballroom. Initially, the Davises had to share their new home with its old tenants; Maksutov and his wife continued to occupy part of the house for six months, until the spring of 1868 when they departed for Russia. Nonetheless, the Davises settled into their new life quickly, and Marietta Davis, who loved to entertain, was soon hosting weekly parties and adapting her usual recipes to accommodate the alimentary limitations of her new environment. The Davises also found the weather far less daunting than they had anticipated. General Davis wrote to a friend that the climate was "much milder than the latitude and longitude of Sitka would indicate. Last winter was not as cold as the winters generally are in Louisville."

Though Alaska officially now belonged to the United States, there were still many issues to sort out. In the days after the transfer ceremony, Rousseau, Maksutov, and Alexei Ivanovich Peshchurov, the Russian commissioner charged with overseeing the transfer, began to determine which buildings in Sitka were public or private and to issue certificates to individual property owners. This proved to be more difficult than it seemed at first blush. According to the treaty, the immovable property of the Russian-American Company would be conferred upon the United States upon the transfer of the territory. The complication came in that many of the city's residents were employees of the company, and it had been the company's practice to house employees in company dwellings over which they, and later their widows and children, possessed ownership. If there were no heirs to the dwelling, it would revert back to the company. This situation was further complicated by the fact that many of the men employed by the company had come to Sitka as single men and had then intermarried with the local Alaska Native women. Rousseau tried to solve this problem by liberally granting certificates of ownership, but General Davis, who had command of the garrison and would assume oversight of such matters after Rousseau departed, wished to interpret the treaty more strictly. Despite these snags, Rousseau reported to Seward that, per his instructions, he had ensured that "all the intercourse between the Russian and American Commissioners should be liberal, frank, and courteous . . . all our communication and association with each other, personal and official, were of the friendliest character, and just such as I am sure you desired."

Rousseau departed Sitka in late October, leaving Gen. Jefferson C. Davis to complete the process of transition as commander of the Military District of Alaska. Davis was less tactful than Rousseau. He demanded the emptying of company warehouses and company homes that were now to house American supplies and troops and complained to the adjutant general in the Department of California that too few buildings had been included in the transfer. Meanwhile, Peshchurov complained to Minister Stoeckl that the Americans had disregarded warnings about the shortage of available homes and had brought too many officials. Moreover, although building materials had been transported from San Francisco, the Americans had yet to begin erecting those structures that would eliminate the housing crisis. The Russian commissioner confirmed Rousseau's report about their pleasant interactions but had less kind things to say about Davis, who had said in his presence that he had no intention of respecting the agents of the Russian-American Company. Consequently, Peshchurov asked Stoeckl to talk to Seward about the matter and request that the secretary of state instruct Davis to deal with the agents more equitably.

Several weeks later, the process of transfer was still underway. On the whole, Peshchurov reported friendly relations with the Americans, but things were far from perfect. The Russian commissioner noted that the Americans were still pressing for a speedy evacuation of the Russian-American Company's warehouses even as they dragged their feet on their own construction projects: "They have not even completed the two unfinished houses which we ceded to them and in which they could easily have stored most of their supplies." Finally, as Peshchurov had anticipated, many of the American soldiers were behaving badly. These men, "composed mostly of riff-raff," had been involved in brawls and theft and "about thirty men of the comparatively small garrison are always under arrest."

Peshchurov's assessment was supported by a report from Sitka published in the *New York Times* at about the same time that declared, "Much ill feeling has been exhibited since our occupation of the city." Not surprisingly, Peshchurov reported in mid-November that not many Russians had chosen to stay in the territory. At that point, only about fifteen had taken the oath of allegiance required to secure American citizenship. Many others were planning to leave. About 150 people had already left aboard the *Tsaritsa*, a ship of the Russian-American Company.

Stoeckl received this news from Peshchurov with some concern and communicated the problems and his recommendations to the Russian Foreign Office. The Russian commissioner had expressed particular concern for the pensioners of the Russian-American Company. There were more of these than he had originally thought, and their circumstances were in danger of growing worse. Peshchurov cautioned, "The company has always been generous with the individuals of this category, but with the rise in prices, which have increased ten-fold since the arrival of the Americans, the allowances for their upkeep as it existed heretofore will become insufficient." Stoeckl had urged the Russian commissioner to provide all of these pensioners who because of age or infirmity could not leave Sitka on their own with the means to travel to one of the ports in eastern Siberia where "among their compatriots they will be able to live at less expense and to lead an existence more in conformity with their customs." Stoeckl recommended to the Russian Foreign Office that the government appoint a consul who could help mediate conflicts and look after the interests of Russian nationals still living in Sitka. Stoeckl was not worried about the Creole population; they would, he believed, readily adapt to their new circumstances under the Americans.

As American and Russian officials completed the process of transfer, the American press still discussed and debated the merits of the purchase. The *New York Times* continued to be supportive, reporting on Alaska's resources and calling it "our Northwest bargain." Similarly, the *Farmer's Cabinet* was optimistic about the future of

Alaska. Relaying information collected from the despatches of the Custom Service's *Lincoln*, the paper confirmed that "the officers express themselves satisfied that the resources of the country in timber and fisheries have not been overated [*sic*]." Its editors still found room for sarcasm, however, referring to "Alaska, Walrussia, or whatever our splinter of the North Pole may be called." Alaska's name continued to be a source of amusement, for its opponents especially. In November, the editor of the *Tribune* noted that the most obvious abbreviation would be the same as that of Alabama, so he suggested "Alas" or "Alak," either of which he believed would fitly signify Uncle Sam's feelings about the new acquisition. By this point, however, the name Alaska had taken hold and was already displayed on the sides of steamships and other vessels. But opposition to the purchase continued through the fall of 1867. The *Times* addressed the continued grumbling with accusations of "narrow jealousies, or still narrower resentments." The paper's editor believed that much of the resistance had to do with hostility toward Seward and the Johnson administration, feelings that should not be allowed to get in the way of the nation's progress and prosperity.

•••••••

Although many in Sitka complained that the U.S. government did not extend enough support to the new territory, there was actually an ongoing attempt by Washington in this first period to create offices and positions that would bring order and organization. In March 1868, the *New York Times* reported that the Military District of Alaska was henceforth to be called the Department of Alaska, with Brevet Maj. Gen. Jefferson Davis as the commanding officer. Meanwhile, Halleck sent three hundred additional troops to Davis, who used the extra manpower to build roads and to man a number of newly established posts like Fort Wrangell, Fort Tongass, Fort Kenay, and Fort Kodiak. Davis also made an effort to see more of the territory he commanded and to make a clear show of America's presence there. In the summer of 1868, with the cooperation of Lt. Cmdr. John G. Mitchell, commander of the Navy's USS *Saginaw*, Davis traveled along Alaska's coast, inspecting a number of forts, meeting with chiefs of various tribes, and displaying the American flag. Davis also began to establish his reputation with the Native Alaskans as a man to be feared and respected but also one who would be their protector and advocate when appropriate. During his time in Alaska, Davis served as mediator and judge for all manner of conflict, between the Tlingit, Americans, Russians, and the remnants of the Russian-American Company (which technically no longer existed). Despite some of his more negative interactions with the Native Alaskans, one of his biographers describes Davis as "genuinely concerned over the condition of the Indians." Others disagree. A less generous interpretation denounces Davis for his policy of "kidnapping Tlingit leaders, hostage taking, imprisoning, bombing villages, and executing Alaska natives. . . . The actions of Davis as the first American governing official encountered by the Tlingit damaged Tlingit-American relations for the next century."

In other matters, Davis's actions were less controversial. Davis was supportive of the establishment of Sitka's first government. Only three days after the transfer, an announcement called for people in Sitka to gather for a meeting to consider the advantages of organizing a civil administration for the territory. Within days a committee had begun to work on a city charter. On November 25, Sitka had its first election. The city charter was adopted, and several councilmen and a mayor, William S. Dodge, were elected. General Davis gave his blessing to the new government, and Mayor Dodge initiated the creation of a public school. Alaska's first newspaper, the *Sitka Times*, appeared in 1867, as well. By December, a Masonic Lodge had been organized and the first American religious service had taken place in a Lutheran church. These early successes were followed by others, and there were small but hopeful indications that Alaska was becoming a part of America, economically and culturally. On July 4, 1868, Sitka celebrated Independence Day, complete with speeches by Davis and Dodge, festive decorations, a parade, fireworks, and a one-mile canoe race of Native Alaskans.

As the residents of Sitka worked to create a provisional government and a permanent and successful settlement, Americans were clearly becoming accustomed to the idea that Alaska was now, and would continue to be, part of the United States. In the fall of 1867, the press in San Francisco reported that the acquisition of Alaska had inspired the establishment of an Orthodox church in the city. The members of the congregation, who numbered more than a thousand, had obtained a priest and begun to hold services and were currently in the process of raising money to build a permanent structure. In November, *Farmer's Cabinet* announced the publication of a sixteen-page pamphlet by *Colton's Journal of Geography* that included a "valuable article" on Alaska with a "fine map." As early as December 1867, Mark Twain used the remoteness and exoticism of Alaska in one of his humorous essays. In the form of an imaginary ad, "Information Wanted," Twain described an uncle who was looking for a quiet place to live. He had tried a variety of places, but in each he had encountered disaster. Twain wrote, "He has tried Walrussia; but the bears kept after him so much, and kept him so on the jump, as it were, that he had to leave the country. He could not be quiet there, with those bears prancing after him all the time." Though perpetuating the uninformed stereotypes about Alaska, Twain's essay nonetheless demonstrated that Alaska was becoming part of the American consciousness.

· · · ● · · ·

The occupation of Alaska by American troops and settlers in the fall of 1867 made it more difficult for Congress to vote against the appropriation bill that would be considered in the coming months. Many believed that Seward had created this situation intentionally to ensure the success of his treaty. The fact that the American flag flew over Sitka did not stop Seward's opponents from resisting the acquisition, however; and for the first half of 1868 the big question facing Seward, Stoeckl, and all the other interested parties in the Alaska deal was whether the House would pass the appropriation bill to pay for Alaska.

WHAT WE MAY LOOK FOR SOON.

"The Hon. TOOKOOLOTO JABINKOKER, Delegate from the Kodink District of the former Russian Possessions, arrived yesterday from New Arehangel. He dined at DELMONICO'S, and ordered the repast in the *haute cuisine* of Kodiak : train oil for two; tallow candles for one; whale blubber for one (but substituted raw pork, as the other was not to be had); asked for a seal's fin, but took India-rubber, *faute de mieux*, with a glass of spirits of turpentine; wanted a rat in an advanced state of decomposition, but had to put up with a bad egg."

There were many comments in the press about what America's new citizens would look like. HARPER'S WEEKLY, MAY 4, 1867. MANY THANKS TO THE STAFF OF THE AUBURN UNIVERSITY AT MONTGOMERY LIBRARY FOR THEIR ASSISTANCE IN SCANNING THIS IMAGE.

CHAPTER V

Paying for the "New National Ice-House:" Approval and Appropriation

hough the American flag now flew over Sitka, there was still the very significant issue of payment. This would be no easy accomplishment. The question of appropriation was tied to the matter of presidential authority and the prerogatives of the House of Representatives. As was already clear, many in the House were angered by the way in which the Alaska deal had been transacted, that is, without consultation or consideration of the House's critical role in approving money for the purchase. Once the deal was ratified by both countries, and especially after the official transfer occurred in October 1867, the House's prerogative to grant or deny appropriation seemed almost nonexistent, yet many representatives continued to push the point, concerned that a dangerous precedent might be set. The debate was further complicated by the tensions between the president and many in Congress over his imperial style in implementing policies of Reconstruction, a tension that would ultimately lead to the country's first impeachment of a president. Finally, the Alaska appropriation was also threatened by a long and protracted claim by an American citizen against the Russian government, a case whose supporters included members of Congress who wanted to link its consideration to the appropriation bill for Alaska.

· · · · ● · ●

The first step in getting the necessary money to pay for Alaska took place soon after the exchange of ratifications. On July 16, 1867, a presidential message was read to the Senate inviting Congress to consider appropriation for the payment to Russia and to propose proper legislation for the occupation and settlement of the new territory. In the Senate, the matter was referred both to the Committee on Appropriations and the Committee on Territories. The message was then read in the House of Representatives on July 19, after which it was referred to the Committee on Foreign Affairs. On July 20, Congress adjourned. By the time they met again in late fall, Alaska was already in American hands.

While Congress was in recess, however, another wrinkle in the Alaska deal surfaced, a particularly thorny matter called the Perkins Claim. The Perkins Claim had a long and litigious history. In June 1855 Capt. Benjamin Perkins, a merchant mariner from Worcester, Massachusetts, met a man who claimed to be an agent and courier of the Russian government tasked with procuring armaments and gunpowder. Over the next few months, Perkins met with various men acting as agents of the Russian government, including Russian minister Eduard Stoeckl, and secured what he believed to be legitimate agreements to provide these materials to the Russian government. In the meantime, Perkins spent a great deal of money acquiring the arms, gunpowder, and other supplies necessary to fulfill the orders. Soon, however, it became apparent that Russia was no longer interested in pursuing these arrangements or obtaining the negotiated war materials. Left in the lurch, Perkins began to try to recover his declared losses through legal means, but he was unsuccessful. When he died in 1862, his claim was pursued by his wife and daughter who, after exhausting all legal remedies, made several appeals to the American and Russian governments. None of these produced any real results, but in 1867 Anna Perkins, destitute and hounded by debts, once again appealed to Congress for help. This time, however, she had an extra bit of leverage—since the United States was in the process of purchasing Alaska from Russia, Anna Perkins and her attorneys asked Congress to withhold the amount of $385,231.31 plus interest from the payment to Russia, at least until her claim was evaluated once more.

This bold proposition elicited strong reactions on both sides. On July 9, 1867, Nathaniel Banks presented Anna Perkins's petition in the House, asking that an amount be withheld from the payment for Alaska until the case had been given proper consideration; Senator Henry Wilson repeated the proposal twelve days later in the Senate. The matter was referred to the Committee on Appropriations and then sat idle until the next meeting of Congress in November. Not surprisingly, Russian Minister Stoeckl was alarmed by the growing momentum of this claim and the attempts to link it to the Alaska Purchase. Late in the summer of 1867 he wrote Seward about his concern that rumors about these efforts might reach the Russian capital and "produce some uneasiness there."

During the next few months, correspondence relevant to the Perkins litigation continued outside of Congress. Seward referred the case to the Bureau of Claims, an office within the Department of State that evaluated such matters. In October 1867, the same month the American flagged was raised over Sitka, bureau examiner E. Peshine Smith expressed his belief that "Capt. Perkins was, and his estate now is, entitled to indemnity from Russia for the top of benefits which he sustained by the fault of her agent in presenting the execution of a valid contract." Smith found the entire contract deal to be a shady one, "a contract which the government could not itself make without breach of its neutral obligations, and which is only tolerated in a private citizen." For this reason, Smith argued, Perkins "had no right what ever, to the interposition of his own government to aid him in obtaining redress." Smith thus concluded that to tamper with the treaty for Alaska would be "inconsistent with our national honor," and "to postpone payment for the further consideration of such a claim, would I think, be to renounce for the future any right to the just confidence in our plighted faith which has been exhibited in this instance." Smith's opinion was clear and, one might imagine, sufficiently decisive as to cease any further discussion of linking the Perkins Claim to the appropriation for Alaska. Not so.

On November 21, a week before Thanksgiving, Congress convened again, but only for a few days since the second session of Congress opened on December 2. Though no bill on Alaska was presented, the question of Alaska was on everyone's mind. On November 25 Cadwallader C. Washburn of Wisconsin put forth a resolution in the House of Representatives proposing that the United States engage in no further purchases of territory, an obvious reference to the recent acquisition. The motion was easily adopted. Five days later, Halbert E. Paine of Wisconsin introduced a resolution that more directly touched on the Alaska deal, asking the Judiciary Committee to report on whether the Constitution gave Congress the right to grant or refuse the appropriation for the payment designated in the treaty with Russia; this proposition also passed.

The second session of Congress resumed business on December 2, 1867, and subsequently met in five separate meetings, or spans of meetings, over the course of the next year. On December 3, 1867, President Johnson gave the annual president's message, which included a brief mention of the Alaska treaty and called for Congress's attention to the appropriation for payment. It was immediately clear that there would be opposition in the House. Several representatives requested that the parts of the president's speech as pertained to the treaty be referred to the Committee on Foreign Affairs and the Committee on Appropriations. In addition, Representative Elihu

Washburne also resurrected the issue of the Perkins Claim, which was referred to the Committee of Claims. There were also clear supporters of appropriation. Republican congressman Thaddeus Stevens, who favored the treaty, made the following statement to his colleagues: "So far as the appropriation is concerned I shall of course vote to make the appropriation. When the Constitution, which is the paramount law of the land, declares that we owe a debt, I should be ashamed to refuse to pay it."

Congress adjourned on December 20 for the holidays and reconvened on January 6, 1868, and remained in session for a little over six months. It was during this period that the real debates over appropriation took place as both sides rallied their arguments and evidence. Seward resumed his efforts to influence public opinion through the use of the press, and he persuaded Robert J. Walker to write a letter in support of the Alaska treaty. In late January 1868, the *Washington Daily Morning Chronicle* printed Walker's letter, and ten days later, the *New York Times* printed an overview of the letter with lengthy quotes. Praising the abundant resources of Alaska, Walker also argued in favor of acquiring the islands of St. Thomas and St. John in the Caribbean, all of which would strengthen America's position vis-à-vis Great Britain. Noting the various missed opportunities of the past, he stressed the importance of seizing the current opportunity to expand through peaceful means. Walker wished to see America "fulfill her destiny, by spreading the blessings of liberty and of the Constitution peacefully over the American continents, placing her beyond the power of any monarchical combinations, with irresistible ability for good, and no motive for evil or aggression." Walker also highlighted the way the acquisition of Alaska would strengthen America's position in commanding "the commerce and exchanges of the world." Walker believed that this competition would be decided in the Pacific market, and the purchase of Russian America would carry the United States "half-way across the Pacific, and within a few days of China and Japan." During roughly the same period, the *New York Times* printed information about Alaska provided by an employee of the Overland Telegraph Company who had spent time there and attested to its mineral, lumber, and fishing resources. The *Times* believed that these kinds of firsthand observations were important since "many and conflicting statements have already been published in regard to Alaska."

Once again, the Perkins Claim played a significant role in the deliberations. On January 7, Representative Halbert Paine asked for the papers regarding the Perkins case to be furnished to the House for further examination. A month later, the House asked that Seward "bring to the friendly notice of the Emperor of Russia the injuries alleged to have been sustained by B. W. Perkins." The continued appearance of the Perkins matter made Stoeckl nervous, and he wrote to Gorchakov in St. Petersburg about the "Perkins roguery" and the persistent support it found in Congress and among members of the press. But the Russian minister made no effort to reexamine the claim or consider its merits.

The Perkins Claim was not the only issue holding up the payment for Alaska, however. Congress's hatred of President Andrew Johnson interfered as well. When John Wilkes Booth assassinated Abraham Lincoln, Johnson became president and was faced with the overwhelming job of reuniting the Union. Like his predecessor, Johnson exercised a strong hand, excluding Congress from the decision-making process and making enemies along the way. Much to the dismay of Republicans in Congress, Johnson's efforts to reintegrate the former Confederate states resulted in more difficulties. Among other things, Johnson pardoned many Confederate rebels and allowed them to reclaim ownership of their land, hampering the congressional mandate of the Freedmen's Bureau to rent confiscated lands to free blacks in the South. Former rebels also resumed positions of political power, leaving former slaves at their mercy. A number of Johnson's policies directly challenged congressional authority and policy. In March 1867, as Seward was completing the Alaska deal, Congress overrode Johnson's plans with a Reconstruction act that made his recently created Southern governments provisional and placed five military commanders in charge of the reconstructed areas. Johnson fought back by removing four of these military commanders and replacing them with men more sympathetic to his position. As one historian succinctly stated, "It was plain by winter, 1867–68, that the president of the United States was consciously and determinedly following a program designed to nullify congressional legislation through the power of executive implementation." His opponents took action and rallied to remove him from office. Passions ran high, as is clear from the fiery words of Representative Reader W. Clarke of Ohio who cried out against Johnson's disregard of law and duty and drew rather chilling comparisons:

> If Washington had been Paris[,] this morning would have found Andrew Johnson a fugitive, fleeing from an infuriated populace, or hanging upon a lamp-post in front of his mansion. For offenses no greater than his[,] the slow but determined English seized upon their sovereign without law, organized a revolutionary tribunal, put him upon trial, adjudged him guilty, and cut off his head.

In late February 1868, the House voted to impeach Johnson for high crimes and misdemeanors in office, and his impeachment trial in the Senate began within twenty-four hours of the vote.

· · · · · · ·

Though discussion of the Alaska appropriation took place in the Committee on Foreign Affairs over several days in mid-March 1868, it became clear that no settlement of the question would be reached at that time. The *New York Times* characterized the discussions of the bill as "decidedly spicy, and somewhat acrimonious." Some representatives, such as William Higby of California, expressed support for appropriation because failure to pay would cause problems for the United States, while others like Cadwallader Washburn declared that the acquisition of new territory was not in the best interest of the country and a decision that Congress alone had the right to make. On March 20, Nathaniel Banks, chairman of the House Committee on Foreign Affairs, wrote to Seward that due to the impeachment trial in the Senate, the committee members had decided to set aside consideration of the Alaska bill for the time being. Banks emphasized that this action "should not be understood to be the result of opposition to the Bill, but a recognition of the inevitable course of public business." Many viewed the postponement with pessimism, however. The editor of the *Daily Alta California* worried that the delay meant that the Committee on Foreign Affairs had "given the Alaska appropriation the go-by," and consequently, "our plighted national faith . . . is to be violated." President Johnson also apparently saw the delay as a negative sign and reportedly said to his secretary, "We have taken possession of the territory and hoisted our flag there, and yet we stand today as a government refusing to pay the money. . . . The treaty has been made in good faith. . . . The government is bound to comply with its conditions, and yet the House of Representatives steps in and, claiming the right under their power over the purse strings of the nation, refuses to make an appropriation to pay for Alaska."

Seward, of course, had to explain the delay to Stoeckl. The Russian minister, who was dismayed by the postponement and not at all optimistic about the outcome, wrote Gorchakov with two possible approaches to dealing with the deadlock. On the one hand, Russia could tell the United States that if it was unwilling to pay for Alaska, it could just have the territory. The second option was to send the United States a polite but strongly worded note that would attempt to tap into American pride. Gorchakov, with the tsar's approval, advised Stoeckl to pursue the second course; both men worried that if Russia offered Alaska for free, the United States might accept it. In late April, Stoeckl notified Seward that the Russian government consented to the delay in payment. Seward replied with his thanks and added, "I think you may rely upon an appropriation being made by Congress in good time." Stoeckl meanwhile tried to dissuade both

Johnson and Seward from intervening on his behalf. As Stoeckl later observed, these men were so unpopular with Congress at present that their intervention "could do more harm than good." He preferred to work through more subtle means. Stoeckl wrote Gorchakov in April 1868, "Seward, for his part, works persistently with Walker and employs all means by which to attract members of the House to our side. . . . Both act with the greatest circumspections and in a manner that will in no way compromise me." At the same time, Stoeckl continued to use all the tools at his disposal to influence the outcome of the vote. Impressed by Robert Walker's articles in the *Washington Daily Morning Chronicle* from earlier that year, Stoeckl offered Walker $20,000 to work for him. Walker accepted, though this information would not come to light until a Congressional investigation of the Alaska appropriation some months later.

Many in Russia were not happy about the delay, however. The U.S. consul in Russia, Eugene Schuyler, reported increasing animosity in Moscow toward the United States during the payment delay. "I feel it my duty to say," Schuyler wrote Seward in early July 1868, "that there is rapidly growing up a feeling against the American arising from the delays and opposition which have been made in the settlement of the Aliaska treaty." According to the American consul, the voluntary ceding of Russian territory was "contrary to all Russian feeling and the mass of Russians were not content with the action of the Government." The only thing that had comforted some Russians was the fact that the recipient of that territory had been the United States, "to whom a genuine friendly feeling was then existing." Since the delay in payment, however, the treatment of Americans had declined in several ways. "In the way of official favors an American gets even less then [sic] others and one is liable to have remarks and questions which, to say the least, are very disagreeable," Schuyler noted. He also cautioned that the tense situation was affecting American businessmen. The carriage manufacturing company of an American named Williams found that "political troubles—the delay in the Aliaska payment—have been very bad for his business," resulting in him being passed over for government contracts that he had expected. Similarly, in the case of the sale of the Nikolai Railroad, which ran from Moscow to St. Petersburg, the offers of American businessmen were disregarded. Schuyler explained, for example, "One great obstacle to Mr. Winans' success was the fact that he was an American."

· · · ● · · ·

As Seward and Stoeckl struggled through this uncomfortable period of deliberation and delay, American newspaper editors put forth their own views of the political wrestling match. In early March, the *New York Times* relayed concerns about the appropriation bill and hoped that the tsar would be patient; still, the *Times* was certain that "The American people will not permit . . . the Star Spangled Banner to be hauled down in the vast territory over which it now waves." Several weeks later, the *Times* reported that rumors had appeared again that the necessary appropriations would be denied. The *Providence Journal*, for example, predicted that America would have to give Alaska back to Russia. The *Daily Alta California*, meanwhile, feared for the future of the commercial interests of coastal merchants and threatened that if the House refused the necessary appropriations, "they will be very likely to lose in the coming election the support of every state of the Pacific Slope—that is, west of the Rocky Mountains." A letter to the editor in the *Washington Daily Morning Chronicle* expressed dismay at the possibility of the appropriation being denied or postponed, adding, "There seems every prospect that the honor of the nation will be compromised." Recalling the good faith of "our ally and friend, the Emperor of Russia," the letter's author argued that it was "the bounden duty of our Representatives in this emergency to *first* sustain the credit of the country by providing for its legal obligation, and *then* they may turn their attention to a modification of the existing law."

There was good reason to worry about international perceptions of the appropriation delay. For some countries, the nasty political dispute in the U.S. Congress was, at the very least, amusing. In particular, the *Neue Freie Presse* in Vienna seemed to delight in the possibility that Russia and the United States might have a falling out. Schuyler in St. Petersburg referred specifically to a long article "filled with falsehoods, which plainly showed a desire to embroil us with our transatlantic friend." In response to this article, two Russian newspapers defended the United States and the strength of the Russian-American friendship. The *Journal de St. Petersbourg* declared that "relations between Russia and America have not experienced the slightest change," and added that, despite the pronouncement of the Viennese press, "the two young giants are still very far from the collision which it announced." The *Moscow Gazette* reacted with equal passion, standing by the United States and adding that in such a political crisis as the impeachment of the president, "the Congress cannot regularly occupy itself with its legislative duties, and . . . it is difficult to attend to the satisfaction of the treaty." The *Gazette* added, "To entertain even for a moment the proposition that Congress wishes to avoid that obligation . . . would be to insult the nation and government of the great North American republic."

In the end, the Committee on Foreign Affairs completed its recommendation before the impeachment trial ended. On May 18, 1868, Banks presented a report that included majority and minority positions. The majority report recommended appropriation based on a very positive assessment of Alaska's potential economic, military, and strategic value; among other things, it would enclose British Columbia within American jurisdiction on all sides and strengthen America's relationship with Russia. The minority report of the Committee on Foreign Affairs roundly condemned the Alaska Purchase and declared that the territory's resources—all of them—were less valuable, less abundant, and less advantageous than reports had indicated. They concluded that it was "inexpedient" to appropriate money for Alaska, declaring that "the right to govern a nation or nations of savages in a climate unfit for the habitation of civilized men was not worthy of purchase." They argued that Alaska would be "a source of weakness instead of power, and a constant annual expense for which there will be no adequate return." Aside from their negative assessment of the value of Alaska, opponents in the House also resented the process by which the treaty had occurred. The opponents of the sale were caught in an impossible situation, however; Alaska was already occupied and formally transferred to the United States, and trade to and from Alaska was being handled as other American trade. In many other ways, Alaska, or at least Sitka, was becoming Americanized. To reject the bill for appropriation was nearly impossible and would cause innumerable problems. On the other hand, approval of the appropriation bill seemed to condone what many perceived as a circumvention of the House's independent right to decide when and if the nation's money would be spent.

After Representative Banks's report of May 18, discussion of the appropriation bill was set aside until the end of June. When the discussion resumed, the Perkins case was raised yet again. On June 27, Representative Henry Paine of Wisconsin inquired whether the matter would be considered before the discussion of the Alaska appropriation or at the same time. Banks answered that the bill must be dealt with separately since the treaty called for payment of a specific sum in a specific manner. Though Banks supported the claim, he could not advocate folding the one issue into the other.

Debate over the appropriation bill began in the full body of the House on June 30, 1868. William Loughridge of Iowa, who supported the purchase of Alaska, proposed a preamble to the appropriation bill that addressed, among other things, a particular stipulation of the treaty that gave citizenship to the inhabitants of the territory, making them "subjects which by the Constitution of the United States are submitted to the power of Congress, and over which Congress has jurisdiction." For this reason, Loughridge argued, it was necessary that Congress must approve said stipulation "before the same can have full force and effect." The following day, July 1, Thomas Dawes Eliot of Massachusetts proposed another amendment stating that henceforth no purchase of foreign territory be made without prior provision for its payment. The amendment added that while the Constitution gave the president and the Senate the power to enter into treaties with foreign governments, it did not include the power to complete the purchase before the necessary appropriation was secured by Congress.

Representative Benjamin Butler, a great opponent of President Johnson and the Alaska Purchase, also submitted an amendment, one that pushed the Perkins case again. Butler asked that $500,000 be withheld until the Russian government agreed to submit to an impartial tribunal to consider claims by American citizens that had been declared valid by the Department of State. Butler's proposal was ruled out of order, so he appealed the ruling to his colleagues, which resulted in a tie vote, and though he tried several more times a week later, all his attempts failed. During the same period that Butler was promoting the Perkins Claim, Seward wrote a memorandum that stated that the Department of State had no knowledge of any agent or citizen of the United States that had "any lien upon the purchase money for Alaska." Nonetheless, Stoeckl was still concerned. He believed that the backers of the case were well organized and had some kind of agreement that they would receive three-fourths of the $800,000, and the other fourth would go to the Perkins heirs. Stoeckl also declared that Butler had an interest in the claim to the tune of $30,000.

The debates surrounding the payment for Alaska echoed the same concerns that had been expressed since the signing of the treaty the previous year. A look at a few of these speeches will suffice to give a general notion of the kinds of things that were said during these often-heated discussions. On July 1, 1868, for example, Leonard Myers of Pennsylvania gave a speech in the House in support of the bill, and his speech expressed many of the arguments made by those in his camp. Myers acknowledged the right of Congress to approve territorial purchases and their payment and added that the actions of the president and Seward in securing the treaty did not bind the House to complete the transaction. Frustration with the administration's handling of the matter, however, was not sufficient reason to reject the purchase out of hand. Russia was a nation that had been "our constant friend, sympathizing in our struggle for the preservation of the Union," Myers said, and this fact was "not without its due influence." But there was more. Alaska was more valuable and hospitable than the opponents would admit. Ridicule and exaggeration had been used to denigrate the deal, but such had been the case with previous purchases of territory as well. These naysayers overlooked the full potential of the Alaska Purchase. "The possession of Alaska is a question of power," Myers asserted, particularly in the relationship with Great Britain. If the United States did not buy Alaska, Russia would look for another buyer, and Great Britain would be the beneficiary. Myers warned, "England never voluntarily contracted *her* possessions. Rest assured, Alaska, if not ours, will be transferred to Great Britain." Myers passionately concluded that the acquisition of Alaska was part of a natural progression already under way, the connecting of the Occident and the Orient. The world would become "more luminous" by this contact. "Alaska must be ours," Myers insisted, "let no man disdain to picture the day, distant though it may be, when over the continent of North America, from ocean to ocean, from the Arctic to the Antilles, the canopy of freedom shall cover one people, one country, and one destiny."

Hiram Price of Iowa had a very different view of things. Price considered the appropriation bill "foolish, insane, and wicked." He questioned how the United States could afford to buy Alaska when it claimed not to have the money to pay benefits to Civil War veterans. Moreover, he argued that the manner in which the deal was carried out, that is, secretly and without the consultation of the House, made it unenforceable. Price angrily declared, "The idea or assumption that this bargain attempted to be made with Russia is a treaty, and therefore, . . . a part of the supreme law of the land, is preposterous in the extreme. . . . No, sir; it is not a treaty, is not a law, and the very fact of coming here to ask for our favorable action is a clear admission on their part that they know this." One of the most outspoken opponents was Cadwallader Washburn, who resented the treaty for a number of reasons. Washburn challenged the enthusiastic supporters of Alaska, particularly Representative Banks, with the accusation of revisionism, declaring that prior to the signing of the treaty "there was not a man in the whole length and breadth of the United States who had even conceived the idea that this territory of Alaska was a valuable territory for the United States to possess . . . not even the gentleman from Massachusetts, though he now declares it to be absolutely necessary to the very safety and existence of this nation." Washburn argued that Alaska was worthless and mocked the purchase with commentary on similarly situated territories: "I believe a treaty is now being negotiated with Denmark for the purchase of Greenland and Iceland. . . . Well, gentleman, laugh at it. I tell gentlemen who go for Alaska that Greenland to-day is a better purchase." Finally, Washburn despised the pressure on the House created by the signing of the treaty and the transfer of ownership. He asked, "Will this House allow itself to be coerced by any such performance?"

The American press closely followed the debates in Congress in June and July. The *New York Times* interpreted the "vexatious delay" over the Alaska treaty as a clear message, "a very pointed and practical hint to the Senate of the necessity, as well as the propriety, of obtaining the sentiment of the House upon a proposed treaty purchase of territory, before ratifying it." While the *Times* was sympathetic to this viewpoint, it nonetheless believed that the House should agree to pay since the government was "honor bound" by the treaty. "If a mistake was made regarding the purchase of Alaska," the *Times* reflected, "it was on our part, not on Russia's." The *Washington Daily Morning Chronicle* agreed, reporting that the bill's enemies might delay the appropriation, which would be worse than an outright rejection because "it would lead to an open violation of a distinct clause of the treaty," the time frame for payment. Equally important, "What will Russia and the Great Powers of the world think of us, should we violate the most sacred obligations, and sport with the feelings and interests of friendly nations [?]" The *New York Sun* presented both sides of the debate, but added "it seems to us . . . that the House of Representatives has a right to dissent from it without exposing the nation to the accusation of violating its contract." To support the treaty would set a dangerous precedent, for it would give "a branch of the Government which, by the express terms of the Constitution, cannot originate a bill for raising revenue, the power of mortgaging that revenue to an indefinite extent . . . and thus take from the popular branch that control over the national expenditures which it ought always to retain."

Even as the American press discussed the legitimacy of the various points of view on appropriation, they also continued to reflect on how the Alaska Purchase would benefit the United States. More than one article pointed to the expansion of trade with Asia. In July the *New York Times*, for example, suggested, "The new steamship line between San Francisco, Japan and China, has attracted our attention to a quarter of the globe whose commercial relations with this country ought to be of the closest and largest and most profitable kind." Other papers remarked on this new possibility as well. The *Washington Daily Morning Chronicle* noted in late July, "It is now certain that we must be the dominant power of the Pacific, and control the trade of China and Japan."

· · · · · · ·

Voting on the appropriation bill was set to take place on July 9, but once again, outside events interfered. The presidential election campaign was already underway, and national party conventions had been scheduled for Democrats in early July; Republicans had met in late May. Banks asked that the vote be postponed for a few days since a number of members were currently absent due to the Democratic convention in New York City. Once the notion of delay was in the air, Paine of Wisconsin attempted once more to interject the Perkins Claim, asking to postpone the vote until December. This suggestion provoked a lengthy and tedious exchange over procedure, during which Butler backed Paine's request. Ultimately, the suggestion went nowhere and the vote was postponed only by a few days. Finally, on July 14, the House Committee of the Whole (a special congressional committee) considered the amendments submitted by Representatives Loughbridge and Eliot, and both passed. In the end, however, when the same amendments went before the House, the Eliot amendment was rejected and excluded. The House subsequently passed the bill 113 to 43, with 44 not voting. It is interesting to note that of the 43 men who voted against appropriation, 41 had supported the impeachment of President Johnson. Several days later, the Senate quickly and harmoniously passed the bill after eliminating the Loughbridge preamble. Over the next few weeks, the bill was shaped into its final form, which appeared on July 27 and stated that Congress approved the appropriation for $7.2 million as stipulated by the treaty for Alaska signed the previous year.

Everyone, it seems, was relieved when the appropriation debates were over. After a very busy and stressful summer, the members of Congress adjourned in early August for a recess until the end of September. Banks was more than a little pleased with his victory and wrote to his wife, "All sides in the House give your husband credit in putting the bill through, and the people observing the activity of Congress will look on this for a long time as a major triumph." Once the appropriation bill had finally been passed, there only remained the actual transfer of money to complete the deal. On July 28, Seward sent a requisition for $7.2 million to the Secretary of the Treasury and four days later Stoeckl received a treasury draft in that amount. Other countries noted the completion of the purchase. The *Western Times* in Exeter, for example, commented with sarcasm that Congress had, "after much hesitation," paid for Alaska.

••••••••

But what of the Perkins case? Banks had told Paine on June 27 that the claim and the payment for Alaska must be kept separate, but he had indicated that he would support a resolution about the matter submitted to the Committee on Foreign Affairs. One might assume, then, that the Perkins Claim would be taken up shortly after the appropriation bill had passed. In fact, the recorded debates in the House indicate that this was the intent. But it did not happen. At the end of July, Banks explained that this omission was due to the interruption in the regular pattern of business at the end of the previous session of the House of Representatives. He did believe that it was appropriate to ask the president to "employ the friendly offices" of the government to seek a fair consideration of the Perkins Claim with the Russian government, but he did not approve of the way the resolution had been used by opponents of the Alaska Purchase to derail the appropriation bill. Ultimately, discussion of the Perkins Claim did not occur until the next session of Congress, which convened on December 7, 1868. Once again, Banks requested permission to offer the resolution asking for government intervention on behalf of all citizens with claims against the Russian government, which he had "promised the House last session should be presented." This resolution was accepted by the House on January 12, 1869, and communicated to the Russian government through Cassius Clay, the American minister at St. Petersburg.

Several months later, once Hamilton Fish had become secretary of state, Banks sought to ensure that the resolution did not disappear into the bowels of the bureaucracy. In May and June 1869, he wrote two letters to Fish that explained the particular circumstances of the resolution of January 1869. He emphasized that it was intended to satisfy a promise to the supporters of the Perkins Claim during the appropriation debates to prevent that issue from interfering with the payment for Alaska, which he considered a separate, and non-negotiable, obligation. He underscored that the promise was made in the House "in public session, with the consent of the Secretary of State, and the Russian Minister." Moreover, Seward had told Banks that Stoeckl "felt great anxiety" about the Perkins imbroglio interfering with the appropriation and had given his assurances multiple times that it would not be forgotten. Banks added, "I do not state that he promised the recognition of the claim in any way, but he said it should be considered and settled upon the facts of the Case— We did not debate the merits of the claim." Banks admitted that he did not know if the case was a solid one, nor did the House intend to argue this point; the goal was simply to ensure that it be referred to impartial arbitration.

Stoeckl retired in January 1869, but interest in the Perkins Claim persisted under his successor, Constantin Catacazy, a diplomat with a scandalous personal life and a strong and sometimes abrasive personality. Catacazy arrived to assume his new post in the United States in late summer of 1869 and quickly developed a reputation as a difficult and dishonest man. The Russian government had instructed him to investigate the Perkins Claim and he did so with great enthusiasm. More than once, Catacazy wrote Fish that the Perkins Claim was not deemed credible by the Russian government because of its "essentially fraudulent character," and he condemned the "entire worthlessness of the so-called claims." In early March 1870, the *Washington Daily Morning Chronicle* published a letter purportedly written by Catacazy, referring to the "fictitious pretensions of the widow Perkins" and suggesting that Perkins had entrapped the Russian agents. Shortly after, another document appeared, an unsigned despatch addressed to the tsar that referred to the claim as an "iniquitous fraud" and its supporters as would-be plunderers of the Imperial government. Perkins's attorney asserted that the document had been written by Catacazy, though Fish did not believe this. Nonetheless, both Fish and Grant were infuriated by the Russian minister's lack of tact and defiance of protocol in general, particularly his insistence on taking matters directly to the press. By the summer of 1871, they could tolerate him no more and requested his recall by the Russian government. Things were not that simple, however. The tsar's son, Grand Duke Alexis, was on his way to the United States and could not make that journey if Catacazy was sent away. Fish and Grant, recognizing the diplomatic significance of Alexis's visit, reluctantly agreed that Catacazy could stay through the end of the grand duke's visit in February 1872. When Catacazy left, the Perkins Claim remained unsettled, and though it was raised in Washington several more times in the 1870s, it was never resolved. The bargaining chip held by Mrs. Perkins and her supporters had been traded for a promise that was never kept.

•••••••

Once Stoeckl received the money from the U.S. Treasury, the political wrestling over the Alaska Purchase should have ceased. That was not the case. By the end of 1868, accusations of bribery and corruption surfaced, leading to a congressional investigation and a persistent sense that Alaska had been bought in more ways than one. Though the report of the investigatory committee was ultimately inconclusive, during the process a number of people were accused of accepting bribes and abusing their political and public influence, and the public's cynicism about government corruption was only reinforced. In the opinion of one historian, the scandal surrounding the Alaska Purchase also had a lasting impact on American foreign policy, discouraging further expansionism for more than twenty years.

The first hint that the Alaska deal might be tainted by corruption arose immediately after the purchase became known to the public. Articles in several American newspapers, such as the *New York World*, suggested that "nobody believes that the whole $7,000,000 will go into Russian coffers." Shortly after, the *New York Tribune* remarked on Seward's "Russian treaty dinner parties" and suggested that he was "employing the machinery of the Associated Press" to push his agenda. Seward had also received help from "the regular Washington Lobby," according to the *Tribune*. These were, however, the bitter insinuations of those who disliked Seward or the notion of American expansion, and there was no proof to support these insinuations.

Accusations reemerged during the deliberation over the payment for Alaska the following year. In July 1868, as the appropriation debate was drawing to a close, Washington was tense with ill feelings over the recent impeachment trial and charges of fraud and corruption against Johnson, Seward, and other politicians. Consequently, when rumors of bribery emerged concerning the Alaska Purchase, there were many who were eager to believe them. The person most responsible for raising the question of corruption was Uriah Painter, a Washington correspondent for the *Philadelphia Inquirer* and the *New York Sun* and a lobbyist for various businessmen and financiers of significant wealth. Many of his friends were anti-Johnson Republicans and men of stature in Washington, and Painter himself owned stock in the *New York Sun* and the Western Union Company and made a comfortable living. Painter was no unbiased cub reporter. Though he had initially supported the Alaska Purchase, he changed his views, and in the summer of 1868, he began to stir up trouble by highlighting various rumors and casting certain facts in a suspicious light, particularly focusing on the presence of Robert J. Walker on the House floor during the appropriation debates. Walker enjoyed this right because he was a former member of the Senate, but his omnipresence bothered Painter. In late June, Painter had also told some of the appropriation bill's opponents that Seward was planning to acquire Greenland and Iceland, exacerbating negative feelings about the Johnson administration and its goals and methods of expansion. Painter sent a despatch to the *Sun* with basically the same information, pointing to Walker's pro-expansionist letter of January 1868 that was being republished as a pamphlet by the Government Printing Office. Painter also pressed Walker's legal partner Frederick P. Stanton and his associate Robert Latham for information.

In the meantime, the appropriation debates continued and drew to a close; the bill passed and on August 1, the Treasury Department issued a draft for $7.2 million to the Russian minister. Stoeckl endorsed the draft over to the bank of George Riggs, who disbursed the money according to Stoeckl's instruction to the London office of Baring Brothers, the bank that handled Russia's foreign accounts. Immediately after the approval of the appropriation bill, Schuyler wrote from St. Petersburg about the tensions over the Alaska payment, "It is to be hoped, now that the purchase of Aliaska is complete, that friendly relations will be restored." Schuyler's hunch was spot on. Once Russia received payment, all negative feelings toward the United States faded into the background. According to Schuyler, "the feeling against Americans to which I referred . . . is rapidly passing away, and . . . the old friendly feeling is returning." This change in mood was also undoubtedly connected to the visit of Admiral Farragut to Constantinople in August 1868 and the resolution of the House demanding free entry for all ships into the Black Sea in July 1868, Schuyler observed.

Just as it appeared that the turmoil over Alaska was drawing to a close, an odd incident occurred that revived rumors of corruption and piqued Painter's curiosity. On August 18, Robert Walker was the victim of a pickpocket while traveling by streetcar in New York City; this was a common enough event, but the amount stolen was $16,000 in gold certificates. The thieves were quickly caught, most of the money was recovered, and Walker declined to press charges. The whole matter might have been forgotten had the victim been anyone else. But Painter had read in a newspaper article that $5 million in gold had been sent to Russia through London which, he deduced, meant that $2.2 million was unaccounted for. Painter quickly drew the conclusion that Walker had been carrying the large sum because he was in the process of distributing bribes to various congressmen who had supported the appropriation bill, and he struck out to confirm his suspicions and confronted Latham and Stanton. Though both men denied knowledge of such a scheme, Painter persisted and began to investigate the disbursement of funds from Washington to London, interviewing the treasurer of the United States, Gen. Francis Spinner, and others in his search for answers. As treasurer, Spinner had prepared the warrants of payment that specified the amount and recipient to be paid.

Meanwhile, others suspected foul play as well, and at least two stories were recorded during this period that supported such rumors. In September 1868, President Johnson composed a private memorandum that has often been quoted in discussions of the Alaska scandal. In it he described a conversation that he and Seward had during a private drive in which the latter indicated that a number of men had been paid off to help the Alaska deal go through, including John W. Forney, a politician and publisher of the *Washington Chronicle*; Robert Walker and Frederick Stanton; and Republican Congressmen Nathaniel P. Banks and Thaddeus Stevens. No one but Johnson would have seen this document given its private nature, but several weeks later, Seward allegedly told John Bigelow, the former U.S. minister to France, a similar story, which Bigelow recorded in his diary. Historians have wrestled with how to interpret these two separate narratives that strongly resemble one another but part ways on several specific points. One historian has suggested that the refreshments that Johnson and Seward shared over this conversation may have been more lively than lemonade and impaired the president's ability to understand or remember the details. Though both of these accounts were recorded privately, one must imagine that if Johnson and Bigelow heard these stories, others did as well. Additional versions did, in fact, circulate in which Banks, Seward, and others had received payoffs.

For most of the fall of 1868 the presidential race took center stage in the media. Once the election ended, however, Painter resumed his investigation and contacted Rep. Benjamin Butler to prompt an official inquiry, emphasizing that only $5 million went to Russia and the rest to bribes. On November 30, Painter also published his alleged findings in the *New York Sun*. His accusations focused on details about how much money went to whom and when, a complicated series of disbursements to Stoeckl in various amounts that, in Painter's view, left room for doubt. Though most newspaper reports and editorials on the allegations raised skepticism and more questions, the story was out and the feeding frenzy began. By early December, *New*

York Sun editor Charles Dana suggested that although the stories were unlikely to be true, it was Congress's responsibility to investigate and put an end to all the unpleasant rumors. At the same time, on December 7, a story appeared in the *Worcester (MA) Daily Spy* that presented all of the Alaska gossip in one place, including suggestions that proponents of the Perkins Claim had been bribed to back down as well. The story was republished in the *Sun* two days later, and other papers followed suit. Finally, on December 14, a resolution was presented and quickly adopted in the House of Representatives calling for the matter to be examined by the Committee on Public Expenditures. Before the investigations could commence, however, another rumor emerged that claimed that former Representative Caleb Cushing had been rewarded for his support of the Alaska deal with a special foreign post, though no one seemed to know where. In fact, Cushing had been sent to Colombia to advance Johnson's cause of creating a ship canal route across the Isthmus of Panama, but the story dovetailed nicely with other accusations that were being tossed about at the time.

The Alaska investigation began on December 16, and during the next two months the committee heard testimony from at least fourteen witnesses, including Secretary of State Seward, Frederick P. Stanton, Robert J. Walker, Secretary of Treasury Francis Spinner, banker George Riggs, and a number of journalists, not the least of whom were Uriah Painter and Richard J. Hinton, the author of the *Worcester Daily Spy* piece. The *Philadelphia Evening Telegraph* gave no credence to the "obnoxious rumors" about bribery and corruption and declared, "It would be difficult . . . to convince many people that Mr. McCulloch, Treasurer Spinner, and Mr. Riggs, the banker, had combined to organize a gigantic fraud upon our own Government and that of Russia."

In fact, the inquiry was significantly hampered by the lack of participation of certain key players. The Russian legation in the United States, for example, did not participate in the investigation in any way. According to the committee, the members of the legation had been offered the opportunity to speak, formally or informally, but "the opportunity so tended has not been embraced." The lack of Russian participation was unfortunate because it was believed that the legation might offer information that would "clear away the clouds of suspicion that in the public mind have gathered around the acquisition of Alaska." The committee was not in the position to demand testimony or evidence from the Russian government, however, and the maintenance of good relations with Russia had made it embarrassing and difficult to unearth everything that had happened surrounding the purchase and the alleged exchange of money. Vladimir Bodisco wrote in a letter to the Russian foreign minister Gorchakov that there was one other avenue that had not been taken: If the investigating committee really wanted to examine the possibility of corruption, "it could have demanded that all of the members of the House and Senate appear before it one after another. It discreetly refrained from this extreme measure."

The results of the Alaska investigation were issued on February 27, 1869, and to no one's surprise, they revealed very little. The committee disagreed on several points and so the summary appeared in the form of a general report and an additional minority statement. The general report focused its condemnation on the *Worcester Daily Spy* journalist Richard J. Hinton, complaining of the "loose morality" of his journalism that he used to besmirch the names of others for "sensational purposes, or to cater to a morbid curiosity." Though the committee complained of the "nebulous gossip" in the newspapers, it made no significant remarks about the alleged corruption of its fellow congressmen and, in fact, drew no conclusions at all about the testimony it heard during the investigation.

The report additionally contained a minority statement by four committee members who felt the general committee statement to be insufficient. Clearly referring to Stanton and Walker, these committee members expressed their disapproval of those who were retained by the Russian minister as advocates or as attorneys for the Russian government "in a case in which their own was so deeply interested, and keeping the fact of their being so retained from the knowledge of those with whom they were brought in contact in conducting the business of their clients." They found this breach of trust particularly problematic when it involved persons who carried great influence in the community because of their former positions within the government. Finally, the minority statement noted that the general report failed to address the matter at hand directly. While it implied that Painter was guilty of stirring up trouble and even seeking secret employment with Stanton and Walker in supporting Russia's interests, it contained "no word of condemnation for those who actually were so employed, and who are at least open to the imputation of endeavoring to divert public attention from their own anomalous position."

The newspapers of Washington and New York reported on the final results of the Alaska investigation but gave it less attention than one might expect. Perhaps their cool approach was a reflection of their pessimism. Even before the investigation had concluded, the *New York Times* had already dismissed it as waste of time. Referring to the members of Congress as "a fierce pack of fraud avengers, in hot pursuit of the official delinquents," the *Times* compared the investigation and its likely results to "one sorry squirrel that ran up a tree." Skeptical that anything would come of it, the *Times* added, that if the "pretended evidence" did not surface, the accuser "must suffer the consequences." Later, when the inquiry had ended, the *New York Herald* published both parts of the report and noted that the committee's inability to obtain all the necessary information meant that "there still remains a cloud over the Alaska Purchase transactions." The *Herald* also urged Stoeckl to divulge the financial details of the Alaska Purchase and concluded, "By his keeping silent we can be assured that where there has been so much smoke there must have been some fire." With these articles the discussion of the Alaska scandal subsided, more or less, and the American public moved on to new concerns with the inauguration of Ulysses S. Grant in early March 1869.

So what can we conclude about the alleged bribery scandal surrounding the Alaska Purchase? It is absolutely true that the entire $7.2
million did not go to Russia. George Riggs testified that at Stoeckl's
request he sent only $7,035,000 to Baring Brothers, leaving $165,000
in the United States. Riggs also reported that he kept $3,600 for his
fee and gave Robert Walker $26,000 in gold. During the following
month, Riggs paid out the remaining $135,400 to Stoeckl in sever-
al disbursements of varying amounts. On the other hand, Painter's
suspicions about the report of only $5 million being sent to Russia
were entirely misplaced. After the original appearance of this information, the *New York Times* reported four months later that this
amount had been transmitted to Russia for a railroad deal, not for
payment for Alaska.

Once Riggs had disbursed all of the money to the Russian minister, the question remains, what did Stoeckl do with it? One historian
has suggested that Stoeckl likely gave money to Bodisco and kept
some for himself as well. Stoeckl had received 25,000 silver rubles as
a bonus for securing the Alaska treaty but thought it was too little,
especially since he had wrangled much more than his government
expected. We also know that Stoeckl distributed some of the money
to Walker and Stanton, as well as Latham, Forney, and other newspapermen. Walker admitted during the congressional investigation
that he received some $26,000 from Stoeckl, $5,000 of which he gave
to Stanton, and the latter admitted receiving that amount. Walker
also testified that he had advised Stoeckl to give $3,000 to his friend
John Forney, proprietor and editor of the *Washington Daily Morning
Chronicle*, in appreciation of his support. Finally, testimony also revealed that M. M. Noah of the *Daily Alta California* received $1,000
in thanks for his active support of the Alaska Purchase. In all cases,
the parties insisted that they were paid after the conclusion of the appropriation debates, and in the cases of Stanton, Forney, and Noah,
the monetary gift was reported to be entirely unexpected. Other
newspapermen denied receiving money at all or of having knowledge about others receiving money.

Painter's accusations about Walker, the money stolen from him in New York, and the alleged bribery of congressmen is impossible to prove, though many have accepted the rumor as fact. No congressmen were registered at the Fifth Avenue Hotel the week that Walker was robbed and, in any event, all of the gold certificates were non-negotiable except one, and Walker immediately stopped payment on that one. Nonetheless, many people, then and later, believed that congressmen were bribed. Historian Frank Golder, who mined the Russian archives in the early twentieth century, could find no conclusive evidence to warrant the indictment of any politician by name but felt certain that some congressmen had been bought off. More recently, other historians have accepted his interpretation, though to varying degrees. One historian, for example, believed that Thaddeus Stevens and Nathaniel Banks received money from Stoeckl but preferred to call it a reward rather than a bribe. He argued that Stoeckl did not need to pay Stevens, who had supported the treaty from the beginning, or Banks, who was an ardent expansionist. On the other hand, both Stevens and Banks had supported the Perkins Claim in 1867 and then changed their stance in 1868 in response to Stoeckl's assurance that the case would be given fair consideration. It is possible that Stoeckl "rewarded" them for their concession, but the timing is peculiar given that Stevens was on death's door in early August and died on August 11. A similar explanation can be applied to the case of Walker, who was a well-known expansionist in his own right. In any event, his letter and pamphlet actually spent little time on the question of Alaska and focused more on promoting the acquisition of the islands of St. Thomas and St. John.

Other historians have attempted to come up with a rough calculation of where the remaining $135,400 went that includes $10,000 each to ten separate congressmen who are never named. These historians admit that their calculations are rough and cannot be verified. And they are right. The very nature of bribery is secretive, and if Stoeckl bribed congressmen only he and they would know for certain what transpired, and it was in neither party's best interest to divulge the details. Bodisco noted this reality during the Alaska investigation in a letter to Gorchakov, remarking that the investigating committee gave the Russian legation the option of testifying on the assumption that it would not. The committee surely knew, Bodisco added, that "foreign missions have funds for intelligence and that no one except the governments to which they answer has the right to know for what they are used." It was only twenty years ago that a historian found an *ukaz* (proclamation) of December 13, 1868, in which Tsar Alexander II declares, "I *command* that the 165,000 dollars spent for the use known to me by . . . Stoeckl be counted as actual expenditure." This document seems to confirm that the Russian minister employed bribery to secure his deal. Still, we are left to wonder who received this money and in what amounts.

There is one other part of the story of how the United States paid for Alaska that should be mentioned. On March 25, 1867, when Stoeckl sent a telegram to Gorchakov with an overview of the terms of the treaty, he included a phrase that indicated that the telegram was being sent at Seward's request and that the U.S. government would be paying for it. This was no small consideration since the charge for the telegram was $9,886.50. Later, in November 1867, Seward received a bill from the New York, Newfoundland, and London Telegraph Company for a number of unpaid telegrams, including the telegram to Gorchakov of March 25, 1867. Seward disputed the manner in which the total was calculated (ciphers versus words) and specifically stated that the Department of State was not accountable for the telegram to Gorchakov. The telegraph company then contacted Stoeckl who stated that Seward had agreed to pay the cost at the time the telegram was sent. Following this, the telegraph company turned once again to Seward, asking that he come to an agreement with Stoeckl on this matter. In January 1868, Seward replied that he had no intention of paying for the telegram, nor was it his place to intervene in any discussion of Stoeckl's obligation to the telegraph company. Indeed, Seward never arranged for the Department of State to pay for any of the telegrams, and nine months later the company sent Seward a bill once again. Curiously, in the summary of charges, one telegram was notably missing—the telegram of March 25, 1867. In February 1870, the New York, Newfoundland, and London Telegraph Company was still seeking payment from the United States and filed suit in the U.S. Court of Claims for the unpaid telegrams. In the breakdown of the money owed to the company, the petition showed that on August 22, 1868, someone had paid for the telegram to Gorchakov. That person was almost certainly Stoeckl, who had received the payment for Alaska earlier that month. This assumption is confirmed by two statements made during the Alaska investigation. The banker George Riggs stated that Stoeckl had indicated to him that he had "paid at one time $10,000 in gold for one telegram." Similarly, Robert Walker claimed that Stoeckl had complained to him "that the whole thing had been very expensive . . . the telegraphs to and from Russia, and other charges which he said were enormous." All of this is to demonstrate that at least some of the money given to Stoeckl was used to pay for this telegram, and not for bribes.

Finally, there is one last difficulty in the payment for Alaska worth noting, yet another blemish on the romantic legend of a smooth, mutually advantageous transaction. When the United States paid for Alaska in August 1868, the payment was three months overdue. At the time, no one seemed to take note of this delinquency, but a little over a year later, the new Russian minister Constantin Catacazy decided to make an issue of it. On October 7, 1869, Secretary of State Hamilton Fish received a memorandum from Catacazy charging the American government 6 percent interest on the late payment for a total of $115,200. Catacazy claimed that Seward had admitted to Stoeckl that the United States owed this interest, and that he, Catacazy, was simply asking for the matter to be settled in the hope that an official request would not be necessary. In fact, it does not appear that the Russian minister had any official instructions to pursue this money, and this appears to be yet another example of Catacazy's meddlesome personality. Nonetheless, Fish seemed to accept the obligation and promised that he would submit it to Congress for appropriation. Soon, however, Catacazy changed his mind, for at the time that he raised the matter of the interest, the Perkins Claim was still alive, and Fish warned him that if he raised the question of interest in Congress, the Perkins matter would surely be interjected in some way. Catacazy subsequently asked that the request for interest be dropped, and it appears that it never came up before Congress.

OUR NEW SENATORS.

SECRETARY SEWARD—"*My dear Mr. Kamskatca, you really must dine with me. I have some of the very finest tallow candles and the loveliest train oil you ever tasted, and my whale's blubber is exquisite— and pray bring your friend Mr. Seal along with you. The President will be one of the party.*"

This is yet another example of the humor that appeared in the press about the purchase. *Frank Leslie's Illustrated* on April 27, 1867. MANY THANKS TO THE STAFF OF THE AUBURN UNIVERSITY AT MONTGOMERY LIBRARY FOR THEIR ASSISTANCE IN SCANNING THIS IMAGE.

CHAPTER VI

Very Uneasy and Vexed: International Reactions to the Purchase

$\mathcal{A}$s surprised as Americans were by the announce-ment of the Alaska Purchase in the spring of 1867, other countries were even more taken aback by the news. In Russia no one outside of official circles, of course, had been aware that the cession of Russian America was even a possibility. Other countries were astonished as well. France, Prussia, Austria, and the Ottoman Empire all, to varying degrees, saw the purchase as an important step in the formation of a Russian-American alliance and an increasing American presence in European affairs. There were concerns about Russian and American activity in Asia as well. Canada and Great Britain also feared an alliance but for different reasons. They worried that American expansion supported by Russia would threaten the future of British North America, and in both countries the press reacted strongly to the news of the treaty. It is important to recognize, however, that the reactions of the press were not always consistent with the official position of the government; moreover, given the complex and tense atmosphere in Europe during this period, other crises often overshadowed the news of the Alaska Purchase. Nonetheless, it is safe to trust the words of Edward Joy Morris, the American minister to Constantinople, who reported to Seward that the major powers of Europe feared a Russian-American alliance; it was a "spectre that oppresses them & haunts their thoughts by day and their dreams by night."

· · · ● ● ● ·

Europe in the late 1860s was a rapidly changing landscape, fueled by nationalism in its various forms and the international rivalry that is usually a by-product of this powerful ideology. As Prussian statesman Otto von Bismarck aggressively pursued his dream of German unification, he provoked a war with Austria in 1866 over the Danish provinces of Schleswig and Holstein and continued to behave in a bellicose manner in subsequent years. In 1867 he antagonized France over the future of Luxembourg. Edward Robinson, U.S. consul at Strasbourg, France, described the mounting tensions over the latter issue in April and May 1867. Warlike preparations in France were underway and some segments of society were even eager for war, namely the army and the Alsatian population. The U.S. consul was both alarmed and amused by the loud cry of patriotism from his Alsatian neighbors, who reminded him of American Southerners before the Civil War: "Then one Southerner could whip ten Northerners; here every Alsatian could conquer the Prussian Army." Robinson was certain that the German people would not allow Luxembourg to be annexed to France, warning that "the whole nation would rise to arms to prevent it." During this same period, Italy was engaged in its own process of unification and eagerly took advantage of the instability in Europe to gain territory from Austria, declaring Victor Emmanuel the first king of a unified Italy. As Germany and Italy consolidated their holdings and power, Austria's fate was decidedly different.

Faced with defeat by Prussia in 1866 and challenged by the Magyar population within its borders, the Hapsburg government compromised in 1867 and created a dual monarchy, the Austro-Hungarian Empire. Henceforth, the empire would consist of two individual states with one ruler, who would be the Emperor of Austria and the King of Hungary. The sudden announcement that Russian America had been ceded to the United States was viewed by many as one more piece of bad news, yet another destabilizing change in the shifting sands of European diplomacy.

Several U.S. officials in Europe remarked that the news had taken everyone completely by surprise. "It is, indeed, astonishing," wrote William Murphy, the American consul at Frankfurt on Main, "what deep and exciting impression the first short and abrupt telegraphic report of that unexpected change of territory produced amongst the different political circles of Europe." Many in Europe feared that the Alaska Purchase and the evolving Russian-American relationship that it foretold was a portent of bad things to come. Murphy reported that while the liberal press of Europe dispassionately viewed the sale as a mutually beneficial agreement between the two countries, the conservative press felt "very uneasy and vexed." In their eyes, the low selling price hinted that there would be "other compensations . . . either actual assistance on the part of the United States, in case she might require such for the satisfaction of her ambitions on another scene of action, or passive garantee [*sic*] upon the demand of some territorial changes on European soil." There were rumors that the Alaska deal included America's promise to back Russia in its ambition to abolish the Black Sea Clause from the Treaty of Paris. At least one European country scrambled to make the most of the new situation. The U.S. minister from Denmark reported in late April 1867 that he had already been approached by one Danish official hoping to strengthen his country's position in Europe with a closer alliance with Russia and the United States.

The primary concern of most European countries about a Russian-American alliance was how it might affect the fate of the Ottoman

Empire and its vast territories, the so-called Eastern Question. The Ottoman Empire had been steadily weakening over the eighteenth century, and by the nineteenth century the Eastern Question was a central theme of European diplomatic relations. The major European powers all had a stake in how, when, and if the Ottoman Empire unraveled, and because they could not agree on how to settle the Eastern Question, each new crisis was accompanied by intense rivalry and suspicion. In September 1866, Murphy wrote to the U.S. State Department that the universal hope was that the resolution of the Eastern Question would not occur "through the sword, but that, . . . all the European powers must take an interest in the maintenance of peace and let the 'sick man' drag on his painful existence for some time longer. . . . The change of the map caused by the solution of that question will certainly cost much blood." Over the course of the nineteenth century, the major powers participated in the slow dismantling of the Ottoman territories, either through direct annexation or the creation or recognition of autonomous or independent regions. One issue of particular concern by all the powers was control of the Bosporus and Dardanelles Straits that connected the Black Sea to the Mediterranean. Control of the straits was critical for the survival of the Ottoman Empire, but its importance for both England and Russia meant that those nations were deeply invested in the determination as well. As the international balance of power shifted and alliances changed, the Ottoman Empire held the uncomfortable position of a country with no clear enemies but no real allies.

Many recognized the role that Russia would likely play in the ultimate fate of the Ottoman Empire and thus any Russian move was closely scrutinized by the other European players. Many European officials had begun to fear that the United States might become involved in the Eastern Question as well. In September 1866, Murphy wrote Seward that "the very friendly relations between the Cabinets at Washington and St. Petersburg have led of late to the apprehension, rather universally expressed, that our Government has taken, too, an interest in the question, which, of course, might render its solution more difficult and dangerous than ever thought of." Only a few weeks later, this fear seemed to be confirmed by the announcement of the Alaska treaty. In early March 1867, American consul Murphy wrote to Seward that though things appeared calm in Europe at the moment, there was still great uneasiness about "the Oriental question, which leads to apprehensions, since Russia evidently endeavors to get reliable Allies to be able to energetically push the matter on to decision."

The European powers had good reasons to be concerned about American intervention in the Near East. The previous year, a rebellion against Turkish power broke out in Crete, a part of the Ottoman Empire inhabited by a largely Christian population. These Cretans, complaining of bad government and high taxation and suffering from the effects of several bad harvests, petitioned the sultan directly for help. In response, the local Turkish governor made moves to dissolve the Cretan Assembly and requested troops from Constantinople. The various foreign consuls posted in the empire, including James Stillman, the American consul at Syros and Crete, did their best to prevent the eruption of an armed conflict. Stillman in particular was trusted by the Cretan people and so featured significantly in the negotiations to maintain peace, urging the rebels to present their grievances peacefully and appealing to the American government to send a warship to help evacuate Cretan refugees, many of whom were women and children dying of cold and hunger. But Turkish officials were cautious and suspicious about American involvement and repeatedly accused Stillman of encouraging the insurgents against the sultan. Ultimately, the Ottoman government would not give permission for American ships to transport refugees and the American government would not act without Turkish permission.

Meanwhile, the U.S. minister at Constantinople, William Morris, was also reporting to Seward on the Cretan crisis and supported Stillman's call for American help with the refugee problem. When violence eventually erupted in September 1866, Seward responded with a passionate despatch conveying American sympathy for the

Christian inhabitants of Crete. Morris made sure that the other European representatives knew of Seward's message, hoping that it would prompt them to intervene as well. In mid-November 1866, Morris wrote, "I flatter myself it [American prestige] never was so widely extended & so firmly established as now." A Constantinople paper, *L'Etoile d'Orient*, apparently agreed, "America is the lion of the day in our capital."

Many in Europe, however, suspected that Washington had other motives. For years, rumors circulated that the United States wanted to establish a fueling station in the Mediterranean. At the end of 1866, Morris wrote Seward that the Ottoman newspapers were convinced of American interest in Turkish affairs, especially in conjunction with Russia, and in acquiring an island in the Greek Archipelago. The press reported this information with such certitude that "they will accept no denials on the subject: Contradiction only seems to excite suspicion." Meanwhile, other European newspapers declared that both Britain and France had warned the sultan that they would not support the sale of any Mediterranean island to the United States. Ultimately, these concerns over American activity in the region and the possibility of a Russian-American alliance prompted the Ottoman government to establish a diplomatic post in the United States in the fall of 1866.

·······

Although Russia was one of the participants in the Alaska sale, opinions in Russia varied about the necessity and benefits of the transaction. Officially, of course, Russia was satisfied with the exchange. Russia's top officials—Tsar Alexander II, Gorchakov, Grand Duke Constantine, and Stoeckl—had initiated, supported, and executed the sale. While other officials may have disapproved, their views were not likely to have been expressed publicly and are, consequently, more difficult to uncover. We know that there was some opposition. In fact, in December 1866, when Gorchakov had submitted the ideas of the committee of Minister of Finance Reutern, Grand Duke Constantine, and Russian Minister Stoeckl to the tsar, there had been one other official with a very different opinion. Baron Fedor Osten-Saken, who worked in the Asiatic Department of the Ministry for Foreign Affairs, was not included in the meeting but attempted to register his views nonetheless. In his memorandum written on the same day as the Reutern-Constantine-Stoeckl meeting, Osten-Saken addressed the major arguments in favor of selling Russian America, but he believed these points were all easily discredited. Though the Russian-American Company had proven unsuccessful, he argued, this did not mean that the territory itself had no value. As to the fear that the territory might be seized by someone else, Osten-Saken dismissed it entirely. Finally, he argued against the notion that the amount of money received for the Russian colonies would be substantial enough to impact the Russian treasury in any significant way. Osten-Saken concluded, "As far as the positive advantages are concerned they belong in reality only to the future, but it would seem that the present generation had a sacred obligation to preserve for the future generations every clod of earth along the coast of an ocean which has world-wide importance." Years later, Osten-Saken explained his reason for writing the above memorandum, recalling that he was "shaken to the depths of my soul" by the news that Russian America might be sold.

Others opposed the deal as well. In July 1867, Stoeckl wrote that the Alaska treaty had elicited strong criticism in Russia, but he did not name names. Stoeckl did, however, stress his own view that Russia's only choice regarding its American colonies was between selling them or losing them. P. A. Valuev, minister of the interior, also opposed the sale, but how widely his views were known at the time is unclear. In his diary on March 22/April 3, 1867, he wrote of the announcement of the sale being a complete surprise, adding with a tone of disapproval, "Strange phenomenon and a depressing feeling. . . . We sell part of our territory on the quiet and do a bad turn to England, whose Canadian possessions now still more exclusively contradict the Monroe Doctrine." Cassius Clay, U.S. minister to Russia, wrote to Seward that the Russians had divided into two camps, those who supported the sale, and those who thought it a mistake. The latter had "attempted to make interest against the administration by attacking the treaty." In general, Clay observed, "Russians are very jealous of foreigners, and traditionally opposed to ceding territory," but given the friendly relations between Russia and the United States, many were willing to say, "Well, we have sold to you too cheaply, but 'tis all in the family."

Meanwhile, Russian newspapers presented a range of views. One newspaper, for example, greeted the news of the sale with disbelief. Doubting that the United States would be interested in buying Russian America, the *Narodnyi Golos* called the despatch from New York a "superb American canard." There seems to have been a general sense that Russia had sold its territory for too little. The newspaper *Bizhevye Vedomosti* called $7 million an insignificant sum, even considering the small benefits of the territory to Russia. Some newspapers were far more critical, the most notable example being *Golos*. Over a period of several days, the editors of *Golos* expressed harsh criticism of the sale by pretending to doubt the veracity of the reports, a tactic that allowed them to discuss the sale and to be critical of government policy. *Golos* declared, "We cannot look upon such an unbelievable rumor otherwise than as the very worst joke on a gullible public . . . they [the rumors] deeply anger all true Russians." The editors argued that Russia had a right to possess this region, conquered and developed with the money, hard work, and "even the blood" of Russians. Indeed, *Golos* bemoaned the loss of other Russian colonies, as well, and appealed to the public's sense of national pride. The paper called the loss of the Ross colony in California more than two decades earlier "an enormous mistake and inefficiency," and asked, "is it permissible now to repeat a similar mistake? . . . does the national self-esteem merit so little attention that it can be sacrificed for some mere 5-6 million dollars?" These were strong opinions in a country where criticism of the government could result in severe punishment.

Other papers were kinder in their assessments. The *St. Petersburgskie Vedomosti*, the semi-official newspaper of the capital, tried to counter and squelch negative interpretations of the sale. Portraying the ratification of the treaty in the most positive light, the paper focused on the strengthening of the Russian-American friendship. The Russian public, the paper claimed, "is not inimical to the cession of the Russian possessions. Many consider it a full rational measure and place on this cession, perhaps not without reason, hopes for a permanent and long-lasting alliance with the Americans." The paper believed that the Russian-American friendship was particularly important in dealing with the Eastern Question and in the current international climate where "almost all of Europe is preoccupied with how to stop our successes and paralyze our influence everywhere." *St. Petersburgskie Vedomosti* explained the underlying message of the Alaska transaction in the following way: "The United States tells Russia that they will condone any increase in her strength in Europe and Asia as long as she does not hinder their strengthening in America; Russia on the other hand declares to the United States that she is ready to give them a free hand and on occasion even give her support in Europe or Asia." The editors did, however, acknowledge that not all Russians were thrilled with the "wise agreement" between Washington and St. Petersburg. To the "sincere and insincere howls of robust patriotism" expressed in the other papers, *St. Petersburgskie Vedomosti* snarked, "We anticipated that the importance of the present transactions would not be understood at once." Meanwhile, Cassius Clay reported from the Russian capital that the Russian-American friendship was very important to the Russian government. He predicted that St. Petersburg would not soon jeopardize this relationship, "for the enthusiasm of the Russian people in the reception of Mr. Fox astonished the government more than it did me; who was really more concurrent with public opinion than they."

The other nations of Europe recognized the significance of the Alaska transaction as well, but how they reacted was largely determined by the recent past and the relationship that each nation had with the parties involved. America's relationships with Prussia, Austria, and France, for example, had been put to the test by the American Civil War. In the case of Prussia, there had been great sympathy for the North and the preservation of the Union. The Prussian government, as a traditional conservative monarchy, opposed all revolutionary movements and had instructed its envoy in Washington to reject any overtures from representatives of the Southern states. When the war broke out, the American legation in Berlin was flooded with support and offers to enlist on the side of the North, so much so that it found it necessary to post a sign on its door that it was not a recruitment office. In the following years, Bismarck worked hard to cultivate a friendship with the United States, aware that Prussia could ill afford the added burden of American animosity when European affairs were so dangerous. Prussia also had been on good terms with Russia, remaining neutral during the Crimean War and supporting the Russian monarchy in other ways in subsequent years. When the Russian government faced an insurrection in the Polish section of its empire in 1863, much of Europe, particularly France, expressed sympathy for the Poles and even raised the possibility of Polish autonomy. Bismarck, however, took the opposite stance; fearing that under European pressure Russia might decide to free Poland, which would undoubtedly lead to demands of autonomy from the Polish section of Prussia, Bismarck signed a secret agreement with Russia to collaborate in suppressing the revolt. Though the agreement was short-lived, his decision in this matter marked a shift in Prussian foreign policy away from France and closer to Russia.

Consequently, when the Alaska Purchase became public knowledge, Bismarck was not alarmed. George Bancroft, who became American minister to Prussia that year, recorded a conversation he had with Bismarck in August 1867. Bancroft recalled that the chancellor spoke favorably of the acquisition of Russian America by the United States. "Russia could not turn it to any account," Bismarck told Bancroft, but "the enterprising men of the United States would do so." Similarly, the British minister to Prussia, Lord Augustus Loftus, recalled that Bismarck was equally nonplussed about the Eastern Question, having stated that the European countries viewed the question with too much passion and feared Russian intentions more than necessary. Bismarck believed that neither Russia nor France would make any serious moves to dismantle the Ottoman Empire. As for Prussia, though the king had sympathy for the Christians in the Ottoman Empire and wanted them to receive fair treatment from the Turks, Bismarck asserted that Prussia had no direct political concern in the outcome of the situation and was only interested in Turkey for commercial reasons.

Not all Germans were as unfazed as Bismarck. The announcement of the Alaska Purchase was used by some Prussians as a platform for the discussion of decidedly more narrow concerns. In the spring of 1867, Prussia was embroiled in a conflict with France over the question of Luxembourg and many drew connections between that situation and the cession of Russian America. William Murphy, the American consul in Frankfurt, relayed that "the news arrived at the very time when the Luxembourg question . . . had aroused and inflamed the minds of the Germans who declared unanimously opposed to the cession of any German territory to anybody and the least and last to France, the 'archfiend to Germany,' . . . when and as long as she is ruled by the Napoleonic dynasty." Members of the various north German parliaments passionately discussed the new American acquisition and pointed out that the transaction clearly illustrated the spirit of the Monroe Doctrine. The United States had persuaded Russia that "America ought to belong to Americans" and in return, Russia would have a free hand elsewhere. The Prussian government was urged to exercise the same principle in reverse, by not allowing "an original and active piece of German soil, being moreover the native soil of some illustrious German Emperors" to be separated from Germany.

Others in Prussia worried about the larger implications. Murphy described concerns among Prussian liberals that the United States was withdrawing from its assistance "in the promotion of republicanism in Europe." They cautioned that "the extremes seem to touch each other and some mysterious sympathy to unite Russia and the United States in their efforts to limit republicanism to America and extend Cossackyism over Europe." Not all Prussians were so alarmed, however. John C. Wright, serving in the legation in Berlin, informed Seward that the news of the purchase was certainly a theme of discussion, but "we have the good wishes of nearly all persons in the purchase, with the exception of those holding sympathies in common with the English and the French."

In the Austrian Empire, there were varying opinions as well. Throughout the nineteenth century, the Austrian state, ruled by the Hapsburg family, combatted the growing flames of nationalism on virtually all sides and its great power status was little more than a mirage. The diplomatic system created after the Napoleonic Wars at the Congress of Vienna was designed to support the legitimacy of existing governments and all monarchies and to suppress revolution wherever it might appear. The Hapsburg Empire's representative at that historic conference, Klemens von Metternich, knew that Austria could not rely on force to retain its position and so, consequently, he pushed aggressively for the policy of legitimacy. It was only through such diplomatic maneuvering that Austria could remain a part of the Great Power system. As a result, the Hapsburg Empire had to play the game well and its relationship with other powers was critical to its success.

Though the United States and Austria had little cause for direct interaction in the first half of the nineteenth century, there was a general disdain on the part of Americans for the Catholic, conservative Austrian Empire. This suspicion and distrust was intensified by the failed revolutions calling for basic civil rights and greater representation that swept through Europe in 1848. The Austrian Empire faced challenges to its government as well, particularly in the Hungarian portion of the empire where the Magyars demanded independence. Americans almost universally supported the Hungarian revolutionaries. The *North American Review*, for example, called Austria a "conglomeration of dissimilar races having no principle of unity but despotism." Despite such opinions, there was no reason for hostility between the two nations until, that is, the United States decided to intervene in Austria's affairs. In the midst of Austria's revolutionary crisis, the U.S. government ordered one of its attachés in Europe to travel to Budapest to assess if Hungarian independence was viable and if it was, to extend U.S. recognition.

In fact, by the time the American attaché reached Budapest the question was moot—the Hapsburg government, with the help of Russia, had crushed the Magyar insurrection. Had this uncompleted mission remained buried within American diplomatic correspondence, the subsequent crisis would have been averted, but instead, an Austrian citizen working for the U.S. consul in Vienna turned over a copy of the attaché's instructions to the Austrian foreign ministry. The Hapsburg government then knew that the United States had been prepared to recognize the Hungarian revolutionaries, violating not only the norms of the Great Power system but also America's own policy of nonintervention in European affairs. The Hapsburg government asked U.S. President Zachary Taylor to disavow his government's actions and apologize, but Taylor refused and there were some in the Senate who called to sever diplomatic relations. Though Taylor died in July 1850, the diplomatic battle raged on, and even as the United States maintained its official position of nonintervention, its actions often communicated a different message. Pro-Hungarian sentiment lingered in the United States and on March 3, 1851, the new president, Millard Fillmore, approved a joint resolution of both houses of Congress to send a U.S. naval vessel to collect the Hungarian revolutionary Louis Kossuth from the Ottoman Empire, where he had been detained since 1849 when he fled the Austrian Empire. Kossuth arrived in the United States in December 1851 and was greeted with much fanfare. He toured the United States and was treated as a hero, the centerpiece for celebrations and balls and speeches in support of Hungarian independence. The Hapsburg government seethed as its worst enemy traveled as a celebrity, every banquet an insult to the sovereignty of the Austrian Empire.

Despite the tensions created by the Hungarian revolution, in subsequent years, the United States and the Austrian Empire remained on cordial terms. At the outset of the American Civil War, the Hapsburg government informed the United States that it would not recognize the Confederacy and maintained that position throughout the war. Thus, Austria's relationship with the United States was not strained by the question of recognition of the South as it was with other European nations. There was another issue, however, that renewed tensions between the two countries. In 1863 Napoleon III of France set up Archduke Maximilian on the Mexican throne. Maximilian was the younger brother of the Hapsburg Emperor Francis Joseph and so the Austrian government was connected to the Mexican arrangement in this sense. For the most part, the Austrian Empire kept out of the whole affair until 1866 when it was clear that Maximilian's government and his life were in danger. The Austrian government felt it could not desert the emperor's brother and agreed to allow four thousand volunteers to go to Mexico to become part of Maximilian's army. News of this enraged Seward, who threatened war if Austrian troops became involved in hostilities in Mexico. Seward's saber rattling frightened the Hapsburg government, which was already on the verge of war with Prussia, and in May 1866, Austria declared that it would not allow troops to sail to Mexico. In the end, the United States and the Austrian Empire navigated these decades without ever severing diplomatic relations, but these crises damaged U.S.-Hapsburg relations and led to a pro-Hungarian stance in popular and official circles that would persist into the next century.

Austria had a complicated relationship with Russia as well. Russia had helped the Austrian Empire defeat the Hungarian revolutionaries in 1848–49, but this spirit of cooperation was narrow in its focus. Only a few years later, when Russian troops occupied much of present-day Romania at the beginning of the Crimean War, Austria could not ignore this aggression. Any growth of Russian power in the Balkans would come at the expense of Austrian influence. Though Great Britain and France could not convince Austria to join them, they did persuade the Hapsburg government to threaten the tsar with war. In doing so, the good relations between the Austrian and Russian Empires came to an end, and in subsequent decades there would always be suspicion over one another's motives in the fate of the Ottoman Empire. Ultimately, this rivalry would play a role in the outbreak of World War I many years later.

On the eve of the Alaska Purchase, the Austrian Empire was in a very tough position. It had been defeated by Prussia in a humiliating war that left it isolated and weak, and the suspension of the constitution in 1865 pending negotiations with the Magyars had created a state of political uncertainty as well. To make matters worse, Austria faced a range of economic difficulties. With a high national debt and the need to pay reparations to Prussia, the Hapsburg state was unprepared to confront floods and harvest failures in the Hungarian portion of the empire. The economic situation was so bad that the government faced the possibility that within a year Austrian bonds would be excluded from the currency exchanges of western Europe. John Lothrop Motley, the American minister to Austria, wrote in November 1866, "This Empire is in a woeful plight. There is deep mortification, dissatisfaction, enormous distress. The poverty is something awful to think of." Consequently, from the fall of 1866 through the spring of 1867, the Hapsburg government was consumed by these problems and the articulation of an agreement with the Magyars to create a dual monarchy.

Despite these domestic problems, the Austrian Empire was in no position to ignore events occurring elsewhere. The rebellion in Crete that had burst forth in the summer of 1866 was one such event. Austria found itself in a difficult situation. It did not want to aggressively push the Eastern Question while it was still weak and recovering, but it could not remove itself entirely from the conversation either. Russia and France both pushed for Crete to be allowed to unite with Greece. Austria was in no hurry to dismantle the Ottoman Empire, however. In spite of everything, the continuation of the Ottoman Empire was a better arrangement for Austria than the alternative—a string of fragile states that would likely end up as Russian satellites. Moreover, a diplomatic success for Russia regarding Crete might elevate Russia's prestige in the Slavic world at large. Thus Austro-Russian relations were strained by mutual suspicion over the Near East: both Austria's determination that Russia should not control the fate of the Ottoman Empire and Russia's suspicions about Austrian designs on Bosnia and Herzegovina.

There was one other reason for tension between Austria and Russia. Galicia was the northernmost province of the Austrian Empire and shared a border with Russia's Polish holdings. After the creation of the dual monarchy in 1867 the Hapsburg government granted virtual home rule in Galicia to placate the Poles, the only group of Slavs whose fear of Russia outweighed its sympathy for the Panslav movement. Russia did not like this generous treatment of the Galician Poles, certain that such action could only give the Poles of the Russian Empire senseless and dangerous dreams. The conflict over this would ultimately lead to the mutual withdrawal of ministers the following year.

Placed in this context, the announcement of the Alaska Purchase could only have been received in Austria with reservations. Though Austria may have cared little about American expansion in North America, it did have reason to worry about any relationship that might influence Russia's position in the Near East. Nonetheless, it seems that few in the government outwardly expressed alarm at the news of the Alaska deal; nor did the American minister to Austria see fit to comment on Vienna's reaction to the Alaska Purchase, focusing instead on the more immediate problems of Prussia's growing strength and the Austro-Hungarian state's precipitous position as its neighbor. According to one historian, only Franz Kuhn von Kuhenfeld, the minister of war, recognized the significance of this treaty and predicted a world dominated by Washington and Moscow.

There were, of course, reports on the sale of Russian America in the Austrian press. The *Weiner Zeitung* reported that next to the Luxembourg matter, the cession of Russian America to the United States was the most significant story in the European press and went on to cite various newspapers on the subject. Similarly, the *Neue Freie Presse* described the "politically important" sale that would put the United States in closer proximity to East Asia and would facilitate its other plans for expansion in the region. A few days later, the same paper suggested that the government of the United States had obligated itself and possibly its navy to support the Russian government in its Asian endeavors. Nonetheless, the *Neue Freie Presse* clearly recognized the potential significance of the Alaska treaty and for several days reported in both its morning and evening editions, giving its own views on the matter in addition to sharing the views of other European papers.

To the south, in Italy, the news was received with similar stoicism. The United States had been on good terms with Italy even before the unification of its various parts. Diplomatic relations had existed with Sardinia since 1838, and during Italy's first war for independence in 1848, both the American public and the American press supported the Piedmont rebellion against Austria. A number of Americans even fought alongside the rebels. In 1860, when Piedmont annexed the Kingdom of Two Sicilies, the United States was the first government to recognize the new Kingdom of Italy, and George Marsh became its first American minister. During the Civil War, the United States and Italy maintained cordial relations. Of course, the United States sought to ensure that Italy would neither recognize nor support the Confederacy in any way. Though there was never an agreement in writing that guaranteed neutrality, the Italian government gave strong assurances that it would not allow Confederate ships in its ports except under the most extenuating circumstances. Meanwhile, the Italian public appeared to wholeheartedly support the cause of the North. When the Civil War broke out in April 1861, the American legation in Turin was inundated with Italians offering to enlist for the

North. So overwhelming was the flood of support that the secretary of the legation, Romaine Dillon, had to post a notice in the *Gazzetta Ufficiale del Regno d'Italia* clarifying that he had no authorization to sign up recruits. This remained U.S. policy even as the war continued and the numbers of war dead increased. When Seward received an offer from Col. Giovanni Battista Cattabeni, a veteran of the wars for Italian Unification, to organize a corps of some two thousand men, the secretary explained that American federal law did not permit the recruitment of foreign nationals. In the end, few Italians went to the United States for the express purpose of fighting in the war, but there were a number of Italian Americans who fought for the Union, including one group affectionately known as the Garibaldi Guard in the Thirty-Ninth New York Infantry.

Even as the American Civil War ended, the United States and Italy shared some common concerns; both countries had to wrestle with the challenges of postwar reconstruction and the political, social, and economic realities of a new unification. In 1866 Italy had acquired Venetia as a consequence of the brief but decisive Austro-Prussian War and was one step closer to complete unification, with Rome still yet to be incorporated. There was great sympathy for Italian unification in the United States, and the American government also intended to officially recognize changes. On March 11, 1867, Seward informed American minister Rufus King that Congress had decided to suspend money to support a mission in Rome. Several weeks later, when the world found out about the Alaska Purchase, King made no comment except to enclose a copy of the *Diplomatic Review* for Seward. The *Review* did have an article on the significance of the purchase; however, the journal was an English publication, not an Italian one, so it sheds no light on Italian opinions. The Italian press, at least, did not react to the news of the Alaska Purchase with great alarm. Primarily, newspapers like *Gazzetta Ufficiale*, *La Nazione*, and *La Stampa* reported the basic elements of the treaty or quoted from other European papers on the possible consequences of the arrangement but provided no editorial responses to the purchase.

There were some diplomatic officials in Italy who shared their own views of the purchase. George Marsh wrote from Florence, for example, "The Russians certainly think they took the stranger in consumedly." J. C. Hooker, the secretary of the legation at Rome, meanwhile, had already expressed a strong distrust of Russia a year and a half before the treaty. Hooker had called Russia "the enemy of every nation that in anyways inteferes [*sic*] with her," and had dismissed the popular notion that Russia was America's friend. Hooker believed that Russia had spies in every country and likely in the U.S. State Department, as well, and concluded, "The Russians are considered the greatest intriguers in Europe controlling presses and shaping public opinion—and my opinion is that they need watching."

France would certainly have agreed with this assessment. Of all the continental European countries, France was probably the most concerned by the announcement of the Alaska Purchase, in part because of its complicated relationship with the United States. During the American Civil War, Napoleon III had at various points seemed ready to intervene on behalf of the Confederacy. In the spring of 1862, for example, he proposed a joint Anglo-French naval expedition to the mouth of the Mississippi to break the Union blockade. In the end, without assistance from Great Britain, French policy remained one of strict neutrality. Napoleon III had also recently set up the puppet government of Maximilian I in Mexico, backed by French troops, and one of his motives in doing so was to check American expansion, at least in the Gulf region. The United States never recognized the government of Maximillian and objected to the permanent presence of French troops there but could do little about it. Once the American Civil War ended, Seward was in a better position to challenge Napoleon and pressured France to withdraw. The situation was sufficiently tense that French officials feared the possibility of war, and Napoleon sought out a mutual assistance agreement with Great Britain as a security against American hostility. The British were not interested, reasoning that in the event of an American invasion of Canada, France could offer no aid. The formation of an anti-American alliance might, in fact, provoke aggression. On top of this failure to pull in Great Britain, Napoleon began to have problems at America's southern border. Specifically, Napoleon came to realize that Maximilian expected France to supply him with military and financial help indefinitely, a commitment he could not make, especially given the increasing discontent with the whole endeavor at home. In the face of these threats and failures, in January 1866 Napoleon announced his intent to evacuate Mexico.

France also had a troubled past with Russia. In the summer of 1866, Napoleon watched as Prussia soundly and quickly defeated Austria, leaving Prussia stronger and Austria weaker than before. Fearful of these developments, Napoleon reached out to Russia, looking for support in western Europe in exchange for concessions in the Near East, especially in the Ottoman Empire. Russia, however, would not agree to any kind of alliance without knowing more of France's intentions. The tsar had reason to be wary; France had fought against Russia in the Crimean War and sympathized with Polish rebels in 1863. Now, only three years later, Russia was still distrustful of Napoleon and his motives. The suspicion was mutual. In the fall of 1866, Gustavus Vasa Fox, wrote to Secretary of the Navy Gideon Welles that he had recently met with the French leader who warned him against trusting Russia. Napoleon told Fox, "Do not be too friendly with Russia. . . . You can stand alone." Fox replied, "When it was doubtful whether we should ever stand again, at a time when the most powerful nations menaced us, Russia felt and expressed her sympathy for us, and America never will forget it." Napoleon responded, "Russia is for herself alone." It seems safe to assume that Napoleon was not happy about the Alaska Purchase or a potential Russian-American alliance.

The French press, meanwhile, was very anxious about the news of the purchase. According to the *New York Times*, the newspapers in France displayed "less indifference than those of England" to the news, and interpreted the deal as "a very clear case of conspiracy between America and Russia to control the affairs of the whole world."

The Paris correspondent for the *New York Tribune* recorded the same mood, explaining "inasmuch as English folks don't like it and are supposed to be offended by it, to that degree it gratifies French folks. For the fundamentalist [*sic*] of all international immoral laws is—hate your neighbor and like what he most does not. Inasmuch as it seems to indicate close relations between Russia and the United States, bearing first on the Eastern, and then on other European and world questions, it is regarded as another in the series of Louis Napoleon's ill-luck—as another proof of his erroneous foreign policy." In angering the United States over the Mexican expedition and Russia over his sympathy with the Poles in 1863, Napoleon III had succeeded in alienating "the two natural political allies of France . . . and throwing them into each other's arms." The newspaper *Le Temps* declared that, "the importance of the event . . . is not limited to the New World." The cession of Russian America was consistent with Russia's emergence from isolation and had gained the growing nation two things, money for its treasury and an alliance. Though the Russian-American friendship dated back to the 1850s, *Le Temps* concluded, "Today's ceding of territory by the Russians cannot fail to strengthen the paradoxical relationship between Tsar Alexander and President Johnson." The journalists at the *Siecle* and *L'Opinion Nationale* agreed, the latter declaring that the contract between the United States and Russia was proof that an alliance had taken place between the governments of St. Petersburg and Washington. The low selling price was also viewed with suspicion. One newspaper, the *France*, apparently believed that the only explanation for Russia's generosity was that it expected compensation elsewhere.

While the nations of western Europe discussed and debated the possible consequences of the Alaska Purchase, politicians in Constantinople also received the news with trepidation. The Ottoman Empire, even more than other countries, feared that a Russian-American alliance would involve the United States taking Russia's side in the Eastern Question. The official Ottoman publication, *La Turquie*, compared the announcement to a bomb bursting "in the midst of very complicated situations charged with tempests." It declared, "All the world knows with what impatience Americans bear with the neighborhood of the English." The paper called the anticipated Russian-American alliance a "common danger" for all of Europe that could seriously impact the outcome of the Eastern Question; specifically, with American blessing, Russia could seize Constantinople and "give a mortal blow to English domination in India." Turkish officials believed that such a relationship would "operate to the serious detriment of Turkey." Even before the purchase, Morris had reported to Seward from Constantinople that people in the Ottoman Empire were uneasy. On December 3, 1866, President Andrew Johnson had mentioned the Eastern Question in his annual address to Congress, noting that American political and commercial interests could potentially be affected by events in that region. On January 2, 1867, Morris wrote, "The allusion in the President's message to Oriental affairs, conjoined with our immensely increased prestige and power since the War—the fear of an alliance between the U.S. and Russia—and the expansive . . . and energetic foreign policy of the Administration—all these and other obvious considerations have induced the Porte to establish a mission in the U.S. straitened [sic] as are its pecuniary circumstances." After the announcement of the purchase, Morris reiterated this statement about the perceived Russian-American alliance and its impact on the Eastern Question.

· · · ● · · ·

As one might expect, the strongest reactions came from Great Britain and Canada. Both countries were suspicious of American intentions in North America, in particular, but in other places as well. Shortly before the Alaska deal, Queen Victoria wrote in her diary, "Talked of America and the danger which seems approaching, of our having a war with her as soon as she makes peace; of the impossibility of holding Canada; but we must struggle for it." When word of the Alaska Purchase reached Great Britain on March 31 and appeared in several London newspapers the next day, the news caught the British government by surprise. Publicly, London gave the impression of indifference but such was not entirely the case. Sir Arthur Buchanen, the British minister to Russia, had reportedly told Gorchakov in St. Petersburg that Russia should have offered Alaska to Great Britain first. In fact, the British government was not particularly interested in acquiring new colonies at the moment, so the offer would have been moot; nonetheless, several officials in the government felt slighted by the oversight. The treaty was only briefly discussed in the House of Commons when someone asked Lord Edward Stanley, the secretary of state for foreign affairs, if the reports were true. Stanley could not reply with certainty, but he informed his colleagues that the Foreign Office had contacted the Russian minister to inquire. The following day, the House of Lords discussed the matter as well, where the secretary of state for the Colonies observed that the Alaska treaty was "likely to cause great feeling and possibly considerable excitement; but I trust it will not be allowed to have undue weight in the minds of Englishmen—for I cannot myself think that the cession or purchase, if it be so, . . . is likely to have any overwhelming influence upon the progress of the colonies sprung from English blood . . . on that side of the world." Beyond one more brief mention of the purchase by Lord Stanley a few days later, it was not discussed in Parliament again.

Others in Britain attributed more sinister motives to the deal between Russia and the United States. Sir Frederick Bruce, British minister to the United States, described his current country of residence as Canada's "arrogant neighbor" with an "aggressive foreign policy." He predicted trouble in the North American provinces and specifically mentioned the various resolutions in Congress against the Canadian confederation. He also felt certain that the American government would try to claim British Columbia as settlement for the *Alabama* claims. Meanwhile, Russia's goal was to "provide the means of neutralizing the efforts of Great Britain in the event of antagonism in the East." Bruce believed that Russia and the United States would come to an understanding "as to the proper period for carrying out simultaneously their projects." Though Stoeckl tried to allay Bruce's fears, the minister could not be persuaded.

The British press approached the news with varying degrees of disquiet. Some papers appeared to accept the announcement with stoicism. The *London Times* suggested that Alaska had been purchased "with a view of asserting the claim of the United States to supremacy of the North American Continent . . . and as a sort of counter-demonstration against our supposed aggressive tendencies." Nonetheless, the paper urged readers to recognize that Great Britain had no right to protest the transaction and that its possessions in North America were in no greater danger than they had been before; moreover, there was no point in fretting over the impact of a Russian-American alliance in a future European war. More than one paper tipped its hat to the United States for recognizing a profitable opportunity when it saw one. The *Manchester Courier and Lancashire General Advertiser*, the *Glasgow Herald*, and the *London Morning Post* all agreed that while the "vague and conflicting" descriptions in the British press indicated a woeful lack of knowledge about Russian America, the people of America clearly had a better understanding of the riches to be found in this remote land. Similarly, the *Belfast News* relayed the facts of the sale, but without emotion.

Other papers reacted to the reports with great alarm. The *Pall Mall Gazette* declared that though the arrangement between the two countries was logical and in accordance with their similar interests, it was for Great Britain "a hint, a protest, a declaration of feeling more effectual and far more politic than anything in the shape of a despatch could be." America's message was that it would not permit the establishment of a strong monarchical state on its border; furthermore, it still anticipated that one day Britain's North American territories would be absorbed. The *Gazette* concluded that even if the rumor proved false, the important thing was "the manifestation of *intention* which the negotiation makes public, and the consideration that . . . we should find ourselves helpless against any serious attempt to carry the intention into effect." The *London Post* considered the treaty as an insult toward Great Britain, a transaction "full of direct hostility, and the intention is so obvious that it cannot be ignored. It is the answer from Washington to the Confederation of our North American Provinces. It is more than an answer—it is a challenge." The *Manchester Guardian* was pessimistic as well. Upset by the secrecy of the deal and suspicious of the motives behind it, the *Guardian* observed that the United States did not need the territory and Russia did not need the money, so there must be some other reason for the agreement between these "eager and unscrupulous" nations. The *London Free Press* warned, "Every foot of ground gained by the United States is a menace to other nations," while the *London Globe* suggested, "Possibly the Yankees even bargain with Russia for a morsel of the 'sick man's' property . . . in order to obtain for their navy a station in European waters." Finally, the *London Economist*, as well as the *Globe*, expressed a common opinion, that the Alaska Purchase offered "a new inducement for the Americans to tempt Canada into annexation."

This belief that the Alaska treaty would encourage or hasten American absorption of British Columbia was a common assumption in many places. A number of American papers commented on it in the weeks after the purchase, for example, the *New York Times*, the *Charleston Daily Courier*, and the Boston literary magazine *Every Saturday*. Even politicians jumped on the bandwagon. In June 1867, Sen. George H. Williams said to a crowd of citizens in Portland, Oregon, that the United States needed British Columbia "to complete its symmetry, to fulfill its advancing destiny." That same month Sen. Cornelius Cole said a similar thing at a banquet in Santa Cruz, California, and later spoke with Seward about acquiring British Columbia. These probes continued in the following months; at least four times during this period a resolution came up in Congress for the purchase of British Columbia. Each time, the proposal went nowhere.

That the Russian-American deal was aimed specifically at Britain was another popular notion in Great Britain and in Europe. The

London Globe declared, "There is a strong party in Congress composed mainly of Republicans who seem bent on picking a quarrel with England." The *Neue Freie Presse* described Russia's desire for territory as a "well-known greed . . . an incurable and chronic disease." Consequently, it was convinced that the real motive for the sale had nothing to do with the distance between Russia and its possessions. Instead, the Austrian paper determined, the real reason for the sale was to cripple British interests. "How else," the paper posed, "can we understand the cession of Russian America to the United States than to endanger British possessions in the West and East?" The Paris correspondent for the *New York Tribune* had indicated that the French seemed to welcome the news for its anti-British character, if for no other reasons. Even Karl Marx saw an anti-British element in the sale of Alaska. He said, "From the economic side, this acquisition for the present is not worth a cent, but, thanks to this, the Yankees will cut England off from the sea from one side and hasten the annexation of all British North America to the United States. That's where the dog is buried." Cassius Clay, writing from St. Petersburg, presented the American side of this portrait of British victimhood. He told Seward that had the Alaska negotiations not been kept secret, he felt certain there would have been the "most energetic protests if not . . . armed intervention to prevent it." The friendly relations between Great Britain and France, Clay believed, began in a common agreement to limit American power on its own continent and elsewhere, but "the strange and unexpected good alliance between Russia and America has taken them by surprise and disabled all their projects."

The Alaska Purchase certainly generated a great deal of agitation in the Canadian provinces. Those in closest proximity to Russian America showed the greatest interest and concern, as did the provinces most committed to confederation. A number of Canadian officials expressed alarm at the news, particularly because there was already tension between British Columbia and the colonial government. More than one official in the colonial office believed that British Columbia's annexation to the United States was inevitable and their fears were exacerbated by outside reports. The British minister to Washington, Sir Frederick Bruce, for example, sent a despatch to the Colonial Office communicating the strong desire of Americans in the West to annex the provinces in that region and adding that Seward gave every indication that he believed British Columbia would one day be American.

Canadian newspapers received the news of the Alaska Purchase with mixed reactions. The *Montreal Transcript* had a tepid response, stating, "It matters little to us that a territory so worthless passes into American hands," and if the United States succeeds where Russia failed in civilizing the area, then "we shall have reason to rejoice rather than to be dismayed." The *Montreal Herald* was glad that Russia had not offered Alaska to Canada for purchase since Canadian politicians would surely have jumped at the chance. The *Herald* was grateful that "a kind of Providence, which it is said keeps watch over fools, has . . . put this piece of progress and aggrandizement out of our reach." The *Toronto Daily Globe*, on the other hand, downplayed the news by declaring Russian America to be of little value, "unpenetrated and impenetrable wild . . . hardly an investment to be coveted by anybody not afflicted with an insatiable craving for useless territory." But one senses that the editor of the *Globe* may have been more troubled than he was willing to admit. The same article acknowledged that the purchase limited British Columbia's access to the Pacific Ocean and declared, with more than a hint of sour grapes, that "the blowing of our neighbors over so sterile an acquisition enables one to form some estimate of the cruel longing that afflicts them for the possession of British America." Many other Canadian papers agreed that there was another intent in the purchase. The *Ottawa Citizen* called it a "bold attempt to show unfriendliness to Great Britain, and the British American colonies," and the *Quebec Morning Chronicle* believed it to be "the most overt demonstration of an aggressive purpose . . . that has yet been made." The *Hamilton Evening Times* similarly announced, "no one will question it as an unfriendly act upon the part of both Russia and the United States." Many conceived that the purchase was part of Washington's plan to assume control of the whole continent. The *Halifax Sun* declared that America's acquisition of "this bleak, barren and fog enshrouded land seems a step in that direction."

Of course, many Canadians worried specifically about the impact of the Russian-American deal on British Columbia, and with good reason. British Columbia was isolated from the rest of the Canadian provinces and by 1867 was facing serious economic problems that led to emigration and a declining population. The British Columbian government lacked the skill and resources to fix these problems and was consequently enormously unpopular. At the same time, Great Britain seemed uninterested in assisting its far-off colony, leaving British Columbia with the choice of joining the Canadian confederation or joining the United States. Though American annexation was an attractive option, in mid-March 1867, the Legislative Council in British Columbia voted to join the Canadian union. Only two weeks later, however, the press announced the Alaska treaty, and the discussion of annexation was resurrected.

Not surprisingly, some officials in British Columbia responded to the news about Russian America with distress. Gov. Frederick Seymour wrote to the Colonial Office in London that although the Americans residing in the colony were excited, many of the English settlers were despondent and worried about the future. Several representatives of the Hudson's Bay Company declared the news unwelcome intelligence, and one, in particular, blamed Great Britain for this new threat. Corresponding with the London office, he called the possibility of annexation "a fitting consummation to the gross neglect & misgovernment which the British Possessions here have received at the hands of the imperial authorities." Others complained of British neglect as well.

Meanwhile, American reports from British Columbia confirmed the presence of an annexation movement. Allen Francis, the American consul in Victoria, reported that British Columbia had initially feared the news of the Russian-American deal but soon reconsidered and many now hoped that union with the United States could improve the conditions of the declining colony. Some American newspapers stoked the fire as well. Soon after the purchase the *New York Times* brazenly declared that British Columbia was now at the mercy of American interests. A month later, the same paper reported that the entire press of Vancouver welcomed the idea of annexation as "the only possible remedy for the political grievances of the Colony." Similarly, the *Charleston Daily Courier* concluded that the purchase of Russian America was but "a preliminary to the acquisition of the intervening territory of British Columbia."

········

In the spring of 1867, then, there were many serious matters brewing in Europe, and the various nations were all engaged in managing both domestic and international threats. Despite these distractions, officials and citizens in European nations took note of the American purchase of Alaska and, for the most part, received the news with alarm. European reactions to the Alaska Purchase reveal a growing awareness of the strength of both the United States and Russia. As the French newspaper *Le Temps* observed, the Alaska deal was a clear recognition of the Monroe Doctrine: "This principle, which yesterday to our great disappointment was triumphant in Mexico, is today triumphant in the voluntary retreat of Russia." Many in Europe worried about the potential of a real Russian-American alliance and what this new arrangement would mean for the Near East and Russian influence in the dismantling of the Ottoman Empire. American minister Morris, however, saw a different significance to be found in the Alaska Purchase, a critical display of American unity after the long and divisive Civil War: "The confirmative action of the Senate shows that upon questions nearly concerning the national dignity and welfare there is but little divergence of opinion among the coordinate branches of the government." Politics would not get in the way of progress.

SITKA, OR NEW ARCHANGEL, CAPITAL OF ALASKA.

This lovely illustration appeared in *Harper's New Monthly Magazine* in 1869. HARPER'S NEW MONTHLY MAGAZINE, 38, ISSUE 227.

CHAPTER VII

That Snowbound Wilderness:
From Treaty to Territory

*O*nce the dust settled from the debate over appropriation and the congressional investigation that followed, America's new acquisition faced the significant challenge of establishing itself in the eyes of the American public and government as a place worthy of attention and investment. Over the course of the next thirty years, Alaska would struggle to create its own government, set up a system of public education, and attract and retain a body of full-time residents. The success of these efforts ebbed and flowed, a combination of the persistent determination of a few motivated Alaska transplants and the influence of outside forces. It was a slow and hesitant process, but by the end of the century most Americans came to realize that Seward's Folly was anything but.

It is perhaps misleading, however, to refer to Alaska as a cohesive unit in this early period. At the time of the transfer, Alaska's white population numbered roughly nine hundred people, including civilians and those affiliated with the U.S. military, as well as another thirty thousand Alaska Natives spread across the entire territory. Sitka was the only permanent white settlement of any significance. In those first weeks of the fall of 1867, others arrived and started claiming land and setting up saloons and stores, but in order for Alaska to grow and prosper, it needed more than itinerant miners and soldiers. The remoteness and challenging climate of the new territory, as well as the general sense that Alaska was still terra incognita, made it difficult to attract the right kinds of newcomers, people who would settle down and help build the region's economy and infrastructure.

In the first years after the purchase, a number of publications appeared that helped Americans learn more about their country's newest territorial addition. In the words of the *Harper's Weekly* literary editor, "Since Alaska is now part of us it is well to know something of that extremity of ourselves." Many of these reports seemed to demonstrate that Alaska had been a worthwhile purchase. In October 1868, the *New York Times* reported that the Treasury Department had received a sample of coal from Alaska, which it declared to be "of good quality." Two months later, the same paper promoted a forthcoming exhibition of archaeological finds collected by Capt. Edward G. Fast while he was stationed in Sitka. Fast's methods will no doubt offend modern readers. According to the *Times*, Fast befriended a number of Native families during his time there and soon discovered that these families had preserved various heirlooms—items like charms, cooking utensils, and weapons—that would have great value elsewhere. Since money was scarce in Sitka, Fast had no problem purchasing items from the destitute owners. As for some of the other relics, "the despolation of the graves of departed heroes would have been a more hazardous and difficult operation were it not for his zeal in the cause, and the influence he held with many Alaskans." The *Times* recognized that the purchase of Alaska had provoked intense interest about the region's earliest inhabitants and predicted it would "probably open a new and wide field of our archaeological friends, and either add to, or end, the vexed question relative to the origin of the American Indians."

Alaska began to pop up in other contexts as well. In two separate articles in December 1868 the *New York Times* referred to Alaska in the most casual and offhanded way as just another place the average person might visit. One peculiar article which, at its core, was arguing against granting women civil rights, raised the concern that women's clothing was too elaborate to allow them to attend to business on an equal footing with their male counterparts, and used this example: "Go into a bachelor's room, note its contents and compare them with those of a young woman—even, of a young woman who is for women's rights . . . and see whether her arrangements are such as to enable her to fly off to Canada or Alaska, when an important telegram is received." Another article waxed sentimental about the importance of family at Christmas but bemoaned the decline of this sacred institution in modern, industrial times when "steam strains and snaps the bonds of the family system." Once, the difficulty of travel had kept even the most restless person at home, but now "with steam transportation, men go a thousand miles in a month in search of gain or pleasure. Have you been to Alaska this Summer, to Italy this Winter, to Japan, to Jericho?—it sounds hardly stranger than it once did to ask last week's news from Buffalo."

Books on Alaska also began to appear. In 1868 Frederick Whymper published *Travel and Adventure in the Territory of Alaska* in London; a New York edition appeared the following year. Whymper, an English artist, had traveled in Alaska between 1865 and 1867 with a group of men who were searching for a path for a telegraph, the so-called Russian-American Telegraph Expedition. Though the enterprise was ultimately abandoned, it did result in a great deal of useful knowledge about the region, much of which is found in Whymper's book. Whymper spent nearly two and a half years in Alaska and gives a detailed but concise account of his travels, describing the land through which he traveled and its resources, as well as the people he encountered, including Russians, Americans, and various Native tribes. Overall, Whymper had relatively good interactions with the Alaska Natives, though he could be a harsh critic at times. Early in his book, he reflected, "Though a partial civilization may have varnished his exterior, beneath the thin crust the savage nature lurks, ever ready to break forth, like those volcanic mountains whose pure snows only hide the molten lava within." He admitted, however, that the influx of white men had been a bad influence, as well, observing, "The least degraded Indians were those who had least to do with the white man." Whymper wrote the book after the United States bought Alaska, and it discusses some of the concerns about and opposition to the purchase, concerns that he did not share. He recognized the potential economic benefit of the new territory, discussing its abundance of furs and salmon and the likelihood that valuable minerals would be found. At the same time, he gave a realistic assessment of its other resources: "A vast deal of nonsense has been published and republished in the newspapers of the United States relative to the agricultural resources. . . . The reader may take my word for it that the culture of a few potatoes and other vegetables is all that has been done in this way, and that the acres of barley mentioned in some of these high-flown paragraphs are purely mythical. There is not an acre of grain in the whole country." Despite the exaggerations, Whymper still believed Alaska was a good deal and its acquisition was in keeping with America's destiny to possess the entire continent.

While much of the country remained ignorant of or inattentive to its newest addition, the Alaska Purchase was still viewed with great trepidation in Europe. In September 1868, Eugene Schuyler wrote Seward about the uneasiness felt in Europe about the Russian-American friendship, particularly in light of the recent visit of Admiral Farragut to Constantinople. His letter contained an excerpt from the *Vedomosti Birzhi* (*Gazette of the Bourse*), an influential St. Petersburg journal that addressed the rumors and speculations at length. According to the *Vedomosti*, European politicians and journalists believed that the goal of Farragut's journey was to demand that Turkey give Crete to Greece and open the Dardanelles to all warships, essentially dismantling the Black Sea clause of the Treaty of Paris of 1856. Across Europe, the press saw Farragut's visit as a declaration of a Russian-American alliance. The *Vedomosti* clearly viewed such an alliance favorably, observing, "If an alliance of Russia with America did not present us evident advantages, or if it was impossible, the foreign press would ignore this alliance and in no way would it consider it a terror for Europe or a treason to European interests on the side of Russia." The article went on to discuss the growing strength of the United States and the likelihood that it would one day decide the fate of Europe. The United States recognized after the French intervention in Mexico that an ocean did not protect it from European encroachment and began to see the need for a strong position in the Mediterranean and strong friends in Europe. In the opinion of the *Vedomosti*, Farragut's visit was "proof that the United States are getting to have their counsel listened to on the banks of the Bosphorus, and that they are to be considered one of the factors in the future solution of the Eastern Question." When it came time to settle this matter, Russia would be able to rely on America's fleet to join in and oppose the fleets of the Western powers. Given this likely outcome, the *Vedomosti* declared, "The voluntary cession of the Russian-American possessions must be marked among the most important and successful acts of our government in the department of foreign politics."

·······

The territory of Alaska faced overwhelming challenges. Travel to Alaska was very expensive and difficult; for example, it took four days by water to travel from the Washington Territory to points along Alaska's Inside Passage. Mail arrived only once a month in Sitka and, as early settlers complained, sometimes it took longer than that if weather or other circumstances interfered. In addition to Alaska's remoteness, early settlers and public officials at all levels underestimated the enormity and diversity of the land. Consequently, it was difficult to attract and keep reliable settlers and employees like teachers, especially when salaries regularly fluctuated with the

economy. At the same time, the influx of adventurers and opportunists of various stripes produced the obvious results—a society that
was a little rough around the edges. The Sitka temperance movement
complained that there were too many thefts, street brawls, and in-
decent episodes with Russian-American and Tlingit women. While
the early advocates of temperance were undoubtedly more critical
than others might have been, most descriptions of early Sitka and
its environs agree that there was a bit of the Wild West to it. In the
fall of 1868, the *New York Times* reported that General Halleck's
visit to the new territory had revealed a number of problems. The
Native population was unhappy with its American neighbors. The
Russian-American Company had managed and cared for the locals
in a patriarchal arrangement, but under the new regime, the people
were "thrown upon their own resources, and they do not understand
the change as yet." Moreover, Halleck found that the influx of white
adventurers, soldiers, and traders into the region often led to the corruption of the Natives. In November the *New York Times* reported
that General Halleck had approved General Davis's suggestion to
establish military posts near the larger villages or groups of Alaska
Natives. The *Times* added, "In this way the whole country will be
gradually opened to our settlers and traders without danger of hostile collisions."

In those first few years Sitka experienced a decline in its population as Russians left for home and early opportunists attempted to
make a go of it, only to decide that they had gotten in over their
heads. Sitka's financial situation declined as well, and, consequently,
public buildings began to fall into disrepair. Eventually, this decline
affected even Sitka's earliest promoters. In 1870 Sitka's first mayor,
William Dodge, had to leave Alaska because he could no longer afford to stay there. Three years later, the Sitka City Council held its
last meeting and the first government ceased to exist. Soon after, the
Sacramento Daily Union reported that California legislators had proposed that Alaska be used as a penal colony. It was not an auspicious
beginning for the new territory.

Sitka's first government did have one significant accomplishment—Mayor Dodge's successful invitation to William Seward to visit the territory he had worked so hard to acquire. Among other things, the mayor hoped that Seward's visit would help to promote the cause of development, but he also had a very specific motive in inviting the former secretary of state. Dodge hoped that that Seward might help solve a problem that was plaguing the territory's new settlers, namely, the inability to obtain titles to land. For the present, no land was available for purchase within Sitka and its immediate surroundings except privately owned property. The rest was federal land under the army's administration. Dodge hoped that Seward might persuade Congress to apply the homestead law to Alaska lands.

In early June 1869, Seward departed his home in Auburn, New York, accompanied by his wife, son, a servant, and a friend. In Chicago, Dodge was there to meet him and escort him across the country by Pullman car along the recently completed Union Pacific Railroad. The party stopped in several cities, including Cheyenne, Denver, Salt Lake City, Sacramento, and San Francisco. Though Seward arrived in San Francisco late in the evening, at eleven o'clock, he was greeted like a true celebrity by enormous and enthusiastic crowds. Before retiring to his hotel, Seward gave a speech in which he echoed his earlier expansionist sentiments: "Where is the power, and whence are the forces to come, to make war upon a people whose boundaries are oceans, and whose people are numbered in the millions?" From San Francisco, the group continued to Victoria, British Columbia, stopping along the way for a tour of the Puget Sound region where Seward and Dodge visited a number of settlements, including Olympia and Seattle. Finally, Seward and his group departed for Alaska aboard the steamship *Active*, arriving in Sitka on July 30.

Seward's visit began with a three-hour walk through Sitka. As he navigated the city's muddy streets, he encountered "Russians in their native dress; United States soldiers in their blue uniforms; Indians in blankets and feathers, and traders and travelers clad in the latest style of Montgomery Street, San Francisco." Sitka had no hotel so Seward and his party initially stayed with Dodge, and then with the family of General Davis in the governor's house. The visitors were both amused and a tad disoriented by the difference in latitude, finding it odd to draw the curtains at ten o'clock at night to block out the sun and equally peculiar to discover the sun rising at two in the morning. Moreover, local residents determined time based on nationality—that is, the Russians kept time with Siberia, while the Americans kept time with New York. In the memoir that Seward's son Frederick wrote more than a decade later, he observed, "Sure enough, here was a place where two Sundays came together! . . . It was a proof of the earth's revolution on its axis that would have delighted Galileo."

During the first part of Seward's visit, he met with the city council, visited both the Russian Orthodox church and the Lutheran sanctuary, toured the Native village near Sitka, and viewed a military parade. Seward and his party were also taken to examine the brewery, the sawmill, the fishery, and a great warehouse filled with the furs of seal, beaver, black and cinnamon bear, otter, and Russian sable. The former secretary of state also traveled north into the territory of the Tlingit, where he met with the head chief of the Chilkat tribe and two to three hundred other tribe members. Seward's son was particularly impressed by the totem poles they encountered at every village: "The emblems of great exploits or ancestral descent—the bear, the seal, the whale, the fox, the salmon, the medicine man, the warrior, and the nondescript monster, are piled, one above another, to the height of twenty or thirty feet. To the civilized eye, it looks like a bit of fantastic savagery. Yet, after all, it is only the same thing, in another form, as those heraldic devices which have excited admiration, pride and envy throughout civilized Europe, for centuries. There, they are borne on shields—here, piled up on sticks."

Seward's visit to the Chilkat tribe is a story of cultural misunderstandings. General Davis had informed the chief of Seward's imminent arrival, but the chief and his tribe interpreted that to mean that Seward himself had purchased and owned the land now known as Alaska. They expected Seward to help them resolve disputes and even presented him with a case in which three of their own had been killed by another tribe. Upon inquiring further, Seward discovered the offended party was willing to settle for thirty-six blankets as reparations for their lost men. Later, the Chilkat chiefs dined aboard the *Active* with Seward and Davis. Similarly, the chief misunderstood Davis's notification that a scientific expedition would be coming as well. The solar eclipse was due to occur on August 7, and on that day, the group of scientists set up their telescopes and other equipment. To the Native residents, however, it appeared "that they were a sort of sharp-shooters taking aim at that luminary." Consequently, when the first line of darkness began to appear on the sun, "stolidity and incredulity gave way to visible anxiety" as the Natives believed that the "Boston men" had taken the sun away, and some fell to their knees in prayer. There were exclamations of relief when the sky resumed its brightness a short time later. Later, when dining aboard the *Active*, the Chilkat chiefs asked Seward to explain the eclipse, which he did using a lamp, an apple, and an orange. The chiefs remained skeptical, and replied that they understood that according to Seward, the eclipse had been produced by "the Great Spirit, and not by man," but "they have noticed, however, that the Great Spirit generally does whatever the 'Boston men' want him to."

Before leaving Alaska, Seward stopped once more at Sitka and gave a speech at the city's Lutheran church. According to the *Alaska Times*, the event was standing room only. Seward spoke favorably of Alaska's various assets, including its scenery, "a varied and magnificent panorama." To no one's surprise, Seward declared that although Alaska's vast territorial expanse had yet to be fully explored, "enough is known to assure us that it possesses treasure . . . equal to those of any other region of the continent." Seward also spoke of the Alaska Native population and the ways in which the influx of Russian, British, and Americans had affected their way of life, dooming them, like other Indian groups, to "merely serve their turn until civilized white men come." With what sounds like a touch of regret, he observed, "When we consider how greatly most of the tribes are reduced in numbers and how precarious their vocations are, we shall cease to regard them as indolent or incapable; and, on the contrary, we shall more deeply regret than ever before that a people gifted by nature, so vigorous and energetic, and withal so docile and gentle in their intercourse with the white man, can neither be preserved as a distinct social community nor incorporated into our society."

· · · · · · ·

Seward's words were prophetic. The first years after the Alaska Purchase were also plagued by difficulties with the Alaska Native population. In 1869 the U.S. military had a number of violent conflicts with the Tlingit near Sitka that ultimately led to an investigation by the Board of Indian Commissioners. The Tlingit had never recognized the sale of their ancestral lands to the United States and consequently viewed the American presence as an occupation. Davis knew of this sentiment, but as a tough, no-nonsense military man, had little patience with the Tlingit when small disagreements or confrontations turned violent. In January 1869, for example, a scuffle between a U.S. Army soldier and three Tlingit leaders quickly escalated when Davis sent troops into the Tlingit village to arrest one of the leaders. Shots were fired on both sides, wounding several men and killing one Tlingit slave. The Tlingit leader ultimately surrendered to prevent the bombardment of his village, but the bloodshed continued the day following his surrender when an army sentinel, for no apparent reason, killed two Tlingit who were departing Sitka. A clan leader attempted negotiations with Davis and in keeping with Indian law, demanded a fee of trade blankets and goods as recompense for the murders. When this attempt failed, the Tlingit exacted the payment they felt owed them by killing two white trappers. By mid-February, with the situation still unresolved, Davis ordered his troops to raid and burn three villages (all of which had been vacated in anticipation of the attack), destroying canoes and enormous amounts of stored food. Although only one Tlingit is known to have perished in what became known as the Kake War, many others died later as a consequence of starvation and exposure. The next winter, in December 1869, the soldiers at Fort Wrangell, near modern-day Wrangell, shelled the Tlingit village there, killing an unknown number and hanging the village shaman.

These conflicts drew criticism on various fronts. In early 1870, Rev. W. Duncan, described as "the most successful missionary among the Indians in British Columbia, near the boundary line of Alaska," wrote to United States Special Indian Commissioner Vincent Colyer: "Military rule among the Indians, while heathen, is, I feel sure, a fatal mistake. It will only breed the troubles it was intended to check." Duncan warned that the military establishment in Alaska would "unless changed or removed, render utterly abortive any measures you may adopt for teaching and civilizing the natives." The special Indian commissioner agreed and in his own report a month later made several notable observations. Colyer relayed that he had already made known his views on "the ill effects of the near proximity of soldiers to the Indian villages, and of the demoralizing effects upon both. . . . Nowhere else that I have visited is the absolute uselessness of soldiers so apparent as in Alaska." Colyer added that both the soldiers and Alaska Natives were fond of whiskey and this led to debauchery and an overall decline in morals. Finally, the commissioner highlighted the principle by which the nearest of kin was expected to avenge the death of his relative, and that "this law was well understood by all the old traders in Alaska." Consequently, American soldiers should know it too.

Even as locals and military advisors wrestled with the difficulties of cohabitation and cultural awareness, positive assessments of Alaska continued to appear in print, helping the reading American public learn more about this far-off land. William Healey Dall, for example, had first gone to Alaska in 1865, employed with Whymper as a member of the same expedition, but stayed on for another several years. In 1870 he published *Alaska and Its Resources*, a hefty tome that contained an enormous amount of information on Alaska's geography, climate, flora and fauna, mineral products, and indigenous peoples, accompanied by lovely engravings and a brief chronological history of exploration and trade in Alaska. Dall argued that many Americans were underselling the territory's current worth and future potential. Alaska was our "key to the North Pacific" and an important contribution to national defense. It could no longer be said that a mere three ironclads could blockade the entire western coast. Dall also noted the irony that many of those who derided the purchase of Alaska because of its cold climate were descended from men who had "wielded the axe in the forests of Maine, or gathered scanty crops on the granite hillsides of Massachusetts." Addressing this specific, and in his view exaggerated, complaint about the cold, Dall challenged his fellow Americans, "Has the race of hardy pioneers died out among us? Do we, as a nation, sigh only for indolent siestas in the canebrakes of Cuba?"

Dall also shared his opinion on the demands for a government in Alaska. He was adamant that the creole (mixed race) population was unprepared to form a territorial government and, in particular, unable to withstand the political and economic dominance of the larger companies already established in the area. Dall believed that the current military government was the best arrangement for the present, adding that since the territory was likely to be sparsely populated for many years, it should be regarded as "a great storehouse of fish, timber, and fur; from which American citizens alone should be allowed to draw supplies, under proper restrictions and on payment of reasonable taxes." Finally, Dall urged his fellow Americans to think to the future. Confident that with time Alaska would prove its worth, he declared, "The oak must weather the storms of many winters before it gains maturity. Alaska is not a California, where cities arise in a night, and may pass away in a day. Meanwhile, we must be patient."

• • • • • • •

Many of Alaska's problems stemmed from a lack of administrative oversight. During the 1870s, it was entirely up to the U.S. military to maintain law and order over this enormous frontier. There was no territory-wide administration to enforce the law, and there was great uncertainty about which laws applied in Alaska and which courts had jurisdiction. When the army first arrived, it had brought with it several hundred men, but in 1870, the War Department ordered that all military posts except Sitka be abandoned, and the garrison there was reduced to 118 men and 13 officers. With insufficient manpower to stop it, the smuggling and trade of alcohol was a major problem, and the constant flow of opportunists looking for quick wealth destabilized the settlements as well. This situation was exacerbated by several other factors. In the years after the Civil War, morale within the army was extremely low and social problems were rife. Military careers were out of fashion and few ambitious and capable men enlisted in the army. In Alaska the various military garrisons also suffered from isolation and boredom, often leading to drinking and bad behavior. Throughout this period, various military inspectors and other individuals writing about Alaska recommended the formation of a sustainable government by Congress, but Washington was not inclined to follow this advice. As a consequence, the U.S. military could do little more than serve as a caretaker for this section of America's growing and developing frontier, lurching from problem to problem with no strategic vision, while the nation's attention was focused on the significant struggles of Reconstruction and the reintegration of North and South.

Despite complaints from early residents that the American government was doing nothing to help the new territory get on its feet, there were, in fact, a number of attempts by the government and its military agencies to get a handle on the circumstances and needs of this new place. In September 1868 the Treasury Department ordered two special agents, Capt. Charles Bryant and H. A. McIntyre, to go to Alaska to examine its resources and the nature of its various tribes. The two men repeated the observances of others before them—that aside from fish and furs, which were more readily accessible and transportable, the other resources of Alaska such as lumber and minerals were hindered by underdevelopment and the inescapable problem of great distances and transportation. Both men highlighted Alaska's great diversity in its physical features and tribes and noted that while vegetables such as beets, cabbages, and turnips could be grown, the agricultural resources in general were limited. McIntyre added that eastern Alaska possessed no arable land whatsoever, and while some of the islands produced luxuriant grasses in the summer months that could feed numerous flocks and herds, the overall rainy and wet climate made it "absolutely impossible to cure any sufficient quantity of this to support the animals that might well be so kept seven months in the year through the remaining five." McIntyre's conclusions about the value of Alaska were grim. As he compared the total cost of Alaska (including the purchase price, total accrued interest, and the expense of the military and naval establishments) to the projected revenue from fur seals and customs, he concluded that the likely income of the new territory was insufficient to balance out the costs, at least for the present time. Only in the event of some extraordinary circumstance, such as the discovery of large deposits of valuable minerals, might Alaska attract enough people and generate enough revenue to justify its expense. Finally, McIntyre had one piece of advice that, along with similar reports, may very well have influenced Washington's stance on establishing a territorial government. The treasury agent advised that "it might not be the worst policy to abandon the Territory for the present, or until some possible change for the better shall have taken place." Noting the small population at Sitka, McIntyre noted, "The establishment of a territorial government for the benefit of so few persons, with the probability of diminution rather than increase of numbers, would, at least, be inconsistent with measures of an economical administration, and for this reason, if for no other, is, perhaps, not advisable."

The government also attempted to gather information about the interior of Alaska. In the summer of 1869 U.S. Army captain Charles

W. Raymond from the Corps of Engineers set out at the request of General Halleck to determine the specific location of Fort Yukon, which had been established several decades earlier by the Hudson's Bay Company within Russian America. Raymond was also tasked with assessing the value of the Yukon River and its tributaries. He reported that it took him twenty-three days to reach Fort Yukon, a distance of some 1,040 miles, and his entire excursion took seven months. Along the way, Raymond noted the potential for timber and salmon production in the future once those items in closer markets had been depleted but seemed less enthusiastic about the region's agricultural and mineral possibilities. He concluded that at present the fur trade was the only well-developed resource and in order to continue a profitable trade on the Yukon, the United States would need to establish and maintain five permanent stations on the river. The captain had also been entrusted with another important mission: as a temporary representative of the Treasury Department, it was his job to inform the representatives of the Hudson's Bay Company that Fort Yukon was now located in the territory of the United States and that they must vacate the buildings as soon as possible and cease all trade with the Natives. Finally, he took possession of the buildings and raised the American flag over the fort.

There was also an effort to assess the condition of the inhabitants of the territory, both whites and Natives. In October 1870 Maj. John C. Tidball, the commander of the post at Sitka, ordered Lt. D. A. Lyle to make a complete enumeration of the non-military inhabitants of the town of Sitka. With the help of a Russian interpreter, Lyle created a detailed chart of 391 residents that included each person's name, sex, age, birthplace, occupation, and an assessment of whether or not the individual was able-bodied and capable of self-support. The report is a fascinating glimpse of Sitka in its early years. The professions for men included merchant, fisherman, tanner, shoemaker, machinist, blacksmith, coppersmith, carpenter, grocer, and even a "thief and rascal." Women were primarily employed as homemakers, laundresses, and midwives, but a significant number were listed as prostitutes. Nearly all of the residents were creoles, the product of intermarriage between the Russians and the Natives. The chart also included rather detailed notes about individuals and their homes. Lyle described one man as a "worthless, drunken wretch," a second man a "worthless cuss," and yet a third a "bilk of [the] worse kind." Some homes were listed as clean, or tolerably clean, but many others were described as filthy, and one was called "dirty and nauseating." Overall, Lyle's assessment of the residents of Sitka in 1870 was not a favorable one.

> I found, as a general thing, a great want of cleanliness, both as regards person, apparel, and place of abode. The houses, with few exceptions, were small, filthy, illy-ventilated, and bore evidence of habitual neglect. There appears to be no energy in them, no desire to look forward to future self-support. A good deal of sickness exists, caused, I think, by their lack of cleanliness, food, and clothing. Their ideas of virtue and chastity seem very limited, and consequently much venereal disease is found among them. A great many complain that they can get nothing to do; that they would work if they could get it. Many of them who are able to work are too lazy, drunken, and worthless to try and make a living. They do not appear to have ever managed their own affairs, but have looked upon their employers and rulers to take charge of them and look after them. Many are destitute, and will require to be fed during the whole of the coming winter.

Lyle, of course, was observing the aftereffects of the Russian departure and the Russian company's practice of supporting the town's residents. He explained that when the Russian-American Company left, it gave its Russian (and, presumably, creole) employees who stayed in Sitka a financial gift, but this money had long ago been spent. As a consequence, local residents were reliant on rations from the commissary department of the military. Lyle was not optimistic that the situation would change any time soon; he saw no prospect of industry that would offer these people employment, and the overall decline in the condition of Sitka as a whole only made this situation worse.

One month later, the assistant inspector general for the Department of the Columbia in Portland, Oregon, Maj. E. H. Ludington, confirmed this evaluation in his own report on the condition of Fort Tongass, Fort Wrangell, and Sitka. Ludington wrote of the extreme poverty and the need to support more than one hundred people with rations else they would starve, and he described the overall material and moral situation in Sitka as a "deplorable state of affairs." Ludington declared that several of the priests of the Orthodox church at Sitka "are often drunk upon the streets, and their lives are anything but good examples to their people." Though he admitted that the presence of the military certainly contributed to the problem of drunkenness and prostitution, he stipulated that "no one having knowledge of these wretched people can believe that they were corrupted by the troops."

The government also took some interest in the conservation of the fur seals of Alaska, though opinions would vary on the sincerity of these efforts. In June 1870, Congress passed an act to prevent the extermination of fur-bearing animals in Alaska by authorizing the secretary of the treasury to lease the right to fur-seal hunting on the islands of St. George and St. Paul for a term of years to private parties. A firm from San Francisco, the Alaska Commercial Company, won the bid and was granted a twenty-year term that stipulated the maximum number of seals to be hunted at one hundred thousand annually. In return for this monopoly, the company had to pay rent on the land and taxes on each seal skin; provide for the needs, education, and protection of the Native inhabitants of the islands; and prohibit the giving or selling of alcohol to the Natives. This prohibition of alcohol would appear regularly in government documents pertaining to Alaska.

Four years later, in 1874, Congress requested that the secretary of the treasury gather information about the fur trade in Alaska. As a consequence, Lt. Washburn Maynard of the U.S. Navy traveled to several islands in the Bering Sea and compiled a lengthy report on the topic. Maynard noted that since the Alaska Commercial Company had leased these islands, approximately 112,000 young male seals had been killed each year. Maynard provided detailed information about the lives and reproduction of fur seals, as well as how they were herded and killed, but he also took up the question of conservation. Maynard argued that government efforts to protect the seal were complicated by natural circumstances: "We do not even know where they are for seven months in each year, while we do know that they have deadly enemies, which make sad havoc, particularly among the pups and yearlings, as a single killer-whale has been found to have fourteen young seals in his stomach when killed." Maynard stated that whether the killing of 100,000 seals was too much was impossible to determine at present because they had no baseline from which to measure. For that reason, he concluded it was impossible to determine if the industry was devastating the population. Perhaps even more could be harvested, but, Maynard warned, to increase the number killed each year at this point would be "a severe and more hazardous experiment, before any results have been obtained."

There was more information gathered in the following year. In 1875 Brig. Gen. O. O. Howard, commanding general of the Department of the Columbia, toured the Alaska territory and reported his experiences. Howard described the villages and the Alaska Natives, including his experience with one group at Fort Wrangell who expected him to compensate them for the loss of their chief who had been taken away by the Americans and then committed suicide in detention. The Natives finally agreed to compensation in the form of one hundred blankets and the body of their chief. Howard also addressed complaints by Jefferson Davis and others against the Alaska Commercial Company, giving voice to accusations that the United States was allowing a monopoly to mistreat the Natives. Though Howard's evaluation of the company was subsequently called slanderous, and Congress could not substantiate the accusations it included, the remainder of his report is useful for his observations about Alaska's administrative needs. He declared, "I could not fail to see that our Government has not carried out in good faith the treaty stipulations made at the time of the purchase of the Territory. Good civil government, as well as religious and secular teaching, is nowhere in heathendom more needed than in Alaska; and yet up to the present there is none." The general recommended that Alaska be attached as a county to the Washington Territory or by some other arrangement "be furnished with such a government as the treaty with Russia, in the transfer, plainly contemplated."

·······

While Alaska's administrative future remained a subject of discussion, there was a separate but related battle also being fought over whether and how to create an education system for the new territory. In 1872 the Honorable John Eaton, U.S. commissioner of education, had noted in his annual report that Alaska was "entirely outside of all organized efforts for education"; despite being an integral part of "the boasted most progressive nation in the world," it was "without the least possible provision to save its children from growing up in the grossest ignorance and barbarism." Eaton made the same complaints in his annual reports for almost a decade. It would ultimately take the perseverance of several determined Presbyterians to get the ball rolling. The first American missionaries began to arrive in 1877 under the guidance and organization of Rev. Sheldon Jackson, Rocky Mountain superintendent for the Presbyterian Board of Home Missions. Their goal was twofold, both to proselytize and to educate. Jackson not only visited Alaska but recruited other missionaries, including the first woman missionary to Alaska, Amanda McFarland, a widow who had already done such work in New Mexico.

McFarland settled at Fort Wrangell and her letters describe some of the difficulties she encountered, as well as some of the "uncivilized" practices of the locals. While focusing on her missionary work, McFarland wrote Jackson of the need of a good doctor and a minister. McFarland had a little schoolhouse in which to work from, but she needed books and a fellow teacher to help her do all she thought necessary. She was troubled by how many Alaska Natives cohabitated out of wedlock, and she stressed to Jackson, "When we have a church organized here I want the minister who ever [sic] he may be to receive none into the church unless they are willing to be married as christians [sic] are." McFarland also worried about the alcohol problem among the Natives. In early 1878, she complained to Jackson, "During the Holliday [sic] the Indians got into a good many troubles. You would not be surprised, if you knew the great quantity of Whiskey that has been made here this winter." Overall, McFarland was glad to be in Alaska and dedicated to her task, but she often felt overwhelmed. She told Jackson that the circumstances required a minister of experience, explaining that Wrangell was "such a stronghold of Sin, and so many things to contend against that I fear a young man would not succeed here. During the Winter season we have quite a large white population, and they are of a kind that it will take a minister of experience and great wisdom to be able to do them any good, or even to get along with them."

· · · · · · ·

In 1877, the same year that Reconstruction ended and federal troops were recalled from the South, the U.S. military withdrew from Alaska. For years, the army had the unfortunate job of trying to administer a large piece of territory with no clear boundaries, regulations, or laws and widely dispersed military garrisons. Now, responsibility for governing Alaska fell under the purview of the U.S. Navy. Cmdr. Lester A. Beardslee was assigned to oversee this massive project. In the summer of 1877, he arrived at Sitka and set up his headquarters on board the *Jamestown* in Sitka harbor. Beardslee faced the same challenges that his army colleagues had, and he was determined to establish authority and instill respect for law and order in Sitka.

Beardslee's reports about his efforts in Alaska offer a vivid snapshot of Sitka in its second decade under the American flag and comment on the state of the town itself, its relationship with its Native neighbors, and some of the obstacles still confronting America's newest acquisition. Beardslee was pleased to discover that the inhabitants of Sitka and the nearby Tlingit settlements, for the most part, coexisted peacefully. There were occasional problems—disputes of various origins and even real or threatened violence—but even these disturbances were the result of cultural misunderstandings and, more often, the influence of alcohol, rather than outright hostility. In describing these clashes, Beardslee emphasized the need to control not only the importation of alcohol into Alaska, but its production within Alaska. Nor did he mince words in his analysis of this ongoing problem, noting, "I do not believe that, uninflamed by drink, the Indians would assault the whites, but they *will* be *crazy* with rum (and that they will so be is almost entirely due to the fault of our government)." Beardslee blamed the government's failure to fully understand the alcohol problem in Alaska, as indicated by the poorly constructed laws in place to control it. He observed that "while the introduction of even a gallon of good or ordinary liquor is sedulously prevented, material from which the most poisonous liquor can be and is made in great quantities is permitted to be imported by the ton."

For his part, the commander did what he could to tackle the problem of illegal alcohol production and its destructive side effects. Beardslee organized raids to destroy illegal stills and enlisted the help of local Tlingits, including the three Tlingit policemen he had appointed when he first arrived at Sitka. One raid alone in July 1879 resulted in the destruction of forty-one stills, most of them in Native residences. Beardslee also visited the salmon cannery, where most of the local Natives worked, to speak to them about the dangers of alcohol and the troubles it usually caused. He intentionally traveled without soldiers to deliver a message of peace and, with the aid of an interpreter, presented his case against alcohol and called for the Natives to help him. By the fall of 1879, Beardslee reported that his experiment seemed successful. In September, as the hunting season and salmon canning season both drew to a close, he had feared the return of the Alaska Natives to their settlements near Sitka, explaining, "The return of each canoe-load of from 8 to 12 men is generally celebrated the same night by a carouse, during which fights occur and great uproar prevails." Beardslee expected some six to eight hundred Alaska Natives at Sitka once all had returned and was worried about preserving order. In the two months that followed, however, he recorded that there was little drunkenness and almost no disturbances. He believed that some of this was due to his intervention: "When we first arrived, every night was made hideous by drunken orgies, and many by fights. I have not had cause to even censure an Indian since the raid upon the cannery ranches by themselves."

Beardslee recognized one other reality that often interfered with peaceful coexistence as well—cultural differences in perceptions of law and justice. Like several others before him Beardslee explained the Native tradition of retribution and compensation for perceived wrongs, which often involved extended groups, not individual families. This tradition not only led to occasional clashes and misunderstandings with the whites at Sitka but also caused disturbances between groups of Alaska Natives that sometimes bled over into Sitka. Beardslee himself had arbitrated such disputes more than once, but he found them frustrating and disruptive: "If this vessel was a steamer, I should have gone too, for these Indian wars are almost interminable and will do much to hazard American interests here."

The commander realized that one reason for Sitka's struggle for stability was the absence of a civil government. Beardslee took it upon himself to call a meeting of citizens to begin the process of electing officials, and a provisional government was established. This new government adopted a preamble and code of laws in August 1879. Within two months, however, Beardslee was complaining of the administration's lack of effectiveness and the ignorance and indifference of its members to their duties. With no unified sense of purpose, a government could not function and, indeed, by early

November, it had ceased to exist, and Sitka was once again without organized supervision.

The news was not all bad, however. The commander reported that the population of Sitka was growing, largely due to the influx of miners attracted by the promise of gold, which was being found in various places. Many of these miners were bringing their families with them and seemed ready to work. The salmon cannery at Sitka was also proving successful, having produced and exported six thousand cans of forty pounds each during the summer, along with a large quantity of corned salmon in barrels. In the end, Beardslee concluded his report with a plea for Congress to establish a court, police force, and government with the ability to regulate and tax liquor sales and to create a procedure for the orderly transfer of lands between individuals and between individuals and the government.

....

As the federal government grappled with how to best manage the problems in Alaska, the debate over the territory's future settled into two camps. One viewpoint, articulated by the American environmentalist and painter Henry Wood Elliott, downplayed Alaska's resources and advocated a slow approach to government development and investment. This position was especially attractive to those in Congress who equated a gradual approach with less money and fewer headaches. The other camp was represented by William Healey Dall, the naturalist who had participated in the Western Union Telegraph expedition. This camp highlighted Alaska's abundant resources and promoted the idea of government involvement. In 1875 after the publication of Elliott's report on Alaska to the secretary of the treasury, Elliott and Dall took their disagreement to the public in a series of newspaper articles in the *Boston Daily Advertiser* and the *Nation*. The two men exchanged accusations and insults, both declaring their expertise and unbiased assessments to be correct. Dall declared that his rival's evaluation of Alaska was full of "multitudinous errors and misconceptions" and was based on an examination of less than 2 percent of the territory. Moreover, it all too clearly reflected the views of the Alaska Commercial Company, particularly with regard to the conditions of the Alaska Natives whom, Dall asserted, Elliott had failed to consult. Elliott, of course, denied these criticisms and attacked Dall's appeal for the establishment of schools for the Natives. Elliott dismissively pronounced, "With regard to the substantial, enduring good of teaching Indian children in our country, I think the 'common sense of the America people' has about made up its mind." Elliott claimed that Dall's various complaints against him were entirely unfounded and challenged Dall to give specific examples and, turning the tables, declared that it was Dall who lacked sufficient experience to write a lengthy tome on Alaska.

The debate continued through the summer and into the early fall. By this point, Dall had accused Elliott of taking their disagreement into the realm of "purely personal controversy," which he refused to engage in, "however tempting the provocation." Nonetheless, Dall did write a lengthy and unfavorable review of Elliott's report in which he reiterated many of his earlier concerns and proclaimed that the government should stop paying people to do surveys of the new territory if they were only going to represent the views of the Alaska Commercial Company. Needless to say, Elliott could not let Dall have the last word and responded a week later, addressing perceived errors in Dall's review and concluding with a pessimistic assessment of Alaska as a new frontier. Elliott proposed to potential settlers: "I think it would be a great deal wiser if their attention was directed to Puget Sound, where the summers are cool and equable and the winters quite mild. Here they can fish, hunt, and cultivate the soil, ship as sailors or work in logging-camps, and, above all, find schools for their children—a future there which the rigorous climatic conditions of Alaska deny."

One could argue that both men made valid points. In the 1870s, much of the economy in Alaska continued to depend on the sale of furs and fish. Each year, approximately 112,000 seal furs were harvested by the Alaska Commercial Company. Similarly, the number of salmon in Alaska was unmatched by those in Washington and Oregon. By the mid-1870s there were eighteen salmon canneries along the lower part of the Columbia River in the territory of Washington; in 1878 two small canneries were set up in Alaska. Mining, which would prove to be so profitable in later years, was still in its infancy in the 1870s and 1880s. The Russian-American Company had engaged in some small-scale mining but had not fully exploited the possibilities of Alaska's mineral riches, being more interested in the profitable fur trade. The company had dabbled in coal mining, and between 1857 and 1860 the annual coal production was 920 tons, but the cost of mining that coal far exceeded its selling price, so the company did not pursue it very aggressively. In the first decade or so after the purchase, there continued to be little mining activity, but there were several minor gold strikes that stimulated interest and excitement, drawing new prospectors to the area. In 1880 several men, among them Joseph Juneau, discovered gold along Gastineau Canal, northeast of Sitka at Gold Creek and Silver Bow Basin. The men staked out their mining claims and laid out a town site, the foundation for present-day Juneau, and the city became the jumping-off point for miners headed north and, eventually, the capital of Alaska. Reports of gold also came out of the Yukon Valley. There was some scouting in the area in the early 1870s, but it was only later in the decade when Chilkoot Pass through the Coast Mountains between Alaska and British Columbia was opened that miners could more easily gain access to this remote region. It was, of course, Chilkoot Pass that would be used by miners during the Klondike gold rush of 1896–99 as the main artery to get through the mountains to the site where gold was found. During the period when the Elliott-Dall debate was dominating the conversation about Alaska, however, no one knew just how much gold lay beneath that beautiful yet harsh landscape.

•••••••

Meanwhile, Rev. Sheldon Jackson, the superintendent of Presbyterian Missions in Alaska, continued to agitate for a government and funding for education in Alaska. Jackson traveled throughout the United States giving lectures in most of the major American cities of the period, as well as speaking to the National Education Association in 1883. These efforts resulted in the NEA passing a resolution that called for educational legislation and funding for Alaska. The resolution circulated to supporters of education and to schoolteachers around the country, and soon, teachers' associations took up the cause and adopted similar resolutions. Finally, Jackson began to see the first signs of success. On December 4, 1882, President Chester A. Arthur said in his message to Congress, "Alaska is still without any form of civil government. If means were provided for the education of its people, and for the protection of their lives and property, the immense resources of that region would invite permanent settlers and open new fields of industry and enterprise." Others also recognized the need for support. Wendell Phillips, the prominent lawyer, abolitionist, women's rights activist, and advocate for Native Americans, wrote to Jackson in 1883: "What excuse the United States Government can offer for leaving Alaska without magistracy or schools passes my conjecture. . . . If it were so poor a country that we dreaded the expense of a government, we might make some pretense of explanation. . . . But Alaska has poured millions into the Treasury, and one-third of what we have annually received would suffice for the whole expense of a government and schools."

In 1884, after years of caution on the part of the federal government and frustration for those residing in the new territory, Congress at last passed the Organic Act on May 17, 1884, which provided a civil government for Alaska. The act declared that the territory known as Alaska constituted a civil and judicial district with a temporary seat of government at Sitka. It further provided for the appointment of a governor with an annual salary of $3,000, a district attorney, and a clerk who would serve as ex-officio secretary and treasurer. The new territory would be given a marshal who would appoint four deputies to represent him in Sitka, Wrangell, Oonalashka, and Juneau City. Four commissioners would also be appointed, one for each of the aforementioned cities, to exercise all the powers and duties granted to justices of the peace in civil and criminal matters, according to the general laws of the state of Oregon, which were now declared to be the law in the new territory. Alaska's first governor was John H. Kinkead. Finally, Congress provided for the education of children in the territory of Alaska and allotted $25,000.

Setting up an education system was the task of John Eaton, the U.S. commissioner of education, and it was an enormous job. Distances in Alaska were great, mail service was slow, schools needed to be built, and under such circumstances it was difficult to find teachers willing to live in Alaska's remote and extreme conditions. Nonetheless, the process was underway and in the following year, Eaton appointed Jackson as the general agent of education in Alaska. By 1890 three secular schools for white children were established in Sitka, Juneau, and Douglas; eleven schools for Native children; and nine church schools.

······

Any discussion of Alaska's evolution from the time of the purchase until it became an official territory would be lacking without some mention of the tourist industry. In 1879–80 the famous naturalist John Muir visited Alaska and penned some of the most picturesque descriptions of the region's resources and natural beauty. Muir wrote of the tens of thousands of salmon swimming upstream: "Nothing that I could write may possibly give anything like a fair conception of the extravagance of their numbers." Muir's visit to Baird Glacier left him equally awestruck in the face of its "sublime grandeur—the noble simplicity and fineness of the sculpture of the walls; their magnificent proportions, their cascade, garden, and forest adornments; the placid water between them; the great white icewall stretching across the middle, and the snow-laden mountain peaks beyond."

The spectacular scenery of Alaska that Muir so beautifully described would eventually catch the attention of the emerging American tourist industry. In 1881 the first large tourist excursion, a group of eighty people, took a cruise through the Inside Passage aboard the steamer *Idaho*. Tourism flourished particularly in the Inside Passage because it was a comfortable and relatively easy way to experience a taste of Alaska's wilderness. There was also a bit of commingling of science and tourism in these excursions; after all, glaciers are objects of scientific and aesthetic interest. Not surprisingly, many early tourists were also amateur naturalists. Tourism, scientific exploration, and eventually mountaineering expeditions would continue to grow in number and disseminate more information about Alaska's glaciers, mountains, and natural beauty. One mountaineering expedition in 1890, cosponsored by the Geological Survey and the National Geographic Society, included not only the explorer John Wesley Powell but also the famous inventor Alexander Graham Bell. By 1890, despite its remoteness, more than five thousand tourists were paying about $100 each to head to Alaska every summer, and 125 years later, that number would grow to nearly 2 million visitors per year.

·······

Alaska's road from questionable investment to official territory was long and bumpy. It took nearly two decades to persuade the federal government to provide Alaska with the tools it needed—a stable administration and funding for education—to grow and develop on par with its potential. Eventually the discovery of gold in the Yukon in 1896 would dispel the myth of Alaska as a barren wasteland and would facilitate other developments. In 1906 Alaska was finally allowed to have one non-voting representative in Congress, and six years later Alaska became an official territory through the Second Organic Act.

Conclusion

*I*n a September 2008 interview, Alaska governor and vice presidential hopeful Sarah Palin responded to a question about what insight she had gained from living so close to Russia with the words, "They're our next-door neighbors, and you can actually see Russia from land here in Alaska." And so began a series of jokes that haunted the McCain-Palin ticket for the remainder of the presidential race. Days later, comedian and actress Tina Fey, in her uncanny imitation of Palin on *Saturday Night Live*, turned the phrase into, "I can see Russia from my house," and an urban legend was born. Palin, with her trademark wink and "Drill, baby, drill!" catchphrase, became a popular Republican figure with a near-cult following and put Alaska at the forefront of American politics and popular culture. Even after the Republican ticket's bid for the White House failed, Palin's presence in various political and media forums—including her television series, *Sarah Palin's Alaska*, which ran in for one season in 2010—kept America's attention on her and her home state.

• • • • • • •

Alaska has been at the center of national attention many times in the century or so since the purchase. In 1900, the same year the capital moved from Sitka to Juneau, copper was discovered near Kennicott Glacier. The richness of what became known as the Bonanza discovery is easier to comprehend when one considers that mines in Arizona and Utah at that time were mining ore with a 2 percent concentration of copper; at the Bonanza mine, the concentration initially measured a staggering 70 percent, though this number eventually settled at an average of 13 percent during the three decades of mining there. At roughly the same period, Alaska became the site of some of the country's earliest natural preservation and conservation efforts. In 1891 Congress passed an act giving the president the ability to set aside forest reserves out of federally owned lands. Over the next ten years, the executive branch converted some fifty million acres (roughly the size of the state of Nebraska) across the nation into national forests. In Alaska these included Tongass National Forest and Chugach National Forest. In 1910 Congress created Sitka National Historical Park and seven years later, Mount McKinley National Park (now known as Denali National Park). Finally, one can hardly talk of Alaska in the early decades of the twentieth century without mentioning the deadly diphtheria outbreak in Nome in 1925. The heroic efforts of mushers and sled dogs—most famously, Balto—to deliver serum to the beleaguered town inspired the annual Iditarod race that is still run today.

In subsequent decades, Alaska's place among the Lower 48 would grow in importance even before it was welcomed into the nation as a state. During World War II, Alaska was an important base of operations, and the Japanese even captured several islands in the Aleutian chain. The federal government recognized the necessity of building bases, airstrips, and roads even before the United States joined the war. When it ended, Alaska continued to benefit from this construction as well as the population growth that resulted from thousands of soldiers who decided to settle in Alaska. Alaska also benefitted financially from the beginning of the Cold War as the federal government decided to strengthen its bases and established a series of radar stations at the northernmost area of the territory as part of an early warning system against a Soviet attack. As Alaska's position in the United States grew during the first half of the twentieth century so did its desire for statehood. On January 3, 1959, President Dwight D. Eisenhower signed the proclamation making Alaska the forty-ninth state. The flag adopted for the new state showed the Big Dipper and the North Star in gold on a blue field representing the state flower, the forget-me-not. A thirteen-year-old schoolboy, Benny Benson, had designed the flag twenty years earlier when he entered and won a contest to give Alaska its own flag.

Alaska has often been at the center of the national debate between energy and the environment. It is ironic that a region that contains some of the country's most valuable energy resources is also home to some of the nation's most spectacular and fragile ecosystems. The battle over how to manage and balance the use of Alaska's natural resources began in various forms in the decades after its purchase with concerns about deforestation as well as declining salmon and fur seal populations. The conflict was exacerbated with the discovery of large oil deposits: the first, in 1957, along the Swanson River on the west side of the Kenai Peninsula, and the second, in 1968, with the discovery of natural gas and oil on Alaska's North Slope at Prudhoe Bay. Several pipelines had been established after earlier oil discoveries, but with the 1968 gusher, a much bigger pipeline was needed. In early summer 1969, the formal application for the Trans-Alaska Pipeline System was submitted to the Department of the Interior. Environmentalists worried about the possibility of spills and other hazards to wildlife and how the transportation of hot oil through a buried pipe would affect Alaska's permafrost. Supporters were more interested in potential profits. What followed was a battle between those who favored protective policies and those wanted to exploit the land's resources and worry about negative consequences later. The same debate continues today. In the end, the Arab oil embargo and the fuel crisis of the early 1970s encouraged the federal government to approve the pipeline; President Richard Nixon signed the Alaska Pipeline Authorization into law in November 1973. In a nod to the permafrost issue, half of the pipeline was built above ground.

There are two other major events that have cast the nation's eyes on Alaska, as well. In 1989, the *Exxon Valdez*, an oil tanker headed for Long Beach, California, struck Bligh Reef in Prince William Sound near Valdez and spilled millions of gallons of crude oil to create one of the worst man-made environmental disasters in history. The consequences of the oil spill on local wildlife were worsened by the remoteness of the area and in 2005 Congress passed an omnibus spending bill that included $442 million for the construction of two bridges in Alaska. One of these was snarkily nicknamed the "Bridge to Nowhere." The bridge, which would have been nearly as long as the Golden Gate Bridge in San Francisco, was intended to connect Ketchikan with Gravina Island, the location of a small town and the Ketchikan airport. Though the bridge was never built, it focused the country's attention on so-called pork-belly spending and government waste.

More recently, Alaska has frequently appeared in the news as politics and science clash in the climate change debate. Numerous reports have documented the melting of glaciers around the world and in Alaska. In 2015 a study published in *Geophysical Research Letters* concluded that in the last nineteen years Alaska's glaciers have dumped seventy-five gigatons (a gigaton is equal to a billion tons) of fresh water into the ocean, which has contributed to an increase in sea levels by two-tenths of a millimeter per year. The scientists who conducted the study monitored 116 glaciers in Alaska, the Yukon, and northern British Columbia to measure the rate of ice loss from calving (ice detaching from the glacier) and melting. Alaska's glaciers have been melting at a particularly rapid rate because they stand at lower altitudes than some of the world's other glaciers and because

Alaska has been experiencing record warm temperatures in recent years. Melting glaciers affect the temperature of lakes and rivers and could negatively impact wildlife. Spawning salmon, for example, are very sensitive to water temperature. Polar bears have also been affected as their main food sources are reduced and the distances between ice floes increase. As one journalist described it, polar bears have been photographed clinging precariously to ice floes, "their fragile grip the prefect symbol of the tragedy of global warming." Not everyone agrees with this assessment, however, guaranteeing that Alaska will remain at the forefront of the global climate change debate.

There are, of course, less somber ways in which Alaska has become part of American culture. Lest we give Palin too much credit, we should remember that she was not the first to create or host a popular television series based in Alaska. *Northern Exposure*, a quirky series set in the fictional town of Cicely, Alaska, had a loyal following and won many awards during its run on CBS between 1990 and 1995. Even more Americans became hooked on the Discovery Channel reality show *Deadliest Catch*, which began airing in 2005. The show follows crab fisherman in the Bering Sea and draws attention to the extreme dangers inherent in the jobs of commercial fishermen. The History Channel's *Ice Road Truckers* aired its first show in 2007 and focuses on the challenges of eighteen-wheeler drivers who transport goods, often over frozen lakes, in the Arctic regions of Canada and Alaska. These shows undoubtedly help to promote Alaska's greatest draw, its wild beauty that attracts nearly two million tourists a year. According to the Alaska Department of Commerce, Community, and Economic Development, these visitors spend roughly $2 billion a year in Alaska.

•••••••

There is one other reason for which Alaska has found itself in the news: ultranationalists in Russia have more than once called for the repatriation of Alaska. The notion that Alaska rightfully belongs to and with Russia, however, predates this recent burst of Russian nationalism. In fact, it was during the era of Stalin that the earliest arguments appeared, massaging and rewriting the story of the Alaska Purchase. As World War II ended and the Cold War began, Soviet Russia sought to condemn the colonialism of its Western rivals and cast its own past in a more favorable light. Consequently, some of the earliest writings on Alaska in this period portrayed Russia's colonization of Alaska as progressive. In this interpretation, Russian colonizers were kind to the indigenous people of Alaska, and conflicts were either nonexistent or the work of foreigners. Several Soviet novels of the early Cold War period similarly embedded a message of Russian imperial glory, complete with "righteous Slavs clashing with foreign (especially American) villains, and with native side-kicks standing and waiting to be blessed by the light of Russian civilization." Even a Soviet march from 1952 contains lyrics referring to Russia's benevolent relationship with Alaska: "Our great-grandfathers ventured / Beyond the Kuril Islands / Making home in those rough lands / Causing trouble to no one."

The notion of Russia as the peaceful bringer of culture, enlightenment, and morality is an essential part of the myth about Alaska that is found in current nationalist expressions. But the myth embodies more than this. In this rewriting of history, Alaska is presented as deeply connected to Russia not only culturally and politically but also through a spiritual bond. This sense of shared Russianness made the sale of Russian America that much more offensive and unnatural and, of course, someone must be held to account. Contemporary Russian nationalists have no trouble finding culprits for this cruel amputation. Some point to the corruptive influence of Western liberalism that infected Russia and its ruler Alexander II; others look to the familiar scapegoats, Jews and Freemasons, backed by the United States and Great Britain. Alexander's brother Constantine, who argued in favor of the sale, is even accused of heading a conspiracy to bankrupt the Russian-American Company in order to make his position more persuasive. This version of events is often compared to the collapse of the Soviet Union in 1991. In the words of one historian, "To patriotic writers, both 1867 and 1991 are examples of a worldwide conspiracy against Russian territorial interests."

This idea of Alaskan repatriation appeared most notably in the patriotic rhetoric of Vladimir Zhirinovsky, longtime leader of the far-right Liberal-Democratic Party of Russia, which achieved unexpectedly high returns in Russia's 1993 parliamentary elections. Despite the party's name, it is neither *liberal* nor *democratic* but seeks to recreate a Great Russia, or Russian Empire. Zhirinovsky has become well-known for his call that Alaska be returned to Russia, and it has been widely noted that his party's emblem includes a map of tsarist Russia that includes Alaska. While one of Zhirinovky's biographers argues that the party's symbol is not meant to be interpreted literally but rather to appeal to the Russian public's desire for a return to glory, many in the West view it with suspicion.

· · · · · · ·

Several misconceptions about the sale of Alaska dovetail with, and sometimes fuel, nationalist rhetoric as well. There is the persistent notion, for example, that the United States never paid in full for its purchase. It has also been argued that the famous treaty was not a sale at all but rather a ninety-nine-year lease that expired in 1966. This is what Soviet schoolchildren were taught during the Stalinist period. In 1994 Zhirinovsky alluded to this during a news conference in Washington, D.C., and added that the October Revolution had nullified all international agreements. In fact, on this at least, Zhirinovsky was correct. Following the 1917 Russian Revolution, the new communist government did renounce all previous international treaties concluded by the tsarist government, including the sale of Alaska. Legally binding treaties are not so easily undone, however, but neither are legends, myths, and rumors.

There are, of course, genuine lingering ties between Russia and Alaska. Approaching Sitka by water, one of the first sights is a large totem pole that embodies traditional Tlingit symbols as well as a double-headed eagle. Nearby is Baranov's Castle, the former residence of Russian-America's governor, and St. Michael's Russian Orthodox Cathedral. Russian Orthodox congregations exist in other towns as well. Similarly, in the small settlement of Ninilchik on the Kenai Peninsula, some older residents still recall a dialect of Russian that several linguistic professors have been working to record. In Nikolaevsk, also on the Kenai Peninsula, a Russian Orthodox village of Old Believers was established between 1968 and 1970. Old Believers, a sect of Russian Orthodoxy that rejected church reforms in the seventeenth century, persisted into the twentieth century but many left Russia over the years because of religious persecution. One small group eventually ended up in Alaska where they set up a community based upon traditional Russian beliefs and culture. The church service in Nikolaevsk, for example, is conducted in Old Church Slavonic and though most people speak English, they are encouraged to speak Russian and Slavonic. In recent years, fractures within that original settlement have led to breakaway villages in other parts of the Kenai Peninsula as well.

Americans have found a great deal of humor in Zhirinovsky's declarations to take Alaska back. In 2005 business columnist Daniel Pearlstein suggested in a humorous article that the United States sell Alaska back to Russia as a way of cutting the federal deficit. Pearlstein pointed out that "with the Kremlin still smarting about losing all those unpronounceable republics, Alaska would be just the sort of strategic acquisition to appeal to President Putin's imperial instincts." Presumably, most people recognized the farcical nature of this essay, but several Russian news sources seemed to have taken the proposition somewhat seriously. Russian newspapers *Trud* and *Novye Izvetia* reported on the story as if it were a serious proposition. More recently, the idea resurfaced. In 2012, an opinion essay in the *Washington Post* by journalist Steven Mufson entitled "To Solve Our Debt Problems, Let's Sell Alaska" was amusing to some but fell flat with others. As the United States once again hit the debt ceiling and approached the perilous "fiscal cliff," Mufson suggested that "selling Alaska could fetch at least $2.5 trillion and maybe twice that amount, enough to lop off a huge chunk of the national debt." Mufson went on to imagine that Russia might be interested, followed by China, or Donald Trump.

As comical as these proposals sound, however, the idea of Alaska being reunited with Russia is taken seriously by many people. In early 2014 a petition appeared on the official White House website calling for the repatriation of Alaska and garnered more than forty-two thousand signatures. Though the petition listed its author as a resident from Anchorage, the *Moscow Times* reported that it was actually uploaded by a Russian organization wanting to point out the weaknesses in the White House petition system. Nonetheless, there are clear indications that some Russians view this idea as a genuine possibility. In March 2014 Vladimir Chizhov, Russia's ambassador to the United Nations, referenced the country's historic tie to Alaska on a BBC talk show, and in the fall of that year, the Russian deputy prime minister for defense issues, Dmitry Rogozin, wrote a foreword to *Alaska Betrayed and Sold: The History of a Palace Conspiracy*, which argues for the return of Alaska. Rogozin was the leader of Russia's nationalist Rodina (Motherland) Party, so one might label him an extremist. But Rogozin is one of Putin's right-hand men, holding a position akin to the U.S. secretary of defense, and in 2015, he was appointed head of Arctic policy for Russia. Ivan Mironov, the author of *Alaska Betrayed and Sold* and also a member of the now-defunct Rodina Party, is a revisionist "historian" with a nationalist agenda. In his article in the *Moscow Times* about Rogozin and Mironov, Georgetown professor Harley Balzer asked, "After the annexation of Crimea in March, which was only part of Ukraine because of a 'historical mistake,' according to Russia, could Alaska be next on Russia's list?" Balzer was not the only one to draw this comparison; various news outlets in the United States have wondered just how far Putin will go in his moves to reclaim lost territory.

Some manifestations of this notion seem relatively harmless. For example, in 1991 the patriotic band Liube released a song entitled

"Don't Fool Around America," which contained lyrics such as, "Only give us Alaska land back / Give us back our dear native land." The band, reported to be a favorite of Putin's, also released a video showing one of the band members in a military uniform looking through binoculars toward America. The campy song seems innocuous enough, but its appearance at the Sochi Olympics could be construed differently. During the closing ceremonies, as the American athletes—smiling and waving to the crowds and cameras—paraded with their medals, the music subtly shifted from Daft Punk's "One More Time" to an instrumental version of Liube's "Don't Fool Around America." The choice of song may have been a joke, but in light of the intensifying Ukrainian crisis, which already contained an element of Russian nationalism, it was in poor taste, at best. The following month there was the claim by Aysen Nikolayev, the mayor of the Siberian city of Yakutsk, that archival documents had recently been found proving that Spruce Island, a small island near Kodiak, rightfully belongs to the Russian Orthodox Church. Several months later, after Russia had clearly become involved in the Ukrainian crisis and Putin had signed a bill to absorb Crimea into the Russian Federation, a Russian candy bar distributed by the company Shokobox featured on its wrapper a map of Russia that included Crimea as "new territory" and other former Soviet states, such as Estonia, Latvia, and Lithuania as "prospective territories." In the latter category, Alaska appeared as well. The story got some play on conservative American media sites but seems not to have been taken too seriously by anyone. Nonetheless, Russian nationalism is nothing to ignore, and Russia's recent involvement in Ukraine is no laughing matter.

Though most people are not worried about Russian aggression toward Alaska, various projects by the Russian government, when or if completed, would bring Alaska and her distant relative closer together. In 2007, for example, Russian mini submarines dove down more than two and a half miles below the North Pole and planted a Russian flag on the underwater Lomonosov Ridge, which Russia has argued for years is connected to its continental shelf. In doing so,

Russia symbolically staked its claim to billions of dollars' worth of gas and oil reserves in the Arctic Ocean. In 2011 Russia reasserted this demand, and in 2012 the Russian Orthodox Church got involved, holding a service near the North Pole and lowering a "holy memorial capsule" inscribed with the blessings of the church's leader, Patriarch Kirill of Moscow, in an attempt to consecrate the Arctic and bolster Russia's case. Though the United States, Russia, and Denmark have made similar claims to the Arctic, only Russia has made these overt symbolic moves, which are not viewed kindly by other countries. Canadian foreign minister Peter McKay was quoted as saying, "This isn't the fifteenth century. You can't go around the world and just plant flags and say: 'We're claiming this territory.'" Similarly, Russia's decision in 2015 to create two floating bases close to the North Pole for the Russian National Geographic Expedition Center was taken as another example of its claim to the North Pole. On the other hand, the announcement in May 2015 that Russia was considering the construction of a superhighway from London to Alaska left most people chuckling and scratching their heads, observing that the cost and complications of such a plan made it unlikely to ever come to fruition. Despite the dreams of Russian nationalists and the revisionism of certain historians and popular authors, the Alaska Purchase was a square deal, and the United States government has no interest in relinquishing some of the most valuable and beautiful land in the country.

Notes

The slash mark appearing in dates refers to the fact that until 1918, Russia adhered to the Julian calendar, which, in the twentieth century, was thirteen days behind the Gregorian calendar. In the nineteenth century, at the time of the Alaska Purchase, it created a difference of twelve days. Once the Gregorian calendar was adopted by Vladimir Lenin after the Russian Revolution, both dates were listed, the "old style" date (O.S.) and the "new style" date (N.S.).

Introduction

Quotes from travel guide found in *Appletons' Hand-Book of American Travel*, 308–10.
Comments of McIntyre found in "Letter of the Secretary of the Treasury," 27, 34.
Quote from Gannett in Cooley, "North Country," 362.

I. Some Mysterious Sympathy

"Most New England houses and ships were put together with Russian nails," quoted from Saul, *Distant Friends*, 26.

"Not only are our interests alike," quote from Nicholas I found in Dallas, *Diary of George Mifflin Dallas,* 209.

Martin van Buren's annual message, quoted from Williams, *Addresses and Messages of the Presidents,* 1098.

Secretary of State Buchanan's statement about American vessels in Russian waters quoted from *Alaskan Boundary Tribunal,* 250.

II. Evident Advantages

Seward in 1846 and 1860, on annexing British North America, quoted in Bancroft, "Seward's Ideas," 85.

Media responses to fictitious sales quoted from *New York Daily Times,* June 8, 1854, and *New York Herald,* July 25, 1854.

Wrangell's assessment of the value of Russian America found in Miller, *Alaska Treaty,* 42.

Alexander's response to Stoeckl's warnings about a Mormon migration quoted in Miller, *Alaska Treaty,* 45.

Stoeckl's comments on the Russian-American Company quoted in Miller, *Alaska Treaty,* 50.

Popov's comment on manifest destiny found in Kushner, *Conflict on the Northwest Coast,* 138.

On the seizure of the *Trent,* quote from Merli, *The Alabama,* 16.

"British knife poised for a thrust," quoted from Warner, Idea of a Continental Union, 3.

Lord Elgin's comments on annexation movements found in Elgin, *Letters and Journals,* 99–103.

Seward's comments on annexation of Canada found in Baker, *Works of William Seward,* 4:123–24.

Averell on Canadian fears of the Fenian movement in letter from Averell to Seward, March 15, 1867, National Archives and Records Administration (hereafter, NARA), Despatches from U.S. Consuls in Montreal, T222, Roll 8.

George Brown's statement that the "Americans are encroaching" found in Pope, *Confederation,* 59.

Averell on opposition to confederation, in letter from Averell to Seward, March 15, 1867, NARA, Despatches from U.S. Consuls in Montreal, T222, Roll 8.

Francis on annexationist sentiment in British Columbia in letter from Francis to Seward, April 13, 1867, NARA, Despatches from U.S. Consuls in Victoria, B.C., Canada.

Stoeckl's comment to Gorchakov on payment clause found in quoted in Miller, *Alaska Treaty,* 50.

III. Seward's Chimerical Project

Welles's comments on Seward's egoism from Welles, *Diary of Gideon Welles,* 75.

Meigs's and Rodgers's opinions quoted in *New York Times,* April 6, 1867.

Stoeckl on the ratification vote quoted in Miller, *Alaska Treaty,* 111.

Initial praise for the purchase quoted in *New York Times*, April 1, 1867, and
   April 9, 1867.
Early support from *Sacramento Daily Union*, April 9, 1867.
Quotes from *New York Times* on manifest destiny, April 11, 1867.
Quotes from the *New York Herald* and the *Bangor Daily Times* found in Reid,
   Purchase of Alaska, 27.
The *New York World* on manifest destiny quoted in Reid, *Purchase of
   Alaska*, 99.
The United States should not "abdicate . . . the empire of the sea," from *New
   York Times*, April 12, 1867.
"British possessions" quoted from *New York Herald* in Welch, "American Public
   Opinion," 488.
Newspaper remarks on potential of Asian market found in *New York Times*,
   March 31, 1867, and April 1, 1867; Seward's speech quoted in *New York
   Times*, July 2, 1867.
"Narrow-minded political bigots" quote found in *New York Times*, April 7, 1867.
"The people don't care who negotiated this bargain," *Sacramento Daily Union*,
   April 9, 1867.
Quotes about Russia's historic friendship from *New York Herald*, April 1, 1867;
   Chicago Republican, April 10, 1867; in Reid, *Purchase of Alaska*, 29; Welch,
   "American Public Opinion," 492.
Opposition point of view from *New York Tribune*, April 1, 1867.
"Mr. Seward's chimerical project," from the *Nation*, April 4, 1867.
"We have heard of people going to Russian America," quoted in Reid, *Purchase
   of Alaska*, 32.
"Russian American folly," attributed to the *New York Evening Gazette* by article
   in *Farmer's Cabinet*, May 2, 1867.
"Certainly not worth seven millions of dollars," quoted in Reid, *Purchase of
   Alaska*, 94.
"Sucked orange," *New York World*, April 1, 1867.
Fable about the frog, quoted in *New York Sun*, April 2, 1867.
"That vulgar sense," from *Harper's Weekly*, April 13, 1867.
"Hurried through the Senate," from *Harper's Weekly*, April 27, 1867.
The *New York Times*'s criticisms of the *Tribune* and the *Evening Post* quoted in
   New York Times, April 2, 1867, and April 10, 1867.
"Influential parties regard it as significant of Russian policy," quoted from *New
   York Times*, April 1, 1867.
Quotes from the Beamon memorandum can be found in Jensen, *Alaska
   Purchase*, 83–86.
Quotes from Sumner's speech are from *Speech of Hon. Charles Sumner of
   Massachusetts*, 12, 13, 16, 48.
Welles's observations about the final vote quoted in Welles, *Diary of Gideon
   Welles*, 83–84.
"The sapient critics," from *New York Times*, April 10, 1867.

"We do not understand the reasons for this secrecy," and "As sailors are sometimes seized with a passion for the land," quoted from *New York Tribune*,
April 10, 1867.

"Impassable deserts of snow," from *New York Tribune*, April 11, 1867.

"Commercially speaking," from *Farmer's Cabinet*, April 25, 1867.

"Time will justify," quoted from *New York Times*, April 11, 1867.

"Beautiful and picturesque islands" and "political and strategical advantages"
quoted in *New York Times*, May 4, 1867.

"Californians are irrepressibly anxious," from *New York Times*, May 30, 1867.

Sumner on the name of Alaska, from *Speech of Hon. Charles Sumner of
Massachusetts*, 48.

Stoeckl on the difficulty of doing business in America quoted in Miller, *Alaska
Treaty*, 92.

IV. No Longer Russian America

Correspondent from *Daily British Colonist* quoted in Neunherz, "The Purchase
of Russian America," 340.

Halleck's instructions printed in the *New York Times*, December 12, 1867.

Descriptions of unseemly opportunism quoted from Bloodgood, "Eight Months
at Sitka,"185–86; Dall, *Alaska and Its Resources*, 241.

Description of Sitka houses from Whymper, *Travel and Adventure*, 97.

Description of the transfer ceremony in George Foster Emmons, *Journal of the
USS Ossipee*, Sitka Historical Society, accessed May 11, 2016. http://vilda
.alaska.edu/cdm/compoundobject/collection/cdmg22/id/3394, 146–47.

Davis's letter about Alaska's weather quoted in Hughes and Whitney, *Jefferson
Davis in Blue*, 374.

Rousseau's report to Seward quoted in Miller, *Alaska Treaty*, 135.

Peshchurov's complaints and comment on "riff-raff" quoted in Miller, *Alaska
Treaty*, 138–41.

"Much ill feeling," from *New York Times*, November 13, 1867.

Peshchurov and Stoeckl on pensioners quoted in Miller, *Alaska Treaty*, 142.

"Our Northwest bargain," in *New York Times*, October 17, 1867.

Comments about Alaska, *Farmer's Cabinet*, November 7, 1867; December 12,
1867.

"Narrow jealousies" from *New York Times*, December 25, 1867.

Positive assessment of Davis quoted from Hughes and Whitney, *Jefferson Davis
in Blue*, 392.

Negative assessment of Davis quoted from Jones, "'Search for and Destroy,'" 8.

Twain's imaginary ad quoted from Twain, *Mark Twain*, 239.

V. Paying for the "New National Ice-House"

Stoeckl's concerns about the Perkins Claim and the "uneasiness" it might produce quoted in Miller, *Alaska Treaty*, 167.

Memo in the Bureau of Claims by E. Peshine Smith, October 24, 1867, Records
of Boundary and Claims Commissions and Arbitrations.

Stevens's statement of support for appropriation quoted in Miller, *Alaska Treaty*, 150.

Walker's letter quoted in *Washington Daily Morning Chronicle*, January 28, 1868.

Quote about conflicting statements from *New York Times*, February 10, 1868.

House request to Seward about Perkins Claim quoted in Miller, *Alaska Treaty*, 151.

Stoeckl's complaint about the "Perkins roguery" found in Bolkhovitnov, *Russian-American Relations*, 301.

Assessment of President Johnson from Benedict, "A New Look at the Impeachment," 504.

Quote by Clarke about Johnson from February 24, 1868, *Appendix to the Congressional Globe*, 199.

"Decidedly spicy," quoted from *New York Times*, March 19, 1868.

Banks's statement on delay quoted in Miller, *Alaska Treaty*, 153.

"Given the Alaska appropriation" from *Daily Alta California*, March 23, 1868.

Johnson's concerns about delay quoted in Miller, *Alaska Treaty*, 153.

Seward's assurance to Stoeckl on payment quoted in Miller, *Alaska Treaty*, 154.

Stoeckl's comments about help from Johnson and Seward found in Bolkhovitinov, *Russian-American Relations*, 301.

Schuyler's comments on treatment of Americans in Russia found in his letter to Seward, July 7, 1868, and July 20, 1868, NARA, Despatches from U.S. Consuls in St. Petersburg, Russia.

"The American people will not," in *New York Times*, March 4, 1868.

Quote about losing elections in western states in *Daily Alta California,* March 23, 1868.

Letter to the editor on the possibility of appropriation being denied, *Washington Daily Morning Chronicle*, March 30, 1868.

Schuyler's concerns to Seward in letter of April 20, 1868, NARA, Despatches from U.S. Consuls in St. Petersburg, Russia.

Quotes from the *Journal de St. Petersbourg*, April 3/15, 1868, and the *Moscow Gazette*, April 7/19, 1868, are also found in Schuyler's letter to Seward.

Arguments of members of Committee on Foreign Affairs about treaty found in "Treaty with Russia."

Loughridge preamble "subjects which by the Constitution" quoted from Miller, *Alaska Treaty*, 158.

Seward's memorandum on Perkin's claim quoted in Miller, *Alaska Treaty*, 159.

Myer's views in *Purchase of Alaska*, 1–4.

Price's views in *Appendix to the Congressional Globe*, 380–81.

Washburn's views in *Appendix to the Congressional Globe*, 392, 394, 399.

"Vexatious delay," "a very pointed and practical hint," and "honor bound" all quoted from the *New York Times*, July 1, 1868.

"If a mistake was made," in *New York Times*, July 2, 1868.

"It would lead to an open violation," in *Washington Daily Morning Chronicle*, June 27, 1868.

"It seems to us . . . that the House," *New York Sun*, June 8, 1868.

Observations about the Asian trade in the *New York Times*, July 22, 1868;
  Washington Daily Morning Chronicle, July 25, 1868.
Banks's boastful letter to his wife quoted in Jensen, *Alaska Purchase*, 122.
"Employ the friendly offices" and "promised the House last session" quoted in
  Miller, *Alaska Treaty*, 162.
Banks's letters to Fish quoted in Miller, *Alaska Treaty*, 164.
Catacazy's extremely negative view of the Perkins Claim quoted from letter
  from Catacazy to Fish, New York, August 12/24, 1870, NARA, Notes from
  the Russian Legation in the U.S. to the Department of State.
Unsigned despatch addressed to the tsar found in Letter from B. Stewart,
  lawyer for Mrs. Perkins, to Secretary of State, Hamilton Fish, Washington,
  April 24, 1870, NARA, Notes to Foreign Legations in the United States from
  the Department of State.
Newspaper comments on likely corruption from *New York World*, April 2, 1867,
  and *New York Tribune*, April 8, 1867, quoted in Stahr, *Seward*, 490.
Schuyler on renewal of good relations, September 19, 1868, NARA, Despatches
  from U.S. Consuls in St. Petersburg, Russia.
"Obnoxious rumors," in *Philadelphia Evening Transcript*, December 17, 1868.
Lack of Russian participation in investigation explained, Committee on Public
  Expenditures, 4.
Quote from Bodisco about the investigation found in Bolkhovitinov, *Russian-
  American Relations*, 316.
Condemnation of Hinton in general report on investigation, Committee on
  Public Expenditures, 3.
Quotes from minority report of investigation from Committee on Public
  Expenditures, 6.
"A fierce pack of fraud avengers," from *New York Times*, February 10, 1869.
Quotes from *New York Herald* regarding Stoeckl found in Holbo, *Tarnished
  Expansion*, 88.
Bodisco's statement about the funds of foreign missions quoted in
  Bolkhovitinov, *Russian-American Relations*, 316–17.
Recently found ukaz about Alaska expenditures quoted in Bolkhovitinov,
  Russian-American Relations, 321.
Statement of Riggs on the March 25 telegram quoted in Committee on Public
  Expenditures, 9.

VI. Very Uneasy and Vexed

Morris's comments on European fears of a Russian-American alliance quoted
  in Braden, "The Eagle and the Crescent," 366.
Robinson's comment about Alsatian bravado found in Robinson to Seward,
  April 4, 1867, and May 15, 1867, NARA, Despatches from U.S. Consuls in
  Strasbourg, France.
Murphy's observations found in Murphy to Seward, March 4, 1867; May 23,
  1867; and September 17, 1866, NARA, Despatches from U.S. Consuls in
  Frankfurt on the Main, Germany.

Morris's reports on opinions in the Ottoman Empire quoted in Braden, "Eagle and the Crescent," 327–28, 369.
Osten-Saken's memorandum and later diary entry quoted in Miller, "Russian Opinion," 524–25.
Valuev's view of the purchase quoted in Zaionshkovskii, *Dnevnik P. A. Valueva*, 195.
Clay's assessment of the Russian view of the purchase found in Clay to Seward, May 10, 1867, NARA, Despatches from U.S. Ministers to Russia.
Quotes from Russian newspapers found in Bolkhovitnov, *Russian-American Relations*, 253–56.
Clay's observation on the Russian public's enthusiasm for America found in Clay to Seward, May 10, 1867, NARA, Despatches from U.S. Ministers to Russia.
Bancroft's conversation with Bismarck quoted in Stolberg-Wernigerode, *Germany and the United States*, 283.
Murphy's and Wright's observations found in Murphy to Seward, May 23, 1867, NARA, Despatches from U.S. Consuls in Frankfurt on the Main, Germany; Wright to Seward, April 4, 1867, NARA, Despatches from U.S. Ministers to German States and Germany.
Quote from the *North American Review* found in Kaufman, "Austro-American Relations," 203.
Motley's dire prediction for Austria quoted in Curtis, *Correspondence of John Lothrop Motley*, 252.
Observation about cession found in *Weiner Zeitung*, April 5, 1867.
"Politically important" in *Neue Freie Presse*, April 2, 1867.
Marsh's and Hooker's comments from Italy found in Ducci, *George P. Marsh Correspondence*, 120–21; Stock, *United States Ministers*, 348.
Fox's conversation with Napoleon III found in Fox to Welles, September 30, 1866, NARA, Despatches from U.S. Ministers to Russia.
American observations about French reactions found in *New York Times*, April 21, 1867, and *New York Tribune*, April 19, 1867.
One reaction of French press found in *Le Temps*, April 3, 1867.
Quote from *La Turquie* and Morris's comment about the concerns raised by the U.S. president's message found in Morris to Seward, January 2, 1867, NARA, Despatches of U.S. Ministers to Turkey.
Quote from Queen Victoria's diary found in Collin, *Theodore Roosevelt*, 155.
Quotes from the House of Commons and the House of Lords quoted in the *New York Times*, April 16, 1867; Neunherz, "Purchase of Russian America," 298.
Bruce's comments quoted in Neunherz, "Purchase of Russian America," 299–300.
"Supremacy of the North American continent," from the *London Times*, April 2, 1867.
Manchester Courier and Lancashire General Advertiser, Glasgow Herald, and *London Morning Post* quoted in *Farmer's Cabinet*, April 25, 1867.
Other British papers found in Neunherz, "Purchase of Russian America," 303–7; Reid, *Purchase of Alaska*, 87–91.

Quote from Sen. George H. Williams found in Neunherz, "Purchase of Russian America," 356

"There is a strong party" found in *London Globe* found in April 1, 1867.

Austrian viewpoint from *Neue Freie Press*, April 6, 1867.

Marx's comment found in Marx and Engels, *Collected Works*, 32:542.

Clay's remark on Anglo-French friendship found in Clay to Seward, May 10, 1867, NARA, Despatches from U.S. Ministers to Russia.

Canadian papers quoted in *The Freeman's Journal*, April 20, 1867; Neunherz, "Purchase of Russian America," 257–61, 268.

Seymour quoted in Neunherz, "'Hemmed in,'" 104.

Annexationist sentiment in the American press quoted from *New York Times*, May 24, 1867; *Charleston Daily Courier*, April 19, 1867.

Alaska Purchase viewed as recognition of the Monroe Doctrine quote from *Le Temps*, April 3, 1867.

Morris's perspective on significance of purchase as display of American unity from Morris to Seward, May 8, 1867, NARA, Despatches of U.S. Ministers to Turkey.

VII. That Snowbound Wilderness

"Since Alaska is now part of us," found in *Harper's Weekly*, March 6, 1869.

Information on Fast quoted in *New York Times*, December 13, 1868.

Casual references about traveling to Alaska in *New York Times*, December 20, 1868, and December 25, 1868.

Whymper's reflections on Alaska from Whymper, *Travel and Adventure*, 36, 37, 76.

Schuyler's report on European concerns and quotes from Russian newspapers found in Schuyler to Seward, September 29, 1868, NARA, Despatches from U.S. Consuls in St. Petersburg, Russia.

Newspaper account of General Halleck's visit from *New York Times*, November 20, 1868.

Seward's speech upon arrival in San Francisco quoted from Hinckley, "William H. Seward Visits," 130.

Descriptions of Seward's experiences in Alaska from his son's book, Seward, *Seward at Washington*, 422, 424, 426, 430.

Seward's speech in Sitka found in Seward, "The promise of Alaska," 5–6.

Duncan's and Colyer's assessment of conditions in Alaska found in "Letter of the Secretary of the Interior," 6–7, 10.

Dall's descriptions of Alaska found in Dall, *Alaska and Its Resources*, 241, 242.

Comments of Captain Bryant and McIntyre found in "Letter of the Secretary of the Treasury," 27, 34.

Lyle's report on condition in Alaska found in "Alaska. Letter from the Secretary of War," 12.

Ludington's report found in "Alaska. Letter from the Secretary of War," 32.

Maynard's comments on the fur seal trade from "Letter from the Secretary of the Navy, A copy of the report of Lieut. Washburn Maynard," 6.

Howard's remarks on Alaska from "Letter from the Secretary of War," 5, 6.

Eaton's comments on the state of education found in *Territory of Alaska, Report of the Commissioner of Education*, 16.

McFarland's observations found in Anderson, "Letters of Amanda R. McFarland," 92, 98, 101.

Beardslee's comments found in "Letter from the Secretary of the Navy, transmitting in response to Senate resolution," 7, 11, 16.

The Elliot-Dall debate can be found in the *Boston Daily Advertiser*, July 15, 1875, August 18, 1875, and August 20, 1875, and the *Nation*, September 9, 1875.

Arthur's message and Phillips letter found in *Territory of Alaska, Report of the Commissioner of Education*, 17.

Muir's descriptions found in Muir, *Letters from Alaska*, 29–30, 72.

Conclusion

Quote about polar bears from Bill Mouland, "Global warming sees polar bears stranded on melting ice," *Daily Mail*, February 1, 2007, accessed June 28, 2015. http://www.dailymail.co.uk/news/article-433170/Global-warming -sees-polar-bears-stranded-melting-ice.html.

Description of Soviet novels and Lyrics of Soviet Army march song quoted in Znamenski, "History with an Attitude," 351.

"To patriotic writers, both 1867 and 1991" quoted from Znamenski, "History with an Attitude," 361.

Humorous proposal to sell Alaska from Daniel Pearlstein, "Alaska Would Be More at Home in Russia," *Washington Post*, November 23, 2005.

Follow-up proposal to sell Alaska from Steven Mufson, "To Solve Our Debt Problem, Let's Sell Alaska," *Washington Post*, December 14, 2012.

Comments about Rogozin and Mironov quoted from Harley Balzer, "Is Alaska Next on Russia's List?" *Moscow Times*, October 14, 2014, accessed June 25, 2015. http://www.themoscowtimes.com/opinion/article/is-alaska-next-on -russia-s-list/509438.html.

Comments of Canadian foreign minister quoted in Tom Parfitt, "Russia plants flag on North Pole," *Guardian*, August 2, 2007, accessed June 28, 2015. http://www.theguardian.com/world/2007/aug/02/russia.arctic.

Bibliography

$\mathscr{O}$ome sources listed here contributed to my research in a general way, but were not listed in the notes because they were not quoted.

Archives and Manuscript Collections

National Archives and Records Administration, College Park, Maryland

Despatches from U.S. Consuls in Frankfurt on the Main, Germany, 1829–1906, M161 (Rolls 16 and 17).

Despatches from U.S. Consuls in Montreal, T222, Roll 8 and T130, (Roll 1).

Despatches from U.S. Consuls in St. Petersburg, Russia, RG 59, M 81 (Roll 7).

Despatches from U.S. Consuls in Strasbourg, France, 1866–1872, T 442 (Roll 1).

Despatches from U.S. Consuls in Victoria, British Columbia, Canada, 1862–1906, T 103 (Roll 1).

Despatches from U.S. Ministers to Denmark, 1811–1906, M 41 (Roll 11).

Despatches from U.S. Ministers to German States and Germany, 1799–1906, M 44 (Roll 14).

Despatches from U.S. Ministers to Great Britain, 1791–1906, M 30 (Roll 90).

Despatches from U.S. Ministers to Russia, 1866–1869, M 35 (Roll 21).

Despatches of U.S. Ministers to Turkey, 1818–1906, M 46 (Rolls 20 and 21).

Notes to Foreign Legations in the United States from the Department of State,

1834–1906: Russia, RG 59, M 99.

Notes from the Russian Legation in the U.S. to the Department of State, 1809–1906, RG 59 (Roll 5).

Records of Boundary and Claims Commissions and Arbitrations, 1716–1979, Record Group 76, Box 2, National Archives, Washington, D.C.

Sumner, Charles. Manuscripts, Massachusetts Historical Society, Boston.

Published Materials

Adams, Henry Mason. *Prussian-American Relations, 1775–1871.* Cleveland: Press of Western Reserve University, 1960.

"Alaska. Letter from the Secretary of War, in Relation to the Territory of Alaska, March 15, 1871," House of Representatives, Executive Document No. 5, 42nd Congress, 1st Session.

Alaskan Boundary Tribunal. Proceedings of the Alaskan Tribunal, Convened at London . . . Vol. 2. Washington, D.C.: Government Printing Office, 1904.

Alduino, Frank W., and David J. Coles. *Sons of Garibaldi in Blue and Gray: Italians in the American Civil War.* Youngstown, NY: Cambria Press, 2007.

Anderson, Charles. "Letters of Amanda R. McFarland: Introduction." *Journal of the Presbyterian Historical Society (1943–1961)* 34, no. 2 (June 1956): 83–102.

Anderson, M. S. *The Eastern Question, 1774–1923.* New York: St. Martin's Press, 1966.

Appendix to the Congressional Globe, 40th Congress, 2nd Session

Appleton and Company. *Appletons' Hand-Book of American Travel.* New York: D. Appleton and Company, 1872.

Bailey, Thomas A. "The Russian Fleet Myth Re-Examined." *Mississippi Valley Historical Review* 38, No. 1 (June 1951): 81–90.

Baker, George E. ed., *The Works of William Seward.* Boston: Houghton Mifflin, 1884.

Balzer, Harley. "Is Alaska Next on Russia's List?" *Moscow Times,* October 14, 2014, accessed June 25, 2015, http://www.themoscowtimes.com/opinion/article/is-alaska-next-on-russia-s-list/509438.html.

Bancroft, Frederic. "Seward's Ideas of Territorial Expansion." *North American Review* 167, no. 500 (July 1898): 79–89.

Barratt, Glynn. *Russian Shadows on the British Northwest Coast of North America, 1810–1890.* Vancouver: University of British Columbia Press, 1983.

Benedict, Michael Les. "A New Look at the Impeachment of Andrew Johnson," *Political Science Quarterly* 88, no. 3 (September 1973): 493–511.

Black, Lydia T. *Russians in Alaska, 1732–1867.* Fairbanks: University of Alaska Press, 2004.

Blagov, Sergei. "Joke About Sale of Alaska Hits a Nerve in Russia." CNS News online, accessed June 12, 2015, http://www.cnsnews.com/news/article/joke-about-sale-alaska-hits-nerve-russia.

Blinn, Harold. "Seward and the Polish Rebellion of 1863." *American Historical Review* 45, no. 4 (July 1940): 828–33.

Bloodgood, C. D. "Eight Months at Sitka." *Overland Monthly* 2, no. 2 (February 1869): 175–86.

Blumenthal, Henry. *A Reappraisal of Franco-American Relations, 1830–1871.* Chapel Hill: University of North Carolina, 1959.

Bolkhovitinov, N. N. *The Beginnings of Russian-American Relations, 1775–1815.* Cambridge, MA: Harvard University Press, 1975.

———. "The Crimean War and the Emergence of Proposals for the Sale of Russian America, 1853–1861." *Pacific Historical Review* 59, no. 1 (February 1990): 15–49.

———. "Obshchestvennost' SShA i Ratifikatsiia Dogovora 1867 g.," *Amerikanskii ezhegodnik* (1987): 157–74.

———. *Russian-American Relations and the Sale of Alaska, 1834–1867.* Kingston, Ontario: Limestone Press, 1996.

———. *Russko-amerikanskie otnosheniia: 1815–1832.* Moskva: Nauka, 1975.

Boraas, Alan. "Russians Look to the East, and That Means Alaska," *Alaska Dispatch News*, March 27, 2015, accessed June 23, 2015, http://www.adn.com/article/20150327/russians-look-east-and-means-alaska.

Borneman, Walter R. *Alaska: Saga of a Bold Land.* New York: Harper Collins, 2003.

Bothwell, Robert. *The Penguin History of Canada.* Toronto: Penguin, 2006.

Braden, Jean Haythorne. "The Eagle and the Crescent: American Interests in the Ottoman Empire, 1861–1870." PhD diss., Ohio State University, 1973.

Bridge, F. R. *From Sadowa to Sarajevo: The Foreign Policy of Austria-Hungary, 1866–1914.* London and Boston: Routledge and Kegan Paul, 1972; reprint, London: Routledge, 2002.

Burley, Edith. *Servants of the Honorable Company: Work, Discipline, and Conflict in the Hudson's Bay Company, 1770–1870.* Oxford: Oxford University Press, 1997.

Callahan, James. *The Alaska Purchase and Americo-Canadian Relations.* Morgantown: West Virginia University, 1908.

Casey, Michael. "Alaska Glaciers Sending 75 Billion Tons of Water into Sea Each Year," CBSnews.com, June 18, 2015, accessed June 28, 2015, http://www.cbsnews.com/news/alaska-glaciers-sending-75-billion-tons-of-water-into-sea-each-year/.

Chang, Kenneth. "The Big Melt Accelerates." *New York Times*, May 19, 2104, accessed June 26, 2015, http://www.nytimes.com/2014/05/20/science/the-melting-isnt-glacial.html?_r=0.

Chastain, Mary. "Russian Chocolate Bar Showing 'Map of Russia' Includes Ukraine and Alaska." Breitbart.com, May 25, 2014, accessed June 25, 2015, http://www.breitbart.com/national-security/2014/05/25/chocolate-bar-displays-russia-in-2015-includes-ukraine-and-alaska/.

Coleman, Marion Moore. "Eugene Schuyler: Diplomat Extraordinary from the United States to Russia 1867–1876." *Russian Review* 17, no. 1 (Autumn 1947): 33–48.

Collin, Richard. *Theodore Roosevelt, Culture, Diplomacy, and Expansion: A New View of American Imperialism.* Baton Rouge: Louisiana State University Press, 1985.

Committee on Public Expenditures, Report, Alaska Investigation, 40th Congress, 3rd Session (February 27, 1869); H.R. 1096, 40th Congress (1868).

Cooley, Richard A. "North Country: A Geographical Study of Alaska." *Journal of the West* 6, no. 3 (July 1967): 362–70.

Crankshaw, Edward. *The Fall of the House of Habsburg.* New York: Penguin, 1963.

Cunningham, Michael. *Mexico and the Foreign Policy of Napoleon III.* New York: Palgrave, 2001.

Curtis, George William, ed. *The Correspondence of John Lothrop Motley.* New York: Harper and Brothers, 1889.

Dall, William Healey. *Alaska and Its Resources.* Boston: Lee and Shepard, 1870.

Dallas, George M. *Diary of George Mifflin Dallas, United States Minister to Russia, 1837–1839.* New York: Arno Press, 1970.

Demirjian, Karoun. "Alaska Day or Time for Annexation? The Russian Jokes That Just Won't Die." *Washington Post,* October 17, 2014.

Ducci, Lucia. *George P. Marsh Correspondence: Images of Italy, 1861–1881.* Madison, NJ: Fairleigh Dickinson University Press, 2012.

Dvoichenko-Markov, Eufrosina. "Americans in the Crimean War." *Russian Review* 13, no. 2 (April 1954): 137–45.

Echard, William E. *Napoleon III and the Concert of Europe.* Baton Rouge: Louisiana State University Press, 1983.

Egan, Timothy. "Alaskans Don't Want to be Anyone's Siberia." *New York Times,* December 19, 1993.

Elgin, James Bruce. *Letters and Journals of James, Eighth Earl of Elgin.* Edited by Theodore Walrond. London: John Murray, 1872. Reprint, New York: Kraus Reprint Co., 1969.

Elliott, Henry Wood. *Our Arctic Province: Alaska and the Seal Islands.* New York: Charles Scribner's Sons, 1886. Reprint, New York: C. Scribner's Sons, 1906.

Emmons, George Foster. *Journal of the U.S.S. Ossipee,* Sitka Historical Society, accessed May 11, 2016. http://vilda.alaska.edu/cdm/compoundobject/collection/cdmg22/id/3394.

Emmons, George Thornton. *The Tlingit Indians.* Edited with additions by Frederica de Laguna and a biography by Jean Low. Seattle: University of Washington Press; New York: American Museum of Natural History, 1991.

Farris, Glen J., ed. *So Far from Home: Russians in Early California.* Berkeley: Heydey; Santa Clara: Santa Clara University, 2012.

Farrow, Lee A. *Alexis in America: A Russian Grand Duke's Tour, 1871–72.* Baton Rouge: Louisiana State University Press, 2014.

———. "Intrigue, Scandal, and International Diplomacy: A Reexamination of the Perkins Claim." in *New Perspectives on Russian-American Relations.* Edited by William Benton Whisenhunt and Norman E. Saul. New York: Routledge, 2016.

Field, Kate. "Our Ignorance of Alaska." *North American Review* 149, no. 392 (July 1889): 78–90.

Fitzgerald, Emily McCorkle. *An Army Doctor's Wife on the Frontier: Letters from Alaska and the Far West, 1874–1878.* Edited by Abe Laufe. Pittsburgh: University of Pittsburgh Press, 1962.

Gerus, Oleh W. "The Russian Withdrawal from Alaska: The Decision to Sell." *Revista de Historia de America,* no. 75/76 (January–December 1973): 157–78.

Gibson, James R. *Imperial Russia in Frontier America, 1784–1867.* New York:

Oxford University Press, 1976.

Goetzmann, William H. *When the Eagle Screamed: The Romantic Horizon in American Expansionism, 1800–1860*. Norman: University of Oklahoma Press, 1999.

Golder, Frank. "The American Civil War through the Eyes of a Russian Diplomat." *American Historical Review* 26, no. 3 (April 1921): 454–63.

———. "Mining in Alaska before 1867." *Washington Historical Quarterly* 7, no. 3 (July 1916): 233–38.

———. "Russian American Relations during the Crimean War." *American Historical Review* 31, no. 3 (April 1926): 462–76.

———. "The Russian Fleet and the Civil War." *American Historical Review* 20, no. 2 (1915): 801–12.

Graef, Aileen. "Russian Mayor Demands Alaskan Island Be Returned to Russia," UPI.com, March 26, 2014, accessed June 25, 2015, http://www.upi.com/Top_News/World-News/2014/03/26/Russian-mayor-demands-Alaskan-island-be-returned-to-Russia/5331395862512/.

Grauman, Melody Webb. "Kennecott: Alaskan Origins of a Copper Empire, 1900–1938." *Western Historical Quarterly* 9, no. 2 (April 1978): 197–211.

Greene, David. "Russia Pushes to Claim Arctic as its Own." NPR.org, August 16, 2011, accessed June 28, 2015, http://www.npr.org/2011/08/16/139577789/russia-pushes-to-claim-arctic-as-its-own.

Griffiths, David M. "Nikita Panin, Russian Diplomacy and the American Revolution." *Slavic Review* 28, no. 1 (March 1969): 1–24.

Grinev, Andrei V. "Russia's Emperors and Russian America (for the Four Hundredth Anniversary of the Romanov Dynasty)." *Russian Studies in History* 54, no. 1 (June 2015): 5–35.

Gusovsky, Dina. "Sochi Closing Song for USA? 'Stop Screwing Around.'" CNBC online, February 14, 2014, accessed June 23, 2015, http://www.cnbc.com/id/101440439.

Halleck, Charles. *Our New Alaska; or, the Seward Purchased Vindicated*. New York: Forest and Stream Publishing Co., 1886.

Haycox, Stephen W., and Mary Childres Mangusso, ed. *An Alaska Anthology*. Seattle: University of Washington Press, 1996.

Herber, Elmer C. "Spencer Fullerton Baird and the Purchase of Alaska." *Proceedings of the American Philosophical Society* 98, no. 2 (April 15, 1954): 139–43.

Hinckley, Ted C. *The Americanization of Alaska, 1867–1897*. Palo Alto: Pacific Books, 1972.

———. "William H. Seward Visits His Purchase." *Oregon Historical Quarterly* 72, no. 2 (June 1971), 127–47.

Hodgins, Thomas. *British and American Diplomacy Affecting Canada*. Toronto: The Rowsell-Hutchison Press, 1900.

Holbo, Paul, *Tarnished Expansion: The Alaska Scandal, the Press and Congress*. Knoxville: University of Tennessee Press, 1983.

Hughes, Nathaniel Cheairs, Jr., and Gordon D. Whitney. *Jefferson Davis in Blue: The Life of Sherman's Relentless Warrior*. Baton Rouge: Louisiana State

University Press, 2012.

Jelavich, Barbara. *The Ottoman Empire, the Great Powers, and the Straits Question, 1870–1887*. Bloomington: Indiana University Press, 1973.

Jensen, Ronald J. *The Alaska Purchase and Russian-American Relations*. Seattle: University of Washington Press, 1975.

Jonassen, Wendi, and Ryan Loughlin. "A 17th-Century Russian Community Living in 21st-Century Alaska," *Atlantic*, May 1, 2013, accessed June 23, 2015, http:// www.theatlantic.com/national/archive/2013/05/a-17th-century-russian -community-living-in-21st-century-alaska/275440/.

Jones, Bruce, and Tom Parfitt, "Russian Reasserts Ownership over the North Pole." *Telegraph*, September 28, 2012, accessed June 28, 2015, http://www.business insider.com/russia-reasserts-ownership-over-the-north-pole-2012-9.

Jones, Howard. *Union in Peril: The Crisis over British Intervention in the Civil War.* Lincoln: University of Nebraska Press, 1992.

Jones, Zachary R. "'Search for and Destroy': US Army Relations with Alaska's Tlingit Indians and the Kake War of 1869." *Ethnohistory* 60, no. 1 (Winter 2013): 1–26.

Journal of the Executive Proceedings of the Senate of the United States of America (1867–1868).

Journal of the House of Representatives of the United States of America (1867–1868); *Congressional Globe*, 40th Congress, 2nd Session.

Journal of the Senate of the United States of America (1867–1868)

Karamanski, Theodore. *Fur Trade and Exploration: Opening the Far Northwest, 1821–1852*. Norman: University of Oklahoma Press, 1983.

Kartsev, Vladimir, and Todd Bludeau. *¡Zhrinovsky!* New York: Columbia University Press, 1995.

Kaufman, Burton Ira "Austro-American Relations During the Era of the American Civil War." *Austrian History Yearbook* 4–5 (1968–69): 203–27.

Keithahn, E. L. "Alaska Ice, Inc." *Pacific Northwest Quarterly* 36, no. 2 (April 1945): 121–31.

Kushner, Howard. *Conflict on the Northwest Coast: American-Russian Rivalry in the Pacific Northwest, 1790–1867.* Westport, CT: Greenwood Press, 1975.

Kutolowski, John. *The West and Poland: Essays on Governmental and Public Responses to the Polish National Movement, 1861–1864*. Boulder, CO: East European Monographs, 2000.

LeFeber, Walter. *The Clash: A History of U.S.-Japan Relations.* New York: W. W. Norton, 1997.

———. *The New Empire: An Interpretation of American Expansion, 1860–1898,* 35th anniversary edition. Ithaca: Cornell University Press, 1998.

"Letter from the Secretary of the Navy, A copy of the report of Lieut. Washburn Maynard, United States Navy, on the subject of the Alaska seal-fisheries." House of Representatives, Executive Document No. 43, 44th Congress, 1st Session.

"Letter from the Secretary of the Navy, transmitting in response to Senate reso-lution of February 26, 1880, information in regard to the present condition of affairs in Alaska, March 5, 1880." Senate, Executive Document, No. 105, 46th

Congress, 2nd Session.

"Letter from the Secretary of War, A report of the commanding general, Department of the Columbia of his tour in Alaska Territory, in June, 1875." Senate, Executive Document, No. 12, 44th Congress, 1st Session.

"Letter of the Secretary of the Interior . . . as relates to the Indian village of Wrangell, Alaska, showing the condition of that village previous to its recent bombardment by United States troops." March 22, 1870. Senate, Executive Document No. 68, 41st Congress, 2nd Session

"Letter of the Secretary of the Treasury," January 20, 1870. Senate, Executive Document No. 32, 41st Congress, 2nd Session.

Lieven, Dominic. *Empire: The Russian Empire and Its Rivals.* New Haven: Yale University Press, 2000.

Loftus, Augustus. *The Diplomatic Reminiscences of Lord Augustus Loftus, 1862–1879.* London: Cassell, 1894.

Lorenz, Lincoln. *The Admiral and the Empress: John Paul Jones and Catherine the Great.* New York: Bookman Associate, 1954.

Luthin, R. H. "The Sale of Alaska," *Slavonic and East European Review* 16 (1937): 168–82.

Marx, Karl, and Friedrich Engels. *Collected Works*, 2nd ed., vol. 32. New York: International Publishers, 1989.

Mazour, Anatole G. "The Prelude to Russia's Departure from America." *Pacific Historical Review* 10, no. 3 (September 1941): 311–19.

Mecutchen, Valerie Stubbs. "Alaska's First Star-Spangled Fourth," *Journal of the West* 6, no. 3 (July 1967): 433–39.

Merli, Frank. J. *The Alabama, British Neutrality, and the American Civil War.* Edited by David M. Fahey. Bloomington: Indiana University Press, 2004.

McPherson, Hallie M. "The Projected Purchase of Alaska, 1859–60." *Pacific Historical Review* 3, no. 1 (March 1934): 80–87.

———. "William McKendree Gwin in the Purchase of Alaska, 1854–1861." *Pacific Historical Review* 3, no. 1 (March 1934): 28–38.

Message of the President of the United States and Accompanying Documents to the Two Houses of Congress at the Commencement of the Second Session of the Fortieth Congress, Washington, D.C.: Government Printing Office, 1868.

Miller, David Hunter. *The Alaska Treaty.* Kingston, Ontario: The Limestone Press, 1981.

———. "Russian Opinion of the Cession of Alaska." *American Historical Review* 48, no. 3 (April 1943): 521–31.

Mouland, Bill. "Global Warming Sees Polar Bears Stranded on Melting Ice." *Daily Mail*, February 1, 2007, accessed June 28, 2015, http://www.dailymail.co.uk /news/article-433170/Global-warming-sees-polar-bears-stranded-melting -ice.html.

Mufson, Steven. "To Solve Our Debt Problem, Let's Sell Alaska." *Washington Post*, December 14, 2012.

Muir, John. *Letters from Alaska.* Edited by Robert Engberg and Bruce Menel. Madison: University of Wisconsin Press, 1993.

Myers, Phillip E. *Caution and Cooperation: The American Civil War in*

British-American Relations. Kent, OH: Kent State University Press, 2008.

Nagengast, William E. "The Visit of the Russian Fleet to the United States: Were Americans Deceived?" *Russian Review* 8, no. 1 (January 1949): 46–55.

Nelson, Soraya Sarhaddi. "Not an April Fool's Joke: Russians Petition to Get Alaska Back." NPR online, April 1, 2014, accessed June 23, 2015, http://www.npr.org/ sections/parallels/2014/04/01/297835873/not-an-april-fools-joke-russian -petition-to-get-alaska-back.

Neunherz, Richard Emerson. "'Hemmed In': Reactions in British Columbia to the Purchase of Russian America." *Pacific Northwest Quarterly* 80, no. 3 (July 1989): 101–11.

———. "The Purchase of Russian America: Reasons and Reactions." PhD diss., University of Washington, 1975.

Nielson, Jonathon M. *Armed Forces on a Northern Frontier: The Military in Alaska's History, 1867–1987.* New York: Greenwood Press, 1988.

Parfitt, Tom. "Russia Plants Flag on North Pole." *Guardian*, August 2, 2007, ac- cessed June 28, 2015, http://www.theguardian.com/world/2007/aug/02/ russia.arctic.

Parry, Albert. "American Doctors in the Crimean War." *South Atlantic Quarterly* 54, no. 4 (October 1955): 478–90.

Pearlstein, Daniel. "Alaska Would Be More at Home in Russia." *Washington Post*, November 23, 2005.

Petrov, Aleksandr Iu. "The Activity of the Russian-American Company on the Eve of the Sale of Alaska to the United States (1858–67)." *Russian Studies in History* 54, no. 1 (June 2015): 61–90.

Petrov, Aleksandr Iu., Metropolitan Kliment of Kalug and Borov, and Aleksei N. Ermolaev, "The Sale of Fort Ross, Russia's Colony in California." *Russian Studies in History* 54, no. 1 (June 2015): 36–60.

Pettersen, Trude. "North Pole Camp for Russian Paratroopers," *Barents Observer*, March 25, 2015, accessed June 28, 2015, http://barentsobserver.com/en/ security/2015/03/north-pole-camp-russian-paratroopers-25-03.

Phelps, Nicole M. *U.S.-Habsburg Relations from 1815 to the Paris Peace Conference.* New York: Cambridge University Press, 2013.

Pierce, Richard A. "Prince D. P. Maksutov: Last Governor of Russian America." *Journal of the West* 6, no. 3 (July 1967): 395–416.

Pletcher, David M. *The Diplomacy of Involvement: American Economic Expansion across the Pacific, 1784–1900.* Columbia: University of Missouri Press, 2001.

Pope, Joseph, ed., *Confederation: Being a Series of Hitherto Unpublished Documents Bearing on the British North America Act.* Toronto: The Carswell Company Ltd. Law Publishers, Etc., 1895.

Purchase of Alaska, Speech of Hon. Leonard Myers, of Pennsylvania, in the House of Representative, July 1, 1868 (n.p.: n.d.).

Reid, Virginia Hancock. *The Purchase of Alaska: Contemporary Opinion.* Long Beach, CA: Press-Telegram, Printers, 1940.

"Report of a Reconnaissance of the Yukon River, Alaska Territory, July to September 1869." Senate, Executive Document No. 12, 42nd Congress, 1st Session.

Richter, F. E. "The Copper-Mining Industry in the United States, 1845–1925." *Quarterly Journal of Economics* 41, no. 2 (February 1927): 236–91.

Russia. Treaty concerning the Cession of the Russian Possessions in North America by his Majesty the Emperor of all the Russias to the United States of America; Concluded March 30, 1867; Ratified by the United States, May 28, 1867; Exchanged June 20, 1867; Proclaimed by the United States, June 20, 1867. (15 Stat. 539), accessed May 16, 2016. https://memory.loc.gov/cgi-bin/ampage ?collId=llsl&fileName=015/llsl015.db&recNum=572.

Saul, Norman. *Concord and Conflict: The United States and Russia, 1867–1914.* Lawrence: University Press of Kansas, 1996.

———. *Distant Friends: The United States and Russia, 1763–1867.* Lawrence: University Press of Kansas, 1991.

Seward, Frederick William. *Seward at Washington as Senator and Secretary of State: A Memoir of His Life, with Selections from His Letters, 1861–1872.* New York: Derby and Miller, 1891.

Seward, William H. "The promise of Alaska." Speech given August 12, 1869, *Promise of Alaska* (January 10, 2009), *History Reference Center*, EBSCOhost, accessed June 30, 2015, http://connection.ebscohost.com/c/opinions/21212996/promise-alaska.

Sherwood, Morgan B. *Exploration of Alaska, 1865–1900.* Fairbanks: University of Alaska Press, 1992.

Shi, David E. "Seward's Attempt to Annex British Columbia, 1865–1869." *Pacific Historical Review* 4, no. 2 (May 1978): 217–38.

Shushina, Lidia. "Unique Russian dialect continues to exist in Alaska." *Russia beyond the Headlines,* July 16, 2013, accessed June 25, 2013, http://rbth.com/science_and_tech/2013/07/16/unique_russian_dialect_continues_to_exist_in_alaska_28123.html.

Smith, Oliver. "Russia Is Considering Plans for a 12,400-Mile Superhighway from London to Alaska," *Telegraph,* March 25, 2015, accessed March 23, 2015, http://www.businessinsider.com/russia-is-considering-plans-for-a-12400-mile-superhighway-from-london-to-alaska-2015-3.

Solovyov, Vladimir, and Elena Klepikova. *Zhirinovsky: Russian Fascism and the Making of a Dictator.* Translated by Catherine A. Fitzpatrick. Reading, MA: Addison-Wesley Publishing Company, 1995.

Speech of Hon. Charles Sumner of Massachusetts, on the Cession of Russian America to the United States. Washington: Congressional Globe Printing Office, 1867.

Stahr, Walter. *Seward: Lincoln's Indispensable Man.* New York: Simon & Schuster, 2012.

Starr, S. Frederick, ed. *Russia's American Colony.* Durham, NC: Duke University Press, 1987.

———. "Scholars from the Soviet Union and America Meet at Sitka to Rehash Old Question of Why Russia Sold Alaska." *Smithsonian* 10, no. 9 (December 1979): 129–44.

Stephanson, Anders. *Manifest Destiny: American Expansion and the Empire of Right.* New York: Hill and Wang, 1995.

Stewart, George R. "The Name *Alaska*," *Names* 4, no. 4 (December 1956): 193–204.

Stock, Leo Francis, ed. and trans. *United States Ministers to the Papal States, Instructions and Despatches, 1848–1868*. Washington, D.C.: Catholic University Press, 1933.

Stolberg-Wernigerode, Count Otto zu. *Germany and the United States of America*. Reading, PA: Henry Janssen Foundation, 1937.

Stone, Kirk H. "Populating Alaska: The United States Phase." *Geographical Review* 42, no. 3 (July 1952): 384–404.

Stuart, Reginald C. *United States Expansionism and British North America, 1775–1871*. Chapel Hill: University of North Carolina Press, 1988.

Tarsaidze, Alexandre "American Pioneers in Russian Railroad Building." *Russian Review* 9, no. 4 (October 1950): 286–95.

Taylor, John M. *William Henry Seward: Lincoln's Right Hand*. Washington, D.C.: Brassey's, 1991.

Territory of Alaska, Report of the Commissioner of Education for the Years Ending June 30, 1918, June 30, 1919, and June 30, 1920. Juneau: Juneau Daily Capital, 1920.

Trauth, Mary P. "Italo-American Diplomatic Relations, 1861–1882: The Mission of George Perkins Marsh, First American Minister to the Kingdom of Italy." PhD diss., Washington, D.C.: Catholic University of America, 1958.

"Treaty with Russia," Report No. 37, May 18, 1868, House of Representatives, 40th Congress, 2nd Session.

Twain, Mark. *Mark Twain: Collected Tales, Sketches, Speeches, and Essays, 1852–1890*. New York: Library of America, 1992.

U.S. Congress, House of Representatives, Alaska, Message from the President of the United States, in Relation to the Transfer of Territory from Russia to the United States, 40th Congress, 2nd Session, 1868, Ex. Doc. 125

U.S. Department of State, Executive documents printed by order of the House of Representatives, during the second session of the fortieth Congress, 1867–68, accessed August 15, 2013, http://images .library.wisc.edu/FRUS/EFacs2/1867 -68v01/M/0458.jpg.

Van Alstyne, Richard W. "John F. Crampton, Conspirator or Dupe?" *American Historical Review* 41, no. 3 (April 1936), 492–502.

Van Deusen, Glyndon G. *William Henry Seward*. New York: Oxford University Press, 1967.

Warner, Donald F. *The Idea of Continental Union: Agitation for the Annexation of Canada to the United States, 1849–1893*. Lexington: University of Kentucky Press, 1960,

Weeks, Albert L. *Russia's Life-Saver; Lend-Lease Aid to the U.S.S.R. in World War II*. Lanham, MD: Lexington Books, 2004.

Welch, Richard E. "American Public Opinion and the Purchase of Russian America," *American Slavic and East European Review* 17, no. 4 (1958): 481–94.

Welles, Gideon. *Diary of Gideon Welles, Secretary of the Navy under Lincoln and Johnson*. 3 vol. Boston: Houghton Mifflin Company, 1911.

Whymper, Frederick. *Travel and Adventure in the Territory of Alaska.* ; Reprint, Readex Microprint Corporation 1966. First published 1868 in London by John Murray.

Williams, Edwin, ed. *Addresses and Messages of the Presidents of the United States, Inaugural, Annual, and Special, from 1789 to 1846,* Vol. 2. New York: E. Walker, 1847.

Williams, Glyndyr. "The Hudson's Bay Company and the Fur Trade: 1670–1870." *Beaver* (Autumn 1983): 4–86.

Zaionshkovskii, P. A. *Dnevnik P. A. Valueva,* Vol. II. Moscow: Akademii nauk, 1961.

"Zhirinovsky Objects to Queries about Alaska, Anti-Semitism." *Toledo Blade,* November 12, 1994, accessed May 13, 2014, http://voiceofrussia.com/2012_03_30/70148263.

"Zhirinovsky: Russia's Political Eccentric," BBB News online, March 10, 2000, accessed June 12, 2015, http://news.bbc.co.uk/2hi/europe/667745.stm.

Znamenski, Andrei A. "History with an Attitude: Alaska in Modern Russian Patriotic Rhetoric." *Jahrbücher für Geschichte Osteuropas,* Neue Folge, Bd. 57, H. 3 (2009): 346–73.

Index

Page numbers with an *f* refer to a figure.

London Post, 142–43
London Times, 142
Loughridge, William, 98, 103
Ludington, E. H., 165
Luxembourg question, 120, 129
Lyle, D. A., 163–65

ℳ

Madison, James, 8
mail, 75, 153
Maksutov, Dmitry Petrovich, 76, 77–79
*Manchester Courier and Lancashire
    General Advertiser*, 142
Manchester Guardian, 143
manifest destiny
    about, xii
    Alaska Purchase as consistent with,
        58, 61
    Popov on, 28
    See also expansionism
mapping of territory, 71, 72
Marcy, William L., 25, 26
maritime power, 2
Marsh, George, 135, 137
Marx, Karl, 144
Mason, James M., 37
Maximilian, Archduke, 132, 137–38
Maynard, Washburn, 165–66
McClellan, George, 14–15
McFarland, Amanda, 167–68
McIntyre, II. A., lx–x, 161–62
McKay, Peter, 187
media reaction
    to appropriations
        delays and, 93–94, 96–97, 101–2
        passage of, 103
        support for, 91–92
    in Austria, 135, 144
    to corruption charges, 106, 109–10,
        112–13
    in Europe, 121, 124, 144
    in France, 138–39, 144

in Great Britain, 142–44
in Italy, 136
in the Ottoman Empire, 139–40
during ratification
    countercriticism of, 62
    criticism of, 60–61, 66
    on international components
        of, 63
    support for, 53–55, 56–60, 66–67
in Russia, 124–27
during transfer process, 81–82
in US, post-ratification, 143
See also publications on Alaska;
    specific newspapers
Meigs, Montgomery, 55, 63
Merli, Frank J., 37
Metternich, Klemens von, 130
Middle East, Russia's interest in, 63
    See also Ottoman Empire
Middleton, Henry, 9
Midway Islands, acquisition of, 23
military presence
    Alaska Natives impacted by, 158–59
    Dall on, 160
    infrastructure construction by,
        82–83
    law and order with, 161
    soldiers' behavior, 80–81
    during transfer process, 74–75,
        77–81, 82–84
military recruiting, British, 14, 29, 36
mining, 171, 173, 178
    See also gold
Mironov, Ivan, 185
Mitchell, John G., 83
Monroe, James, 10
Monroe Doctrine, 10, 125–26, 129, 147
    See also expansionism
Montreal Annexation Association, 39
Montreal Herald, 145
Montreal Transcript, 145
Mordecai, Alfred, 14–15
Mormon invasion, 27
Morrill, Justin, 65

O

October Revolution (1917), 183
oil reserves, x, 179–80
Old Believers (Russian Orthodoxy sect),
  184
L'Opinion Nationale, 139
opportunism
  destabilization from, 161
  influx for, 153–54
  land seizures, 73
  Perkins Claim and, 99
  during Russian property liquidation,
    76
Oregon territory, 34–35, 45
Oregon Treaty, 35
Organic Act (1884; 1906), 174, 176
Orthodox churches, ownership of, 50
Osten-Saken, Fedor, 125
Ottawa Citizen, 145
Ottoman Empire
  Alaska Purchase as shock,
    139–40
  Austria as supportive of, 133–34
  Farragut's visit and, 153
  fracturing of, xii, 121–24, 147
  Prussian neutrality toward, 129
  Russia's interest in, 63

P

Pacific Northwest
  conflict resolution, 10
  fur trading disputes in, 8–9
  Russians in, 5, 7
  three-way rivalry in, 34
Pacific telegraphic cable, proposed,
  17–18
Pahlen, Fedor, 4, 8
Paine, Halbert E., 90, 92, 102–3
Paine, Henry, 98
Painter, Uriah
  accusations about Walker, 114

allegations by, 109
congressional report and, 112
corruption question raised by, 107
funds disbursement investigation,
  108
questionable conclusions of, 113
testimony from, 110
Palin, Sarah, 177
Pall Mall Gazette, 142
Panama Canal, promotion of, 110
Paris, Treaty of, 15, 121, 152
Patriot War, 39
Patterson, James, 63
Paul I, 4, 6
Pearlstein, Daniel, 184
Perkins Claim
  about, 88–90
  bribe rumors, 110, 114
  in congressional deliberations, 91,
    92, 98, 99, 102–3
  fate after appropriations victory,
    103–6
  late payment interest vs., 117
Perry, Matthew, 45
Peshchurov, Alexei Ivanovich, 79, 80–81
Philadelphia Evening Telegraph, 110
Philadelphia Inquirer, 57–58
Phillips, Wendell, 174
Polish holdings
  home rule in, 134
  uprising, suppression of
    in 1830–31, 11
    in 1863, 16–17
    Prussian-Russian collaboration
      in, 128
    US noninterventionist stance
      in, 22
Politica, Pierre de, 9
Polk, James, 34–35
Popov, Andrei, 28
popular culture, Alaska in, 177, 181
population
  about, 149–50
  decline in, 154

W

Walker, Robert J.
  during appropriation debates, 107
  bribes paid to, 109
  disbursement to, 113
  letter supporting Alaska Purchase,
    91
  as pickpocket victim, 108
  self-interest of, 111
  as Stoeckl's employee, 95
  on telegram costs, 116
  testimony from, 110
  visit to Canada, 41
War of 1812, 8, 33
Washburn, Cadwallader C., 90, 93–94,
  100–101
Washburn, Elihu, 90–91
Washington Daily Morning Chronicle
  on appropriations delay, 96, 101
  on trade with Asia, 102
  Walker's letter in, 91
Washington Treaty (1871), 38
Webster-Ashburton Treaty, 33
Weed, Thurlow, 46, 54
Weiner Zeitung, 135
Welles, Gideon, 54, 65–66, 73–74, 138
Western Hemisphere, European
  interference in, 9–10

Western Times, 103
whaling vessels, 13
Whistler, George Washington, 11–12
Whymper, Frederick
  on Alaska Natives, 152
  Russian-American Telegraph
    Expedition and, 159
  *Travel and Adventure in the Territory
    of Alaska*, 151
wildlife, climate change impact on, 181
Wilkes, Charles, 37
William H. Webb Shipyards, 15
Williams, George H., 143
Wilson, Henry, 89
Worcester (MA) Daily Spy, 110
World War II, Alaska in, 178–79
Wrangell, Ferdinand von, 26–27

Y

Young, Brigham, 27

Z

Zhirinovsky, Vladimir, 183, 184